Painting and Drawing Animals

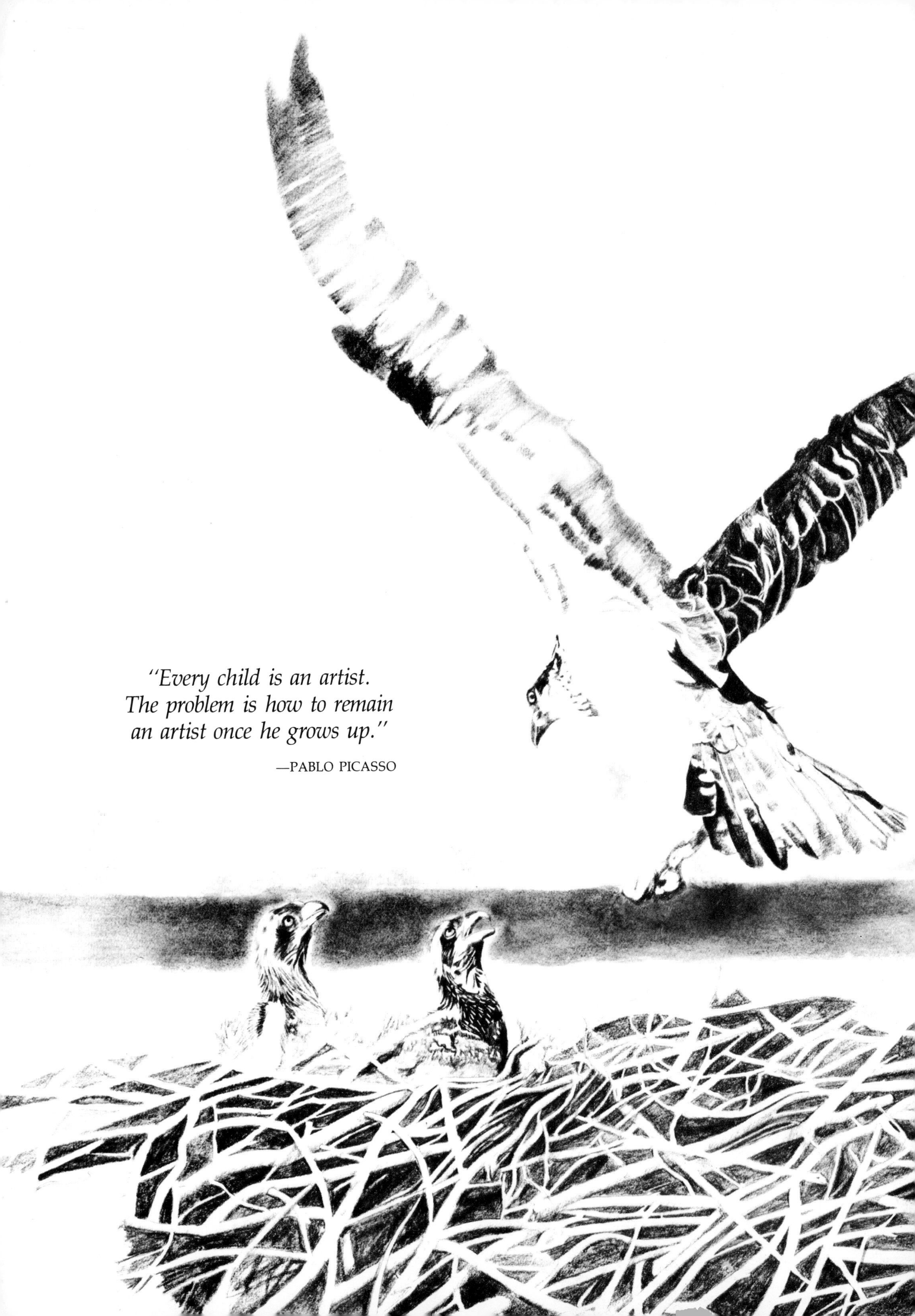

"Every child is an artist.
The problem is how to remain
an artist once he grows up."

—PABLO PICASSO

Painting and Drawing Animals

by Graeme Sims

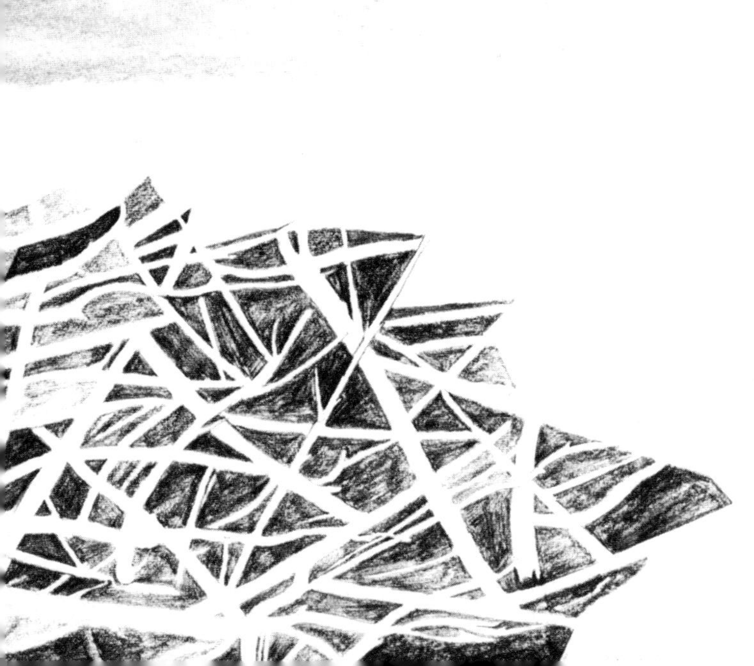

WATSON-GUPTILL PUBLICATIONS
NEW YORK

To my family—after all the glitter and frustration of the outside world, I have this warm and creative place to come home to.

First published 1983 in New York by Watson-Guptill Publications,
a division of Billboard Publications, Inc.
1515 Broadway, New York, N.Y. 10036

Library of Congress Cataloging in Publication Data

Sims. Graeme.
Painting and drawing animals.
Includes index.
1. Animals in art. 2. Art—Technique. I. Title.
N7660.S65 1983 751.42′2432 83-14497
ISBN 0-8230-3556-5

Distributed in the United Kingdom by Phaidon Press Ltd.,
Littlegate House, St. Ebbe's Street, Oxford.

Manufactured in Japan

1 2 3 4 5 6 7 8 9/88 87 86 85 84 83

Edited by Bonnie Silverstein
Designed by Bob Fillie
Set in 11-point Palatino

Acknowledgments

I would like to thank the following people and organizations for their help: at Watson-Guptill, David Lewis, for his help and support; Bonnie Silverstein, for arranging and editing the material; and Bob Fillie, for the design of the book. Michael Petts, who photographed all of my paintings for this book with a craftsmanship seldom seen today. Michael Lyster, the resident photographer of London Zoo, for the superb animal stills that were beyond my own photographic ability. Marwell Zoo and The Cat Survival Trust for allowing me to get so close to my subjects.

Finally, thank you to my daughter Fiona, who typed when she should have been out enjoying herself, and who shouted, "Hooray, finally," when she typed. Thank you, too, to Michael and Helen, who helped.

Contents

Part Four. Exercises and Demonstrations 67

Part Five. Working Out a Composition 106

Part Six. Twenty Painting Projects 123

Part One

The Basics

I BELIEVE in the sanctity of all life. In this book I will try to describe the things I have noticed and learned about animals and how observation and logic firmly demonstrate the interdependence of every creature on this earth, including an animal called "man." But this is a book about painting, not about conservation, and so I will concentrate on teaching you the craft of painting and drawing animals rather than dwell on problems concerning their survival. However, I do want you to be aware that the subjects of this book are increasingly under pressure from our encroaching civilization. It is my hope that the paintings produced by wildlife artists, be they amateur or professional, will remind us that man is just an animal and shares this world with other animals on an equal-rights basis.

I hope you enjoy this book and that it will pass on the technique and observation lessons that I have learned. I have tried hard to make it a real teaching work, hopefully removing much of the mystique and "arty grandeur" associated with painting, because I firmly believe that every one of us has a painter locked inside, just waiting to be encouraged out.

I ask you, too, every time you pick up this book or practice an exercise from it, that you spare a thought for the creatures depicted, because unless we all care, they will end up as no more than rendered memories of animals that once lived. The pictures in this book should make their own powerful plea, as well as provide you with a series of techniques and methods that will give you good results and a lot of absorbing pleasure.

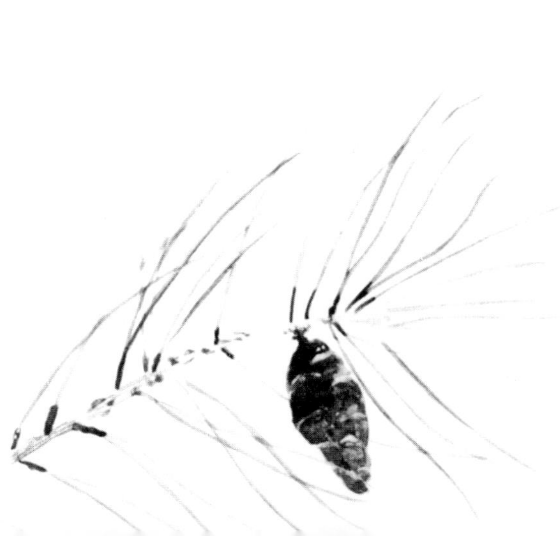

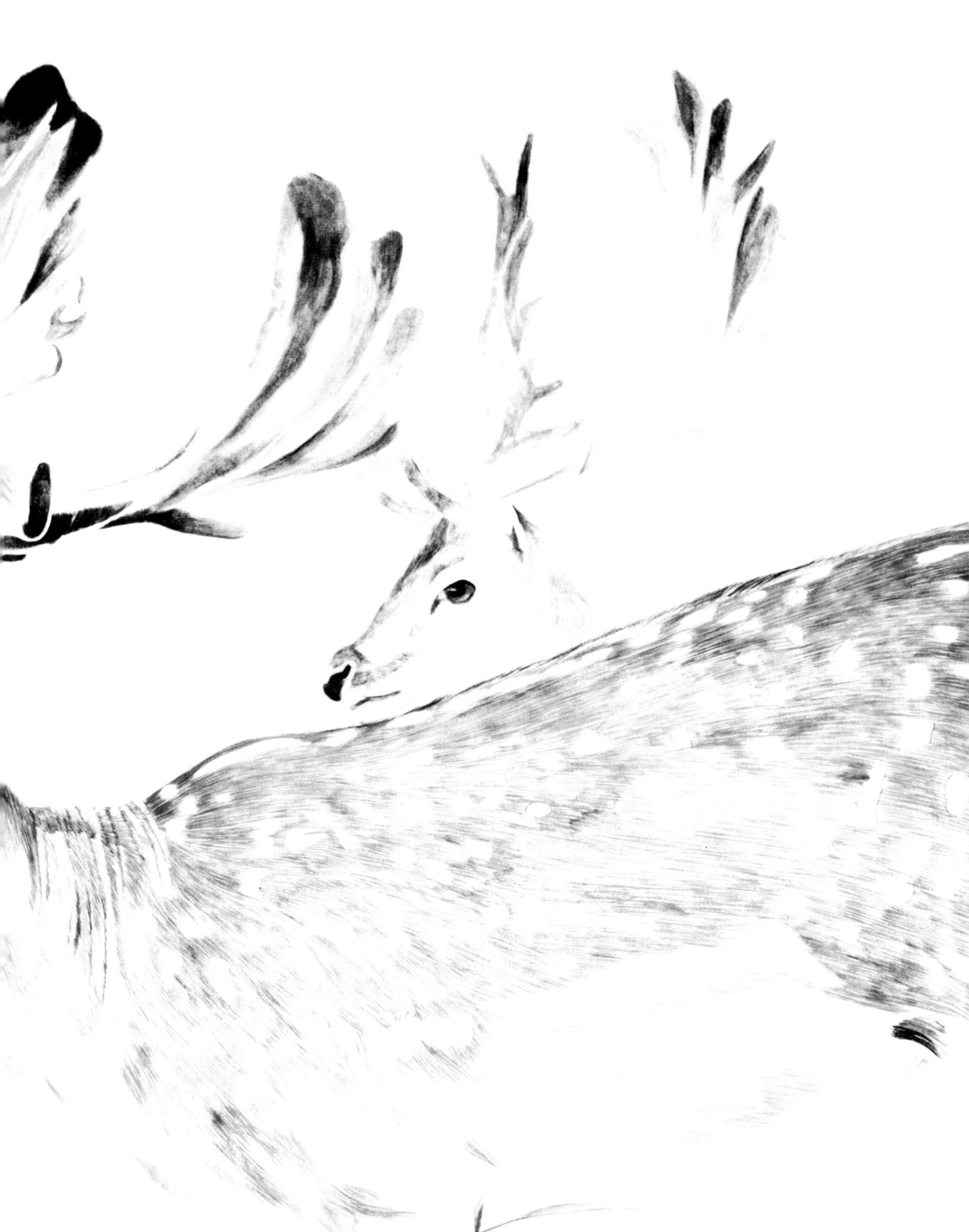

Gathering Reference Material

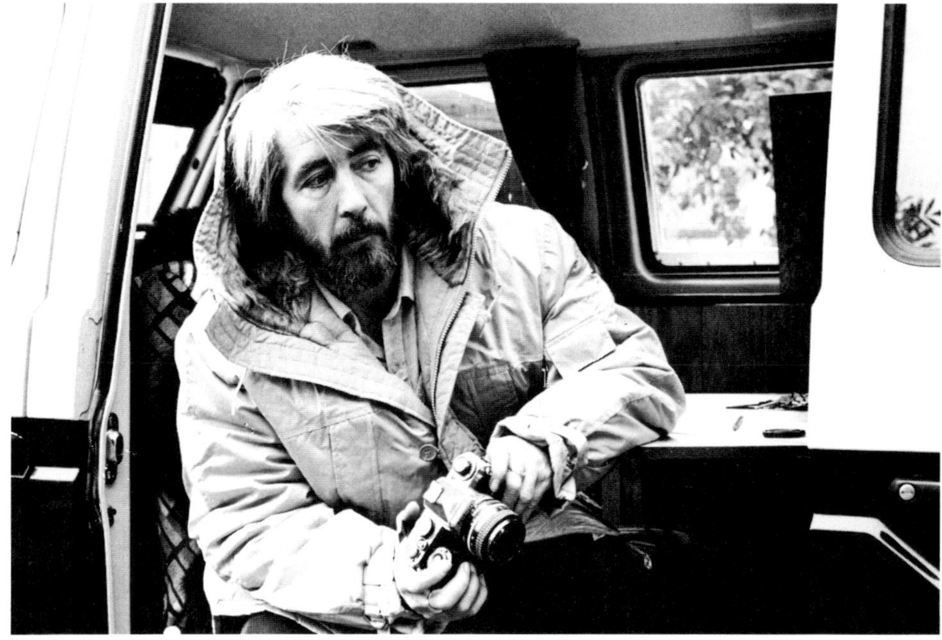

There are three ways to get reference material. You can photograph the animals at a zoo or wildlife park—or in the wild. You can draw sketches of the animals as you watch them move or sleep. Or you can collect pictures of animals from magazines.

Photographing and drawing animals from life is the best way to gather reference material, however, because it allows you to get out into the open air and study the real animal—the way it moves and the characteristic way it holds itself. And, in the long run, in order to draw and paint wild creatures accurately and sympathetically, you must spend time watching them. Even if you can't manage a trip into the wilderness, you can still observe them first-hand in zoos, wildlife parks, and aquariums. And because the animals are on show, you can be sure of returning with many images on film or in your sketchbook—or both.

When you watch an animal in action, your mind's "filing system" will be surprisingly able to retain sequences of movement, just as film or video does, and you will find that you can play it back later.

I usually prefer to photograph animals rather than sketch them. It's difficult to draw properly at a zoo. It is usually crowded, and people are curious and may bother you and prevent you from concentrating. When I do draw at zoos, it is usually in the dead of winter when it's less crowded. And even then, I sketch quickly, concentrating only on the essential movement, shapes, and lines—and fill in the details later in the comfort of my studio.

Sometimes you can sketch the animals at a wildlife park from your car—a few places even will let you stop your car as you move through the park. But for the most part, it's easier to capture an animal totally, in full color, at 1/250th of a second and draw it at your leisure later.

Hints on Photographing Animals

Since automatic cameras do almost everything for you nowadays except press the button and focus, using photographs for reference does not involve a lifetime of study. With a little practice, you can create a photograph of sufficient quality to refer to it when painting or drawing.

Telephoto lenses are a great help in photographing wildlife. I use either a 250mm or 500mm lens. Both are powerful enough to give me a large print of the animal itself, eliminating the extraneous background.

When photographing in zoos, you will want to eliminate the wires or bars between you and the animal. To do this, make sure you're some distance from the wire, then focus tightly on the animal. Because the cage is not in focus, the animal will be reproduced miraculously, without any bars showing.

Since clear focusing is the most important ingredient, while it is not too difficult to hand-hold a camera with a 250mm or 500mm lens, you'll get even better results if you use a sturdy tripod—particularly under overcast skies when you'll need a longer exposure time. For that reason, I suggest using a very fast film, one with an ISO or ASA of 400, for example. Also, remember that a fast-moving animal needs to be photographed at a shutter speed of 1/250 of a second or higher, while an animal that is standing still will probably require only 1/125 second.

Don't be tempted to photograph the animal every time it moves. Be prepared to wait, with camera ready, for the one pose worth using as the basis for a painting. I always follow this golden rule when selecting a photo for painting: The animal's eyes should be clear and, ideally, have a strongly defined highlight or reflection—and the pose and composition should be striking enough to stir up real inspiration.

Photographing Animals in the Wild

There are several ways of photographing wild animals. You can move quietly and hope you'll be lucky enough to come across a creature worth photographing—and stealthy enough to capture it on film. Or you can employ a more painstaking "waiting" method, which is the approach most likely to yield the best results.

I usually do the latter. In choosing a waiting spot, I note where certain creatures have been seen or observe the ground for evidence of their presence. Then I position myself and wait for them to appear. Meanwhile, I set up my camera on the tripod so I am ready to shoot the photograph should an animal appear. I begin filling my sketchbook with drawings of the environment—trees, plants, and the landscape—including the lighting effects.

Here's an example of how I work. Recently, I noticed a buzzard perched on a telegraph pole. I drove past it and parked my car some distance away. Then, quietly, under the cover of some trees fringing the road, I returned to the spot and got several good photographs of it. On the following day, knowing roughly where the buzzard would be, I returned and waited for it to appear—with my camera pre-set to include a good landscape background as well.

Instead of actively searching for an animal, you can try to lure it to a pre-selected spot with food. Birds—particularly seagulls or garden birds—can be attracted to your camera this way, and I've often waited in the branches of a tree for a badger or deer to appear, with excellent results. Telephoto lenses are a great aid then and allow you to get good shots of birds and animals by just sitting quietly in your car. For some reason, these creatures completely ignore a parked car, viewing it not as a threat, but as a piece of the natural landscape. In short, with common sense and some practice, I'm sure we all have enough "animal" in us to know instinctively what to do to get close enough to a bird or wild animal to photograph it.

Drawing with the "Identikit" Method

One of the biggest worries in drawing is getting the various elements in the right position, in the right relation and proportion to each other, without, say, having the eyes too far from the nose or too big for the outside shape.

Over the years, I've developed a quick method of composition that removes much of the worry and risk of getting a composition that doesn't work—a risk I can ill afford when I'm painting a commission with a fierce deadline and need to paint accurately, without many time-wasting, confidence-sapping false starts. I call my method "the identikit method."

To show you how it works, I've chosen two photographs of a male and female lion, photographed by the London Zoo's resident photographer. I acquired them for a small sum, and the prints were so beautifully clear and dramatic that you could see, even at this early photo-selection stage, that the finished work stood a good chance of being excellent.

It's very important to start with a good reference photograph, one that contains plenty of details, because you won't be able to imagine them later. In this case, the sunlight came from the right on both lions, which made it easier to combine both photographs into a single painting. The width of the spacing between the bars of the cages was also the same, which meant that each animal was the same distance from bars and camera and their proportions would be correct for a combined portrait.

Working Area

My studio is carefully organized to streamline my work. Almost all my painting and drawing is done at a Formica-topped, inclined drawing board I've found amazingly versatile for painting watercolors. All the items I need are on a table next to the drawing board so I can reach them quickly. Every pencil is sharp, every brush carefully pre-pointed, and all photographic (or real) references are at hand. (I even had nearly an entire lichen-covered birch tree in my studio for reference!)

I work under the steady light of a bank of color-corrected fluorescent tubes. (Since paintings are so often viewed under artificial light, it seems more sensible to paint them under the same conditions.) I also have on hand a series of sketchbooks containing reference material for future paintings, so that when I need to paint a particular animal, the information has already been worked out and is at hand. The idea is that, with everything organized, the painting can be done quickly, with a minimum of effort.

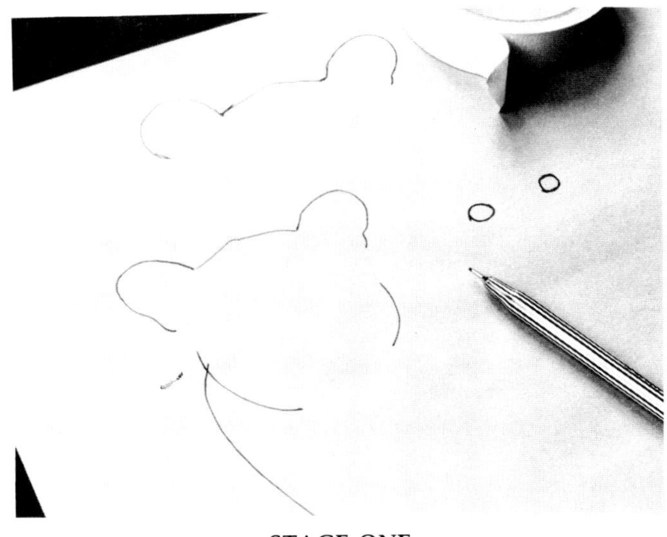

STAGE ONE

First I tape both photographs securely with masking tape to the Formica-faced drawing board in order to prevent the images from moving. Then, ignoring the color and detail, look for the simplest line on the two images. In this case, the simplest form is the lioness and the simplest line is at the top of her head and the ears. Trace it with a long, unbroken line. (I notice that many art students tend to draw with a series of short, sketchy lines rather than longer, more definite ones. Try to break this habit. A single line is stronger and will give a more fluent shape and greater force to your drawings.)

Now check the outline of the head and ears carefully for accuracy, then draw the outline of the rest of the head.

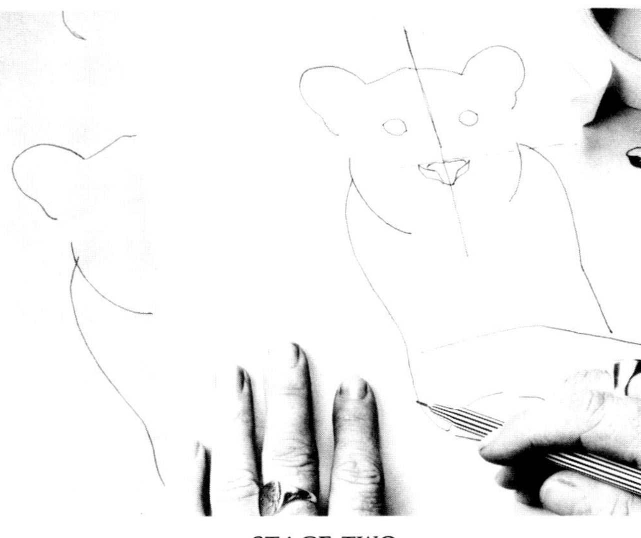

STAGE TWO

Divide the head with a faint, ruler-drawn line to decide where to position the nose and eyes. Draw them on a separate sheet of tracing paper. This is when you'll begin to notice how much easier this system makes your life. Now the eyes and nose can be placed beneath your first tracing. And you don't have to worry about the outside shape because you've already drawn it in stage one.

You'll notice on my drawing that the vertical line divides the nose into halves and the horizontal line bisects the centers of the eyes, not the pupils but the eye outlines. If you're getting a good result and feel confident, go on to sketch the body shape. But there's no rush–you can do it later if you wish.

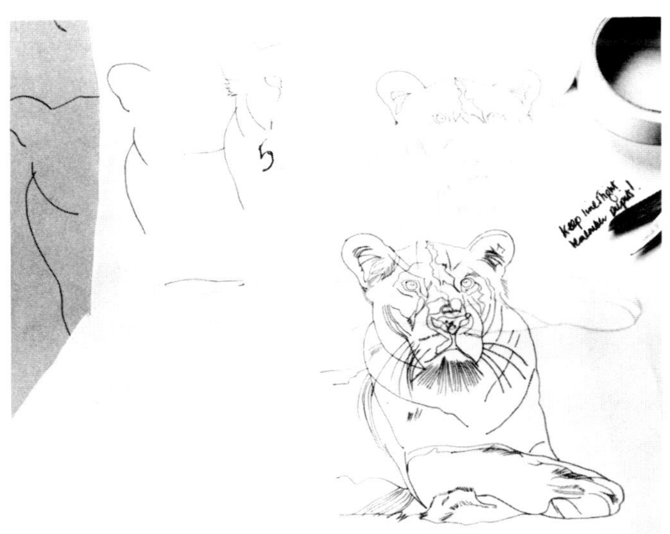

STAGE THREE

Now draw the mouth, again just concentrating on the shape. Don't block in areas, just draw outlines. Again don't worry about how many sheets of paper the parts of the drawing are on, how messy they are, or how long the whole process is taking.

As you see, with the identikit method, you can combine two or more drawings faster and with better results than more traditional methods. At the very least, you will have a good working plan, with all of the component parts in the right position. And even if things go wrong, you will still have the various parts of the drawing on different pieces of tracing paper so you can correct the drawing without starting over.

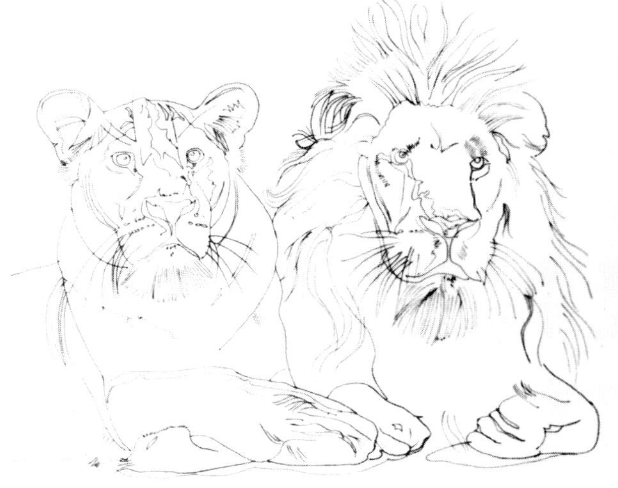

STAGE FOUR

Now sketch the lion. Ignore the hairs in the mane and pay attention to the general shape and arrange them into a composition. I decide to put the lioness on the left. She has a much better paw line, and it can be used to overlap the left-hand side of the male to efficiently link both images into a single arrangement. I also decide to tilt the lion's head a bit to the right to give him a slightly inquisitive air. As I make these decisions, I lay one sheet of tracing paper over the other and adjust the position of each in relation to the other until I'm satisfied. Then I tape them down and trace them onto the watercolor board. (Later you'll see how these lion portraits were painted.)

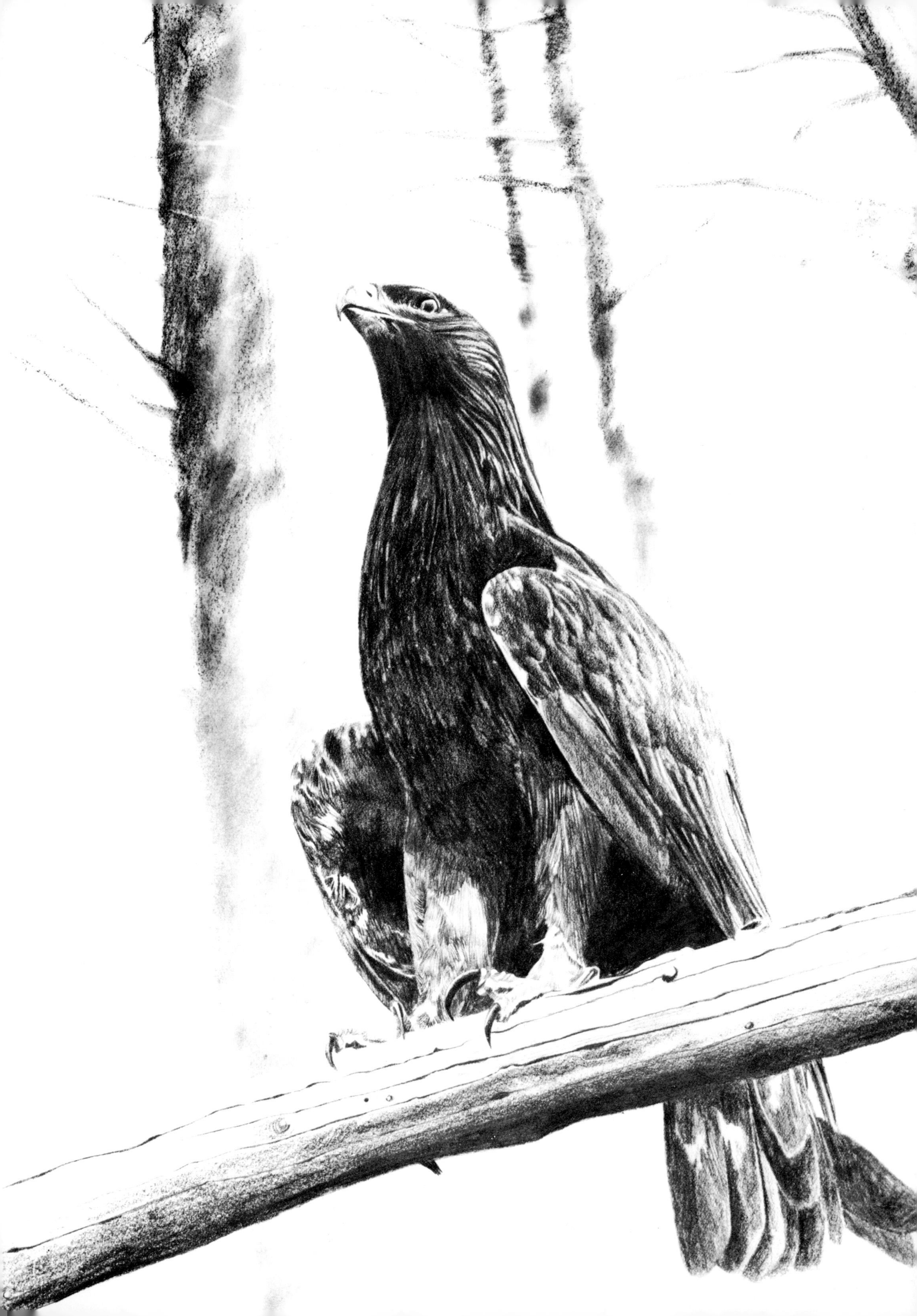

Part Two

Drawing Animals

YOU DON'T NEED tricks or gimmicks to draw animals, just a lot of practice. To learn to draw them, begin with animals that have simple shapes, such as birds and fish, and gradually move on to more complicated animals, those that walk on four legs and those with humanlike shapes, apes and monkeys.

Since I want you to concentrate on getting the basic shapes before you add the details, I have deliberately separated the drawings into two different types. First there are quick sketches of animals drawn with an HB pencil on hard-milled paper, a rather unsympathetic combination of materials that has the advantage of showing the drawing process without flattery. I want you to notice the different shapes of these animals and the weight of the lines forming these shapes.

I have also drawn more detailed sketches of the animals on rough-grained Kent paper using a 2B pencil, with solid graphite pencil for the darkest areas. These are finished drawings rather than preparatory sketches, and so here the pencil work is more important. This time pencils and paper are better suited to each other, which means that really good results can be obtained.

A 2B pencil has an enormous range of shades and densities, but because it is soft and smudges, it is hard to keep the paper clean. One way to do this (if you're right-handed) is to work from the upper left to the right and top to bottom as you fill in the detail. You should also keep a kneaded eraser nearby and continually use it to remove stray smudges from the paper and the outside edge of your drawing hand.

Birds

Shapes

When you really look at birds closely, you will notice that they're constructed out of a series of linked curves that elongate and change in terms of line according to each bird's function. For example, parrots have a strong bill for cracking nuts and seeds; geese have elongated bills and long necks so they can reach food and filter out water; owls have large, well-developed eyes for seeing small rodents in the dark, a head that can turn almost a full circle, and a beak ideal for tearing meat. Doves, on the other hand, show the soft lines of a domesticated bird primarily bred for eating, while the predator has evolved to streamlined hunting perfection, with a fierce beak for tearing; an ever-aware, far-seeing eye; and a muscle and bone system that shows obvious striking power at the back of the neck. Capturing these characteristics is far more important than mastering the detailing. Start by copying these shapes. But don't hurry. Look for a long time and really think about them and how they differ, before you draw. That is how you will learn.

Details

I have not attempted to finish any of the drawings here, except one, because I want my technique to remain clear. Also, since the heads of the various birds contain the real essence or character of each species, I have put more attention into these and other essential parts that sum up their character. The strength and sureness of my line also varies with the nature of the bird.

The predator has a watchful, alert expression and I have tried to capture it by making the features uncluttered. I have also emphasized the intensity of the eye and the fierce lines of the beak. Notice how the strength, direction, and boldness of my line emphasizes the character of the bird. A fierce pose needs strong treatment. Too many fine details will flatten the drama.

The owl, too, is treated in an "unfussy" manner, with all of the attention going into its beak, eyes, and ear tufts. I have deliberately left my lines indefinite because I want to suggest that its head might suddenly turn to the left or the right at any moment.

The two geese are drawn in different ways. The bill of the one on the left, its most prominent feature, is detailed by lightly shading some areas and then smudging the pencil with a flat bristle brush. The bill of the goose on the right is composed of a series of very fine, short lines.

Notice how the shape and character of the two goose heads are suggested by the direction and the softness of the lines. I describe a predatory bird with positive, firm, and rapid flicks of the pencil, but for a "gentle" bird I use shorter, finer strokes.

The parrots' charm is built into their pose and so they need less drawing then some of the other birds. But again notice that most of the attention has gone into their main feature—the strong, hooked, seed-cracking beak.

The crow on the right is handled differently from most of the other birds. Much of the drawing is centered on the eye and the reflection of trees in it, which gives both a wild and watchful quality to the bird. Because it is a strong bird and a dark black, the strokes and pencil pressure are very definite.

The two tiny birds are treated gently and simply. Too much attention to detail can freeze a drawing of a bird and make it appear stuffed.

Practice the weight of your strokes and their direction. Never press too hard or overwork an area too much. And don't feel duty-bound to finish the whole drawing. A high finish on main-featured areas and a light sketchy quality on others will give your drawing more force and more contrast. I usually start my detailing on the eyes because once these are mastered, the character of the bird is fixed and acts as a good guide to the sort of treatment needed in the rest of the picture.

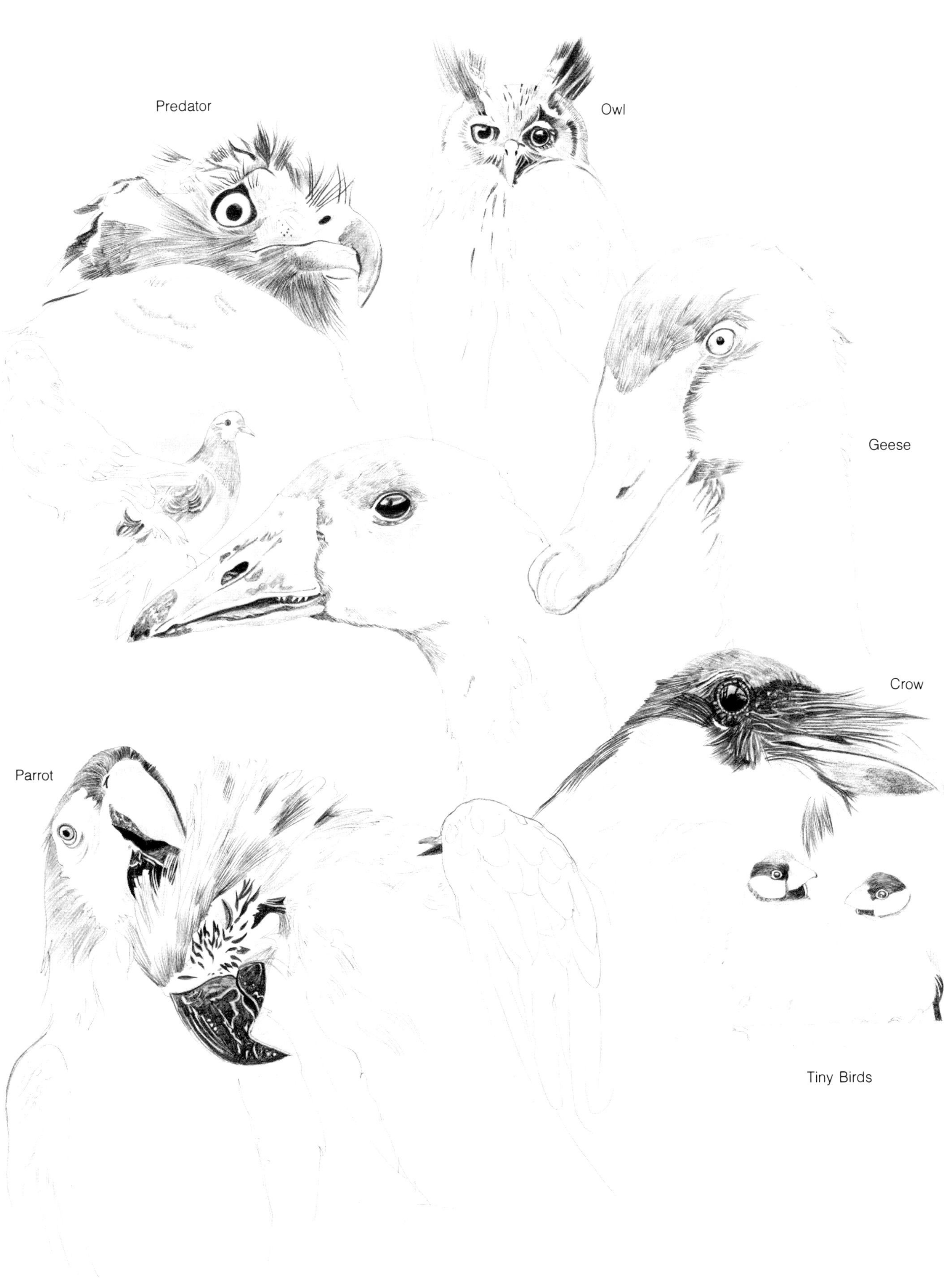
Predator
Owl
Geese
Crow
Parrot
Tiny Birds

Water Creatures and Fish

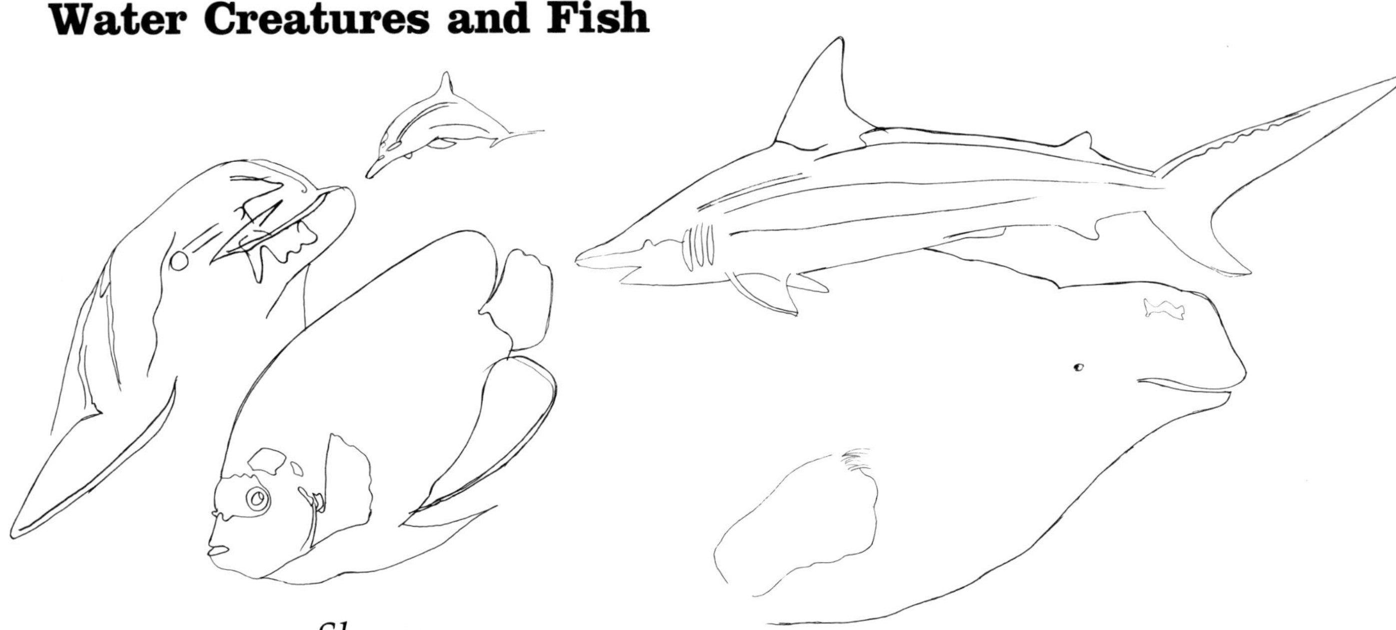

Shapes

Fish and sea creatures are beautifully aerodynamic (or should I say "water"-dynamic). In a way they, too, are capable of flight, but flight through the medium of water rather than air.

If ever you have been skin-diving, you will have experienced a strange sensation of appearing to fly in a watery sky, above the rocky, sandy landscape of the ocean floor. From a drawing point of view, water creatures are challenging and beautiful to draw, and a quite different series of techniques is needed to capture their particular characteristics.

A school of highly intelligent dolphin (their brains are one and a half times bigger than man's) make a balletlike study of fluid grace, while the great gray-white brooding majesty of the white whale can be impressive. Sharks are perfect peaks of evolutionary animal design, with a shape that allows them to practice their predatory role with speed, style, and muscular fluidity.

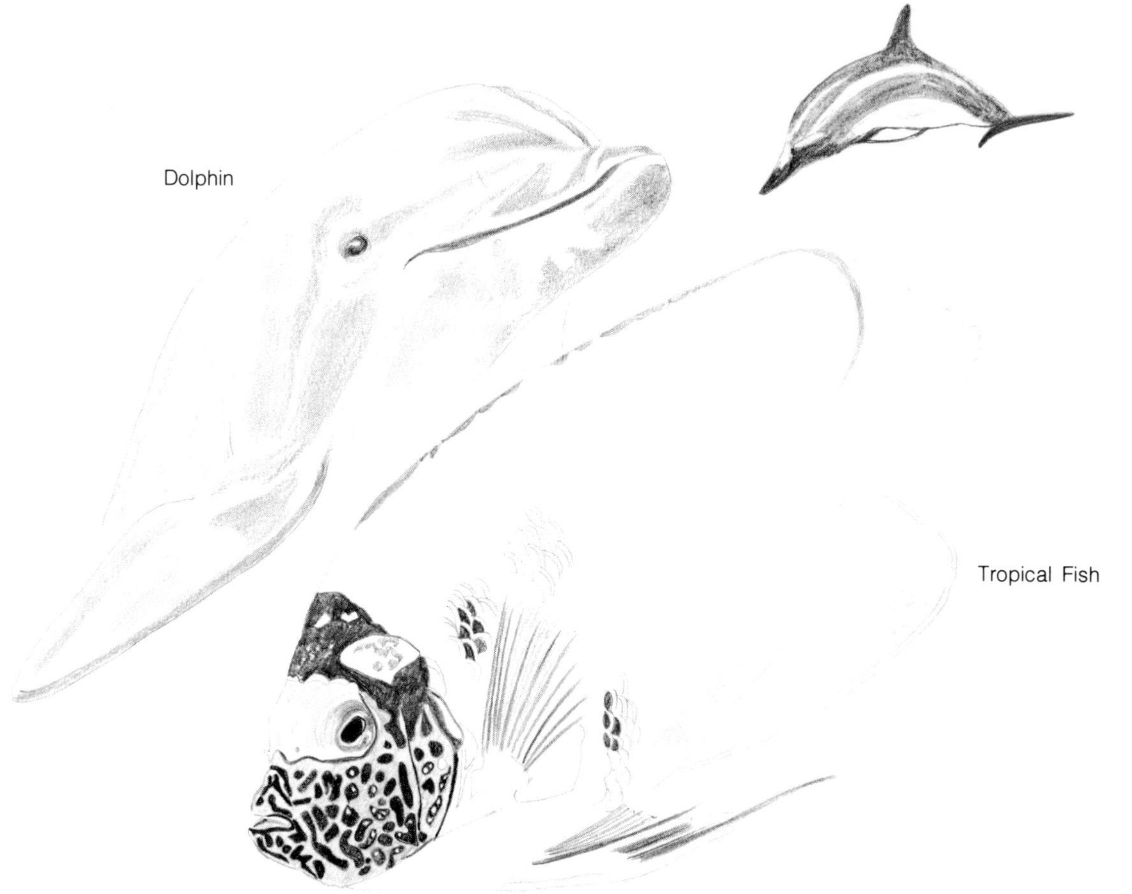

Details

These sea animals are excellent to practice on because they all require different techniques. Their shapes are simple, but after thousands and thousands of years of evolution, they have been honed to perfection. Fish shouldn't really be drawn without a background because as just a tone-rendered shape, they look strange against the white paper. Therefore, for all water creatures (except tropical fish), getting the effect of water and light on the shape is as important as an accurate drawing.

The dolphin is smooth-skinned, with a very soft, rounded, almost feature-free body. I started with the eye and the mouth to give me definite points of reference and drew the rough areas of light and shadow. Then, with the side of the pencil, I gently darkened the shadow area. I then rolled a tiny piece of absorbent cotton between my fingers and used this to gently smudge the shadow areas into a soft tone. Finally I lifted out water reflections and highlights with a small piece of kneaded eraser.

Tropical fish require a totally opposite technique because they are geometrically patterned with almost mathematical accuracy. Accurate drawing and filling in of the pattern shapes is of prime importance here. Draw the patterns first with a very sharp pencil. If you intend to draw all the scales (if you have the patience), then lightly sketch them in. Remember, each scale overlaps the other, with the curve of one row coinciding with the dips in the other (see my diagram). I recommend that you draw no more than I have unless you want to drive yourself to distraction. Once the pattern shapes have been drawn, gently smudge in the shadowed tones of the body shape with a piece of graphite-covered absorbent cotton or with your finger.

The shark must be treated decisively to capture the feeling of this fast, cold-eyed killer. But don't get carried away as I did and treat it too firmly. I started on the fin and edged this strongly in black, since it is one of the shark's essential features. Then, with the side of my pencil, I smudged in long, firm strokes to indicate the shape of its body. When you're doing this, work from the front to back because, even after smudging, the direction of lines give the impression of speed and movement. Then smudge the shaded area very firmly with your finger. I made the shark's eye indefinite (in fact, I've given the impression of having two eyes on the same side) in order to achieve a more frightening, malevolent, machine-like appearance.

I used a no. 00 sable brush, with the bristles cut very short to smudge the smaller areas of shadow. Then I wiped most of the moisture off the brush and applied some irregular smudges of graphite with the damp brush. Most of the finishing work—including minimizing the effect of my overly vigorous patches of wet graphite, and cutting out highlight and water-ripple effects—was done with a rolled piece of kneaded eraser. Smudging the edge of the fin adds an impression of speed, but don't overdo this or it will become too prominent.

The beluga whale at the bottom of the page is included to demonstrate how surface-wave reflections can lend shape and features to what would otherwise be an expressionless blob. The only firmly rendered features are the eyes and mouth. The rest of the creature is shown by lightly sketching patches (see the left-hand side), and then blurring them with a chopped-off sable brush, and finally cutting out ripple effects with a roll of kneaded eraser.

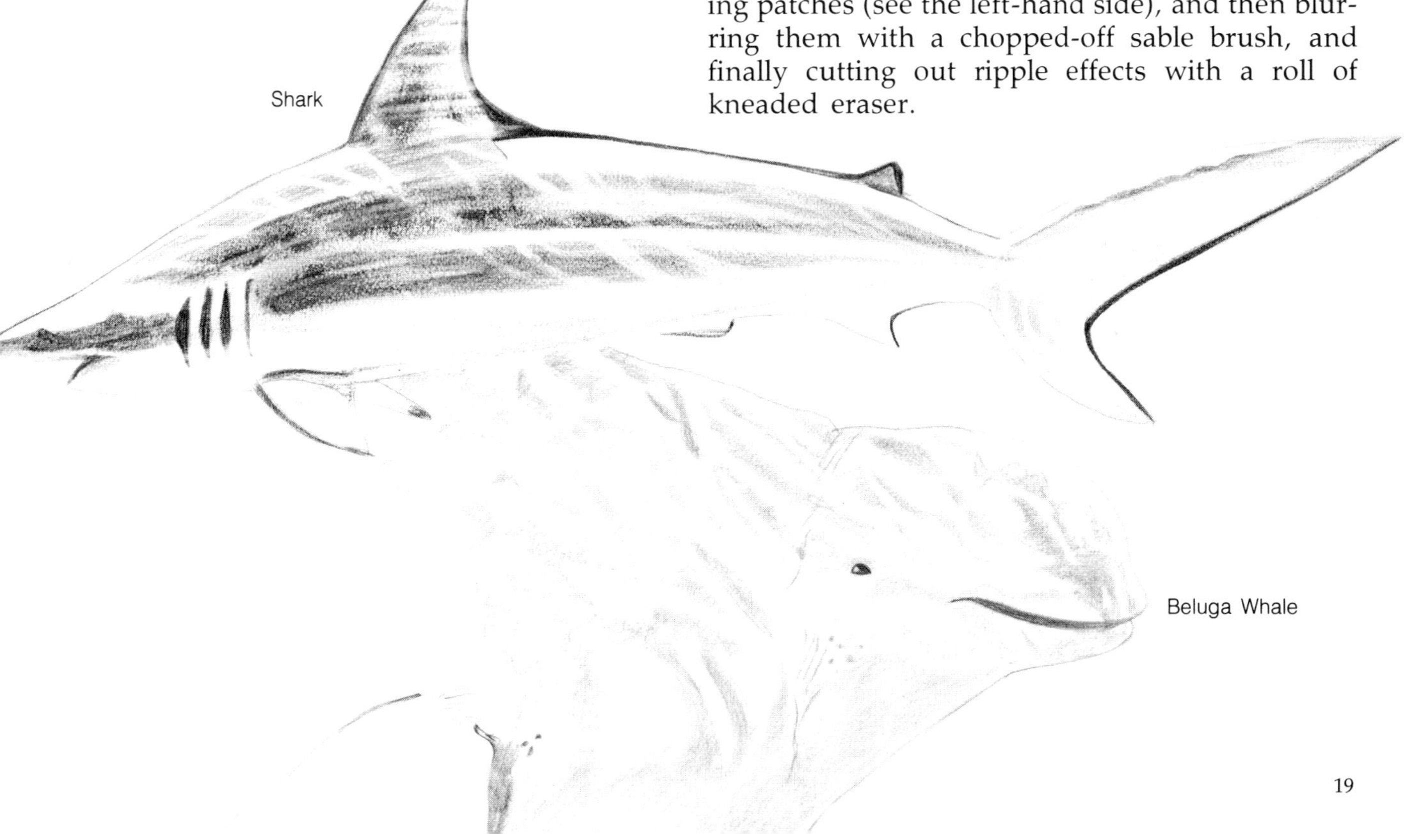

Four-Legged Animals

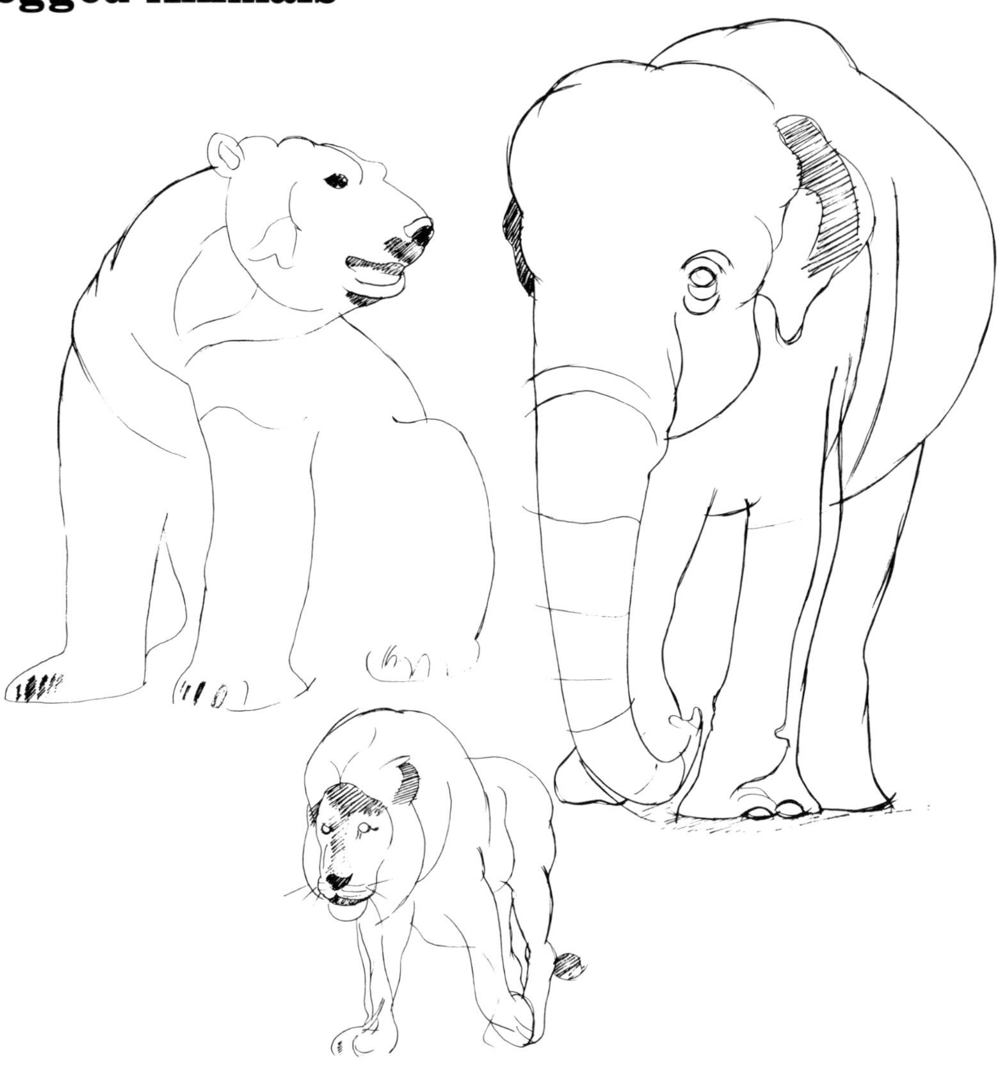

Shapes

Here are three entirely different characters. The shape of each animal is determined by the role they play and the climate they inhabit.

The polar bear has a mass of muscle, but its shape is softened by a layer of fat and a shaggy coat that protects it from the fierce cold. Its big, flat feet enable it to move across snow or ice at an ambling gait.

Look at its basic shape. The head and the feet are very large and the frame of the animal is sturdy. Its fatty covering and shaggy coat soften and pad its angles so its body and the legs lack dramatic curves. The fat covering the skull is less generous than it is over the body.

The elephant has a massive frame to hold its vast bulk. The skin looks like a leathery bag and its head, with its strong but sensitive trunk, is also large. The legs have less shape than those of most four-legged animals, and the feet are flat and round.

The lion is a formidable predator and looks it! Its head and mane are impressive and its body is heavily muscled and very strong.

Details

Each of these three animals is useful as a drawing exercise since each involves keen observation and totally different drawing techniques.

The polar bear must be drawn with a soft, but deft, touch. Notice how the direction of the hairs reveals the shape of the animal. The bear has just come out of the water. Note how the hairs have formed clumps rather than individual, fine-hair shapes. Since the bear is white, its fur must not be overworked. Gradation of tone is important in shadow areas, but let the white of the paper work as highlights. Draw a contour map of the hairs and, with the point of the pencil, softly shade in the shadow areas between the hairs. A white animal on a white background is difficult, so smudge in a "holding" tone on parts of the outline.

Since the head is the most interesting area and needs the most emphasis, work on this part more than any other. Cold-climate animals have small ears, eyes, and nostrils as protection against fierce cold, and I have therefore featured these character-shaping features. The eye is black and gives a squinting appearance, and the ear is closed up against the cold. The nose has been worked on to look moist, shiny, and cold.

The elephant has a baggy, ill-fitting leathery skin that is covered with spare folds and wrinkles. The body folds and crevices are directional and run with the shape of the body. Light strikes the ridges of wrinkles and throws shadow into the hollows. I have rendered just enough of the elephant for you to be able to see the drawing techniques. After capturing the shape of the elephant, I concentrate on drawing a contour map of the various lines that crisscross the animal's surface, and then I fill in the hollows between the raised ridges of the wrinkles. A very sharp pencil is not needed. Aim for a gentle building up density of pencil. Pressure of stroke achieves a clumsy effect and should be avoided. Don't forget that where the hollow is deepest, the shadow will be strongest. It can be hard to accurately capture the wrinkles and folds and achieve a solid mass of area at the same time. So after faintly drawing the contour lines, I lightly shade in the flat planes with the side of my pencil and then smudge them gently with my finger. This technique enables black lines and erased white lines to crisscross the solid tone.

A kneaded eraser is very helpful and can be used to pick out shape highlights and soften tones. Pull off a small piece of eraser and roll it between your fingers until it becomes roughly like the end of a pencil, and then use it with long definite strokes to cut out lines, or with short "dabbing" strokes to

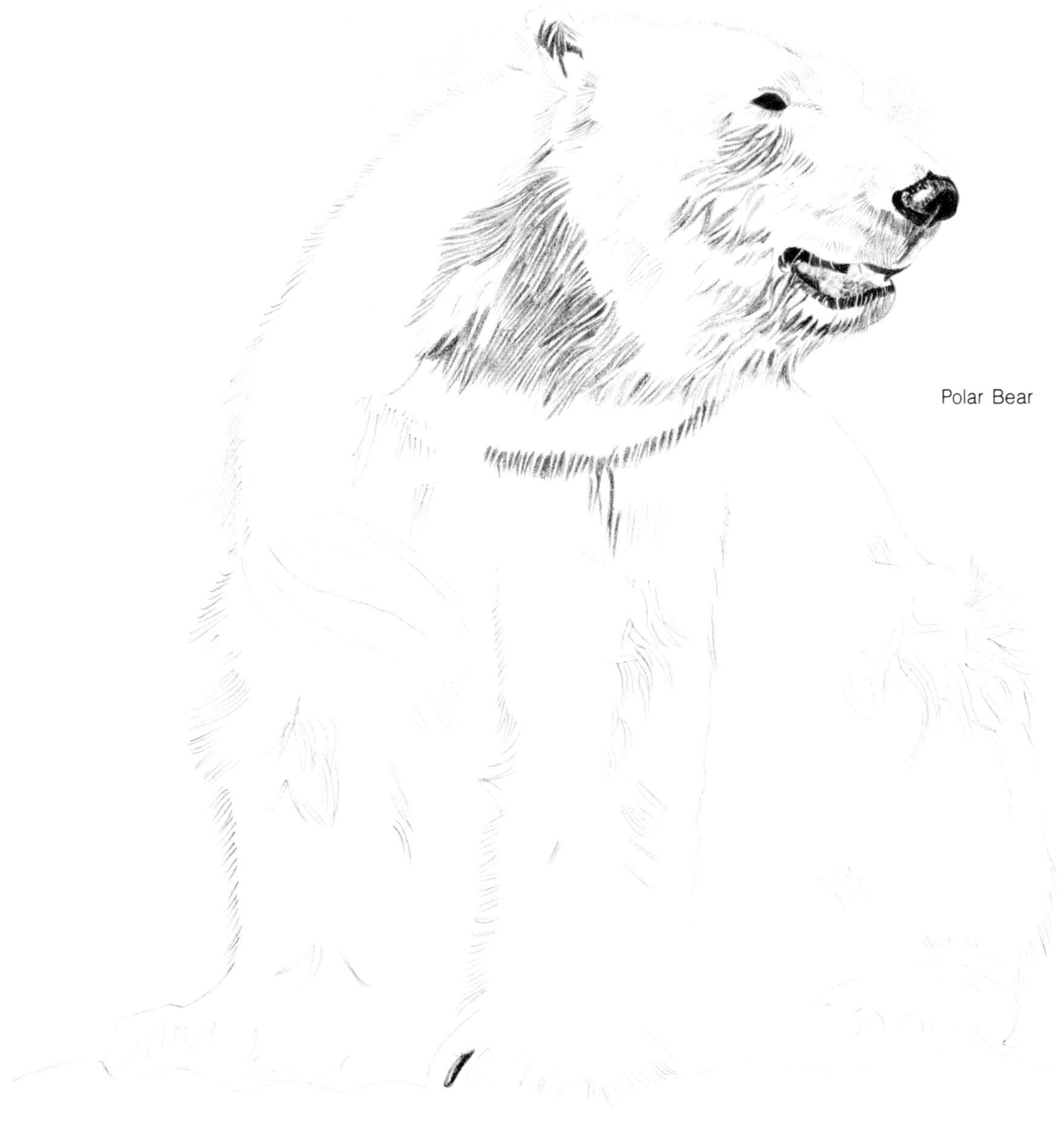

Polar Bear

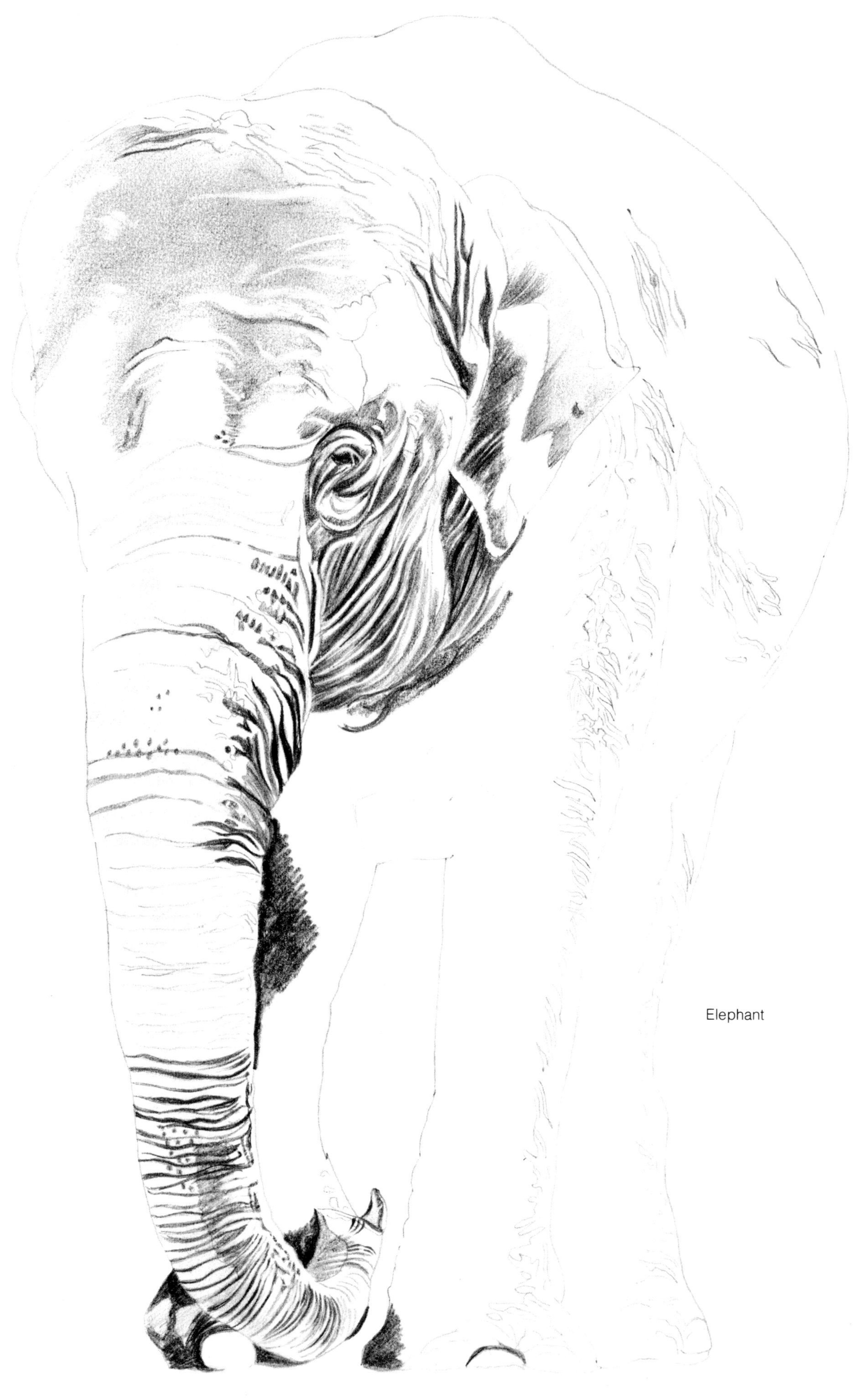

Elephant

soften areas of pencil tone. It can also be used to remove small mistakes and keep white areas clean.

The male lion is one of the most difficult animals to draw because the hairs in its body vary so much in length and texture. So I concentrated here on capturing the male lion's most dominant features—its large, noble head and the impressive mane that sets it apart from the rest of the cats.

First I sketched the lion's basic shape, taking great care to get the legs in exactly the right position. On the left, the front and rear legs are supporting the whole body weight, while both legs on the right are moving. Look at how the almost scaffold-straight front leg supports the whole of the lion's head and shoulders.

In drawing the mane, resist the temptation to symbolize a dark mane with either heavy strokes or solid shading. Here I drew very faint lines on the head and mane to separate areas of dark and light.

The hairs on the lion's face are very short and their direction describes its contours. To show this, use very gentle, short strokes with the point of the pencil, and direct them along the shape of the face as I have done. The hair on the mane is long and of varying color. Use the point of the pencil gently to draw long hairs that move roughly in the same direction, but by different paths. The mane touches the face at the top like a sudden outcrop of hair. Many artists use the side of the pencil to portray large areas of short hair, but I prefer the point of the pencil as the result is cleaner, better defined, and more lifelike.

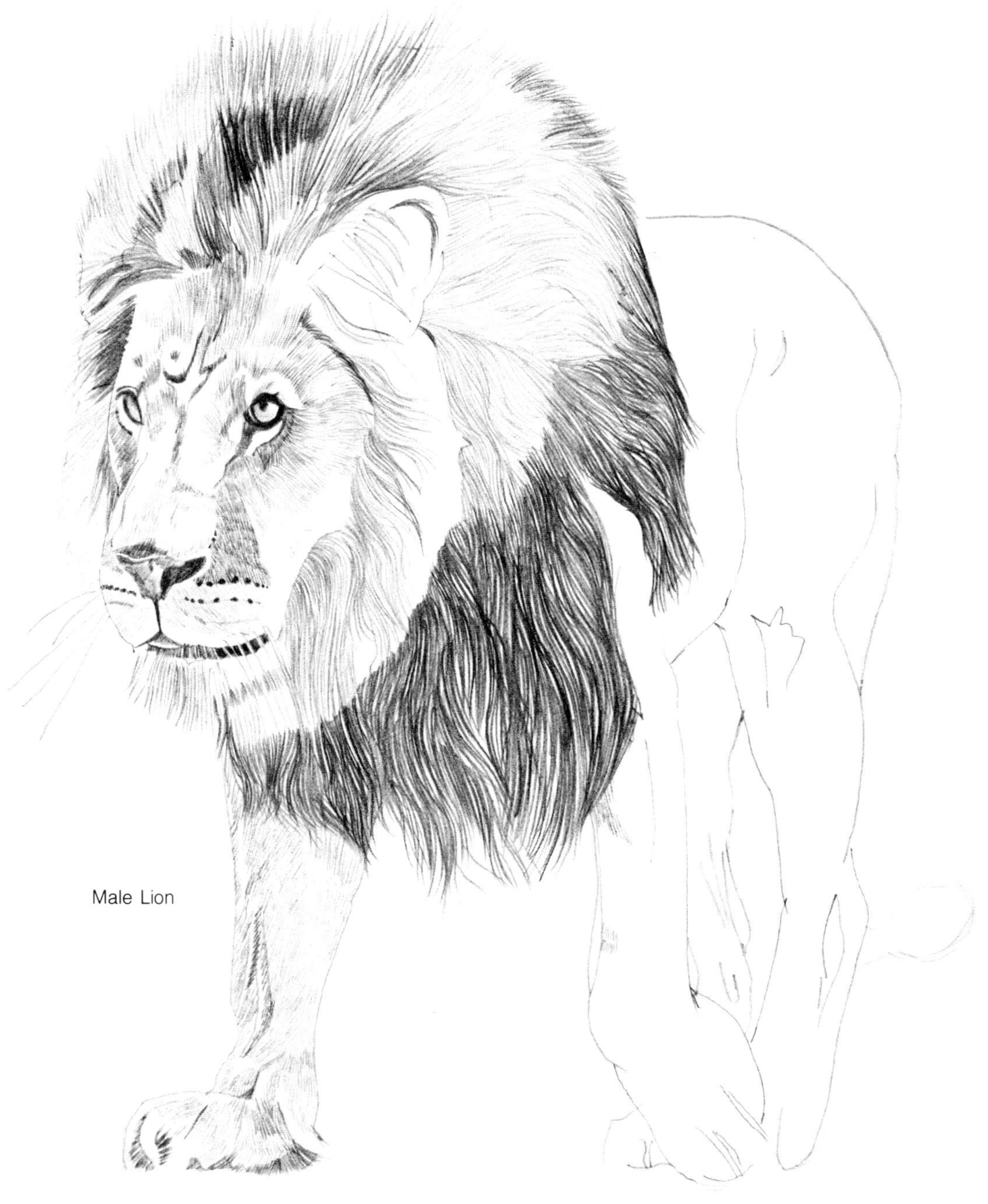

Male Lion

Apes and Monkeys

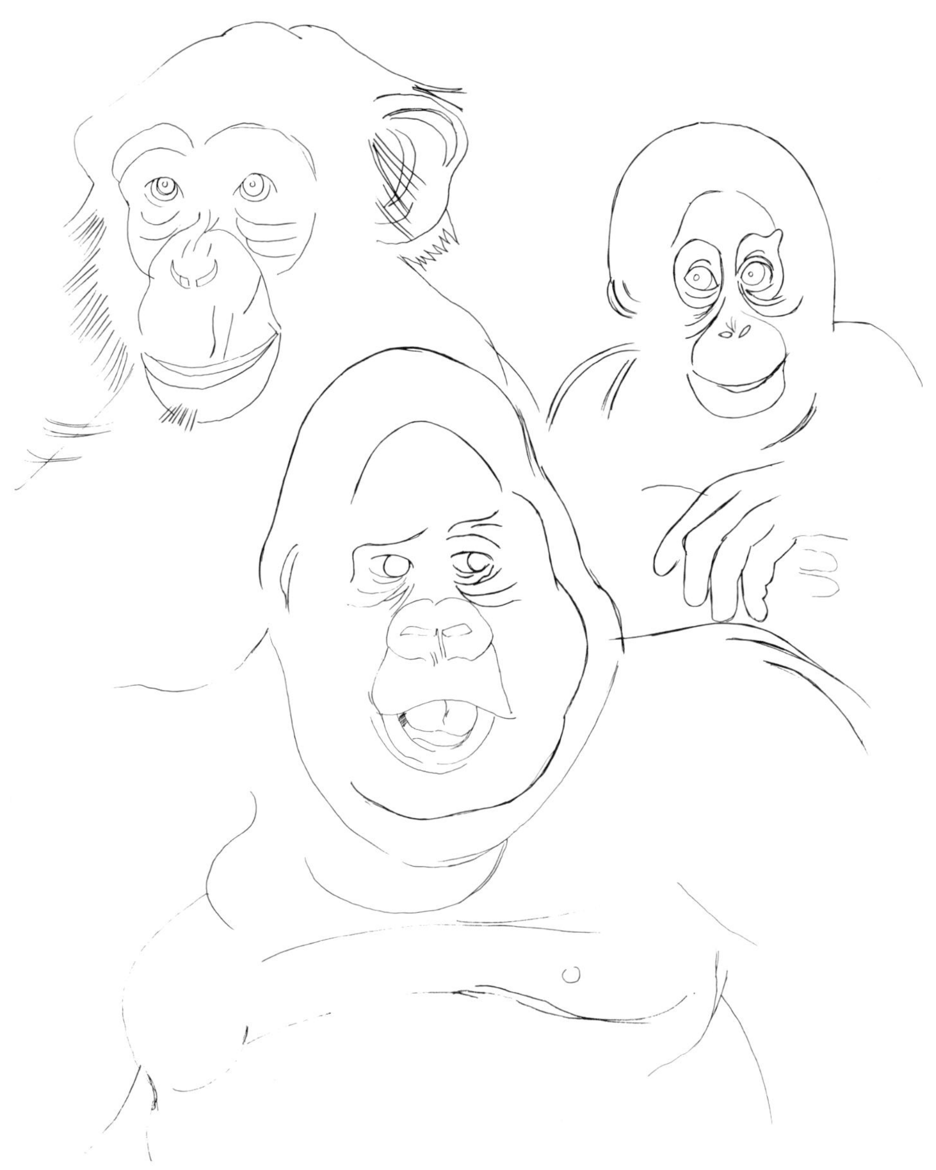

Shapes

I love drawing apes because of their similarity to man. Gorillas, in particular, are fascinating because their vast bulk and strength is combined with a gentle sensitivity. Imagine a chest measurement of 6 feet, an arm span from fingertip to fingertip of over 9 feet, 23½ inches of unexpanded bicep, a neck 36 inches in circumference, and a weight of 420 pounds—and all this packed into a stooping height of 5 feet 8 inches, and combined with a peaceful and passive nature.

Chimpanzees and orangutans are fascinating, too. The chimpanzee's eyes are lustrous and totally expressive, and the orangutan grows through all of the visible "seven stages of man."

Details

Chimpanzees are beautiful. Somehow they remind me of a distant uncle, but without any of the nastiness that humans so often demonstrate.

I started by very carefully drawing the shape, paying a lot of attention to the exact placement of the features and the expression, and then lavished a great deal of care on the eyes. Chimp eyes are a lot more lustrous than human eyes, and because the pupils are so black and the surrounding pigment colors so deep, the eye's expression has a depth that is fascinating, with childlike purity.

The difficulty in drawing any of the apes is in rendering a mixture of hair and sometimes a human-type skin texture. It's like drawing a human portrait! I drew guidelines for the wrinkles and furrows on the fleshy part of the chimp's face and then gently etched in the darker tones of the shadows. The hair sections were done with single strokes of the pencil and I avoided using solid shading because it wouldn't allow the light to show between separate pencil strokes. I was unable to achieve sufficient depth and shine to the eyes, so I cheated and added an almost water-free gouache white highlight to the pupils with a no. 00 brush. I also picked out the white hairs on the chimp's chin, where they extended over the black area of his chest with a fine brush and some process white.

The orangutan pictured here is just a baby. But even so, he also has many of the expressions and characteristics of an older orangutan. I gently sketched in a contour map of wrinkles and features plus an indication of the dark and light areas. Then I concentrated on the eyes because again, if these lack character, the drawing won't look right. In order to get a deep effect I used a block of solid graphite (a rectangle of graphite without a wood casing) and filled in the blueprint lines sketched earlier, taking care not to fill in the pre-drawn eye highlights. The gray area bordering the eye was softly rendered with a 2B pencil. The skin of the forehead and cheeks is fairly dark and covered with small, pale freckles. I had already drawn these freckles, so the next job was to softly shade the area around them.

Then I made a mistake. Before applying hairs, I impatiently shaded in the head area of the orangutan with the side of my pencil instead of ren-

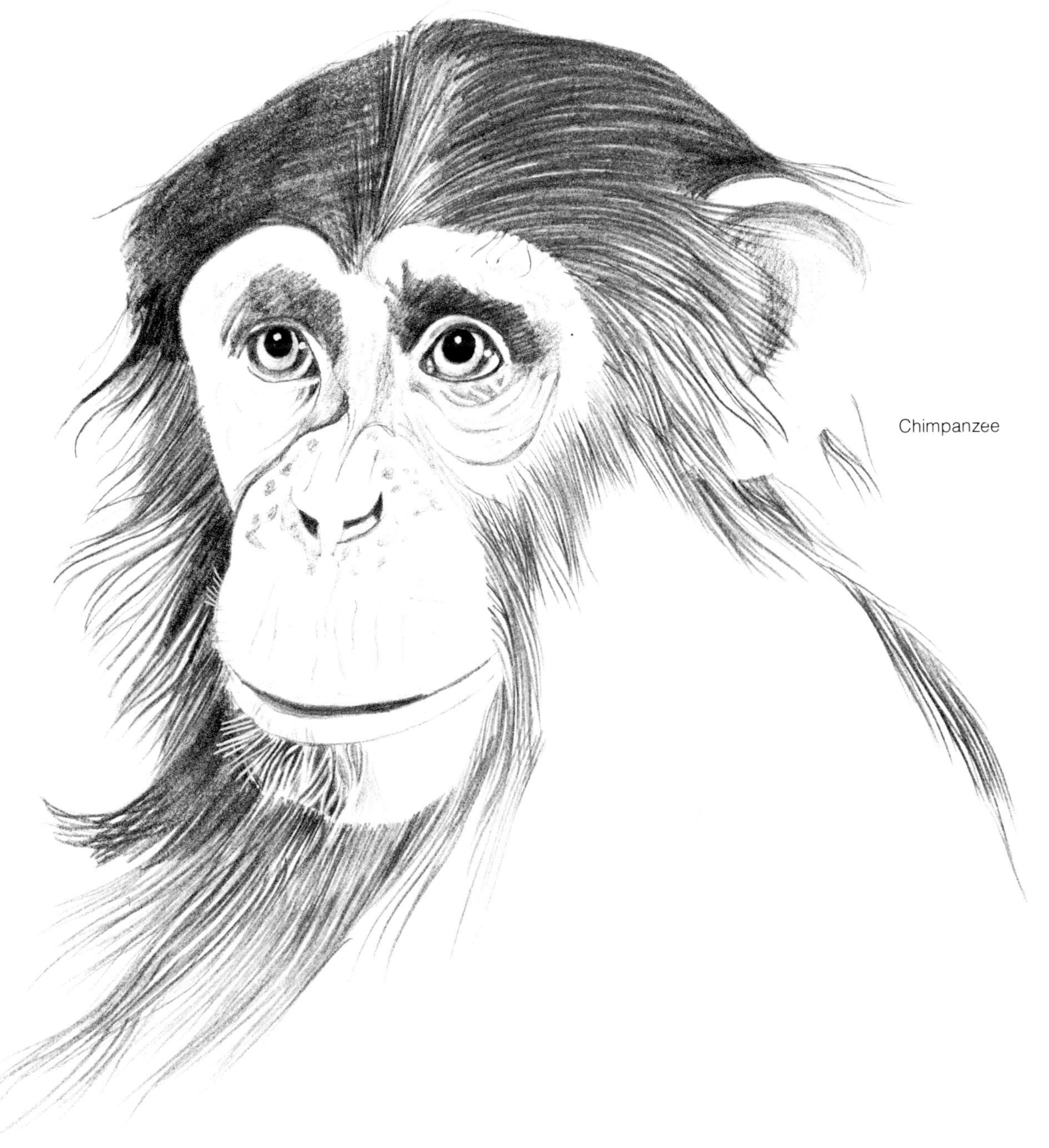

Chimpanzee

dering each hair individually on a white ground. As a result, the drawing is smudgy and ill-defined. If you compare this drawing to the next one you will see what I mean. The moral of the story is that professionals make plenty of mistakes, so don't be discouraged when you do. The charm of art is its uncertainty. Because I earn my living by painting, I can't afford to wait for the right mood, but if you can, it is best to draw or paint when you feel right. There are definitely good and bad days.

This gorilla is the only finished picture in the drawing section. The original is about 3 feet × 2 feet (91 × 61 cm), so the rendering is close to life-size. It is a portrait of Guy, the London Zoo's Cameroon lowland gorilla, and hangs in the Zoological Society's art collection. I included it because I wanted to demonstrate exactly how far you can go with just a pencil. An enormous amount of care and attention has gone into this picture because I wanted to capture the true essence of this now-endangered relative of man.

All of the techniques have been used: fine, short strokes; gentle etching; hard, definite strokes; and highlights picked out with a kneaded eraser. Perhaps when you finish reading this book you may feel that pencil drawing suits you more than watercolor. For my part, if I never ever produce another good painting, this picture is justification enough for choosing art as a career and hobby.

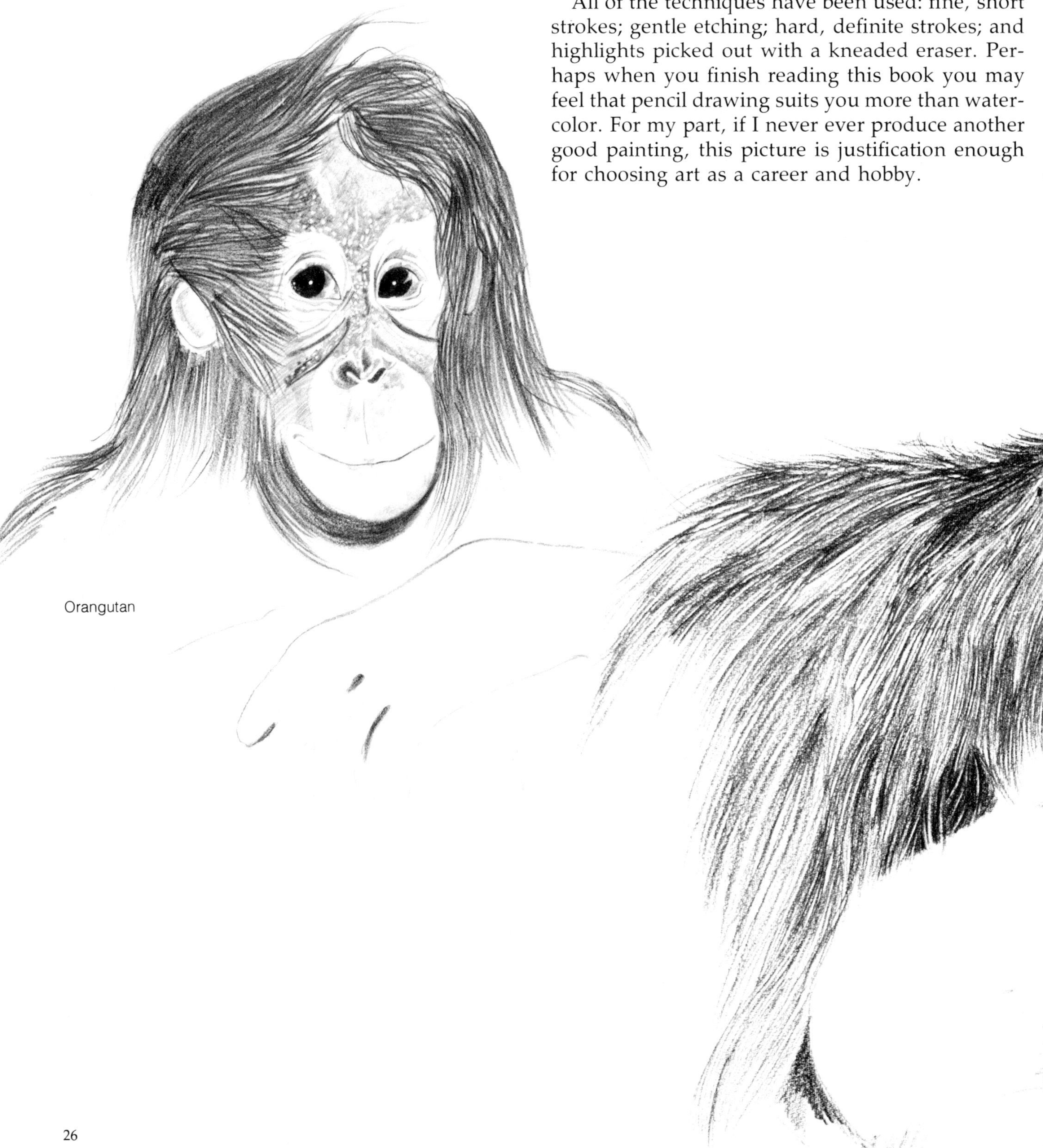

Orangutan

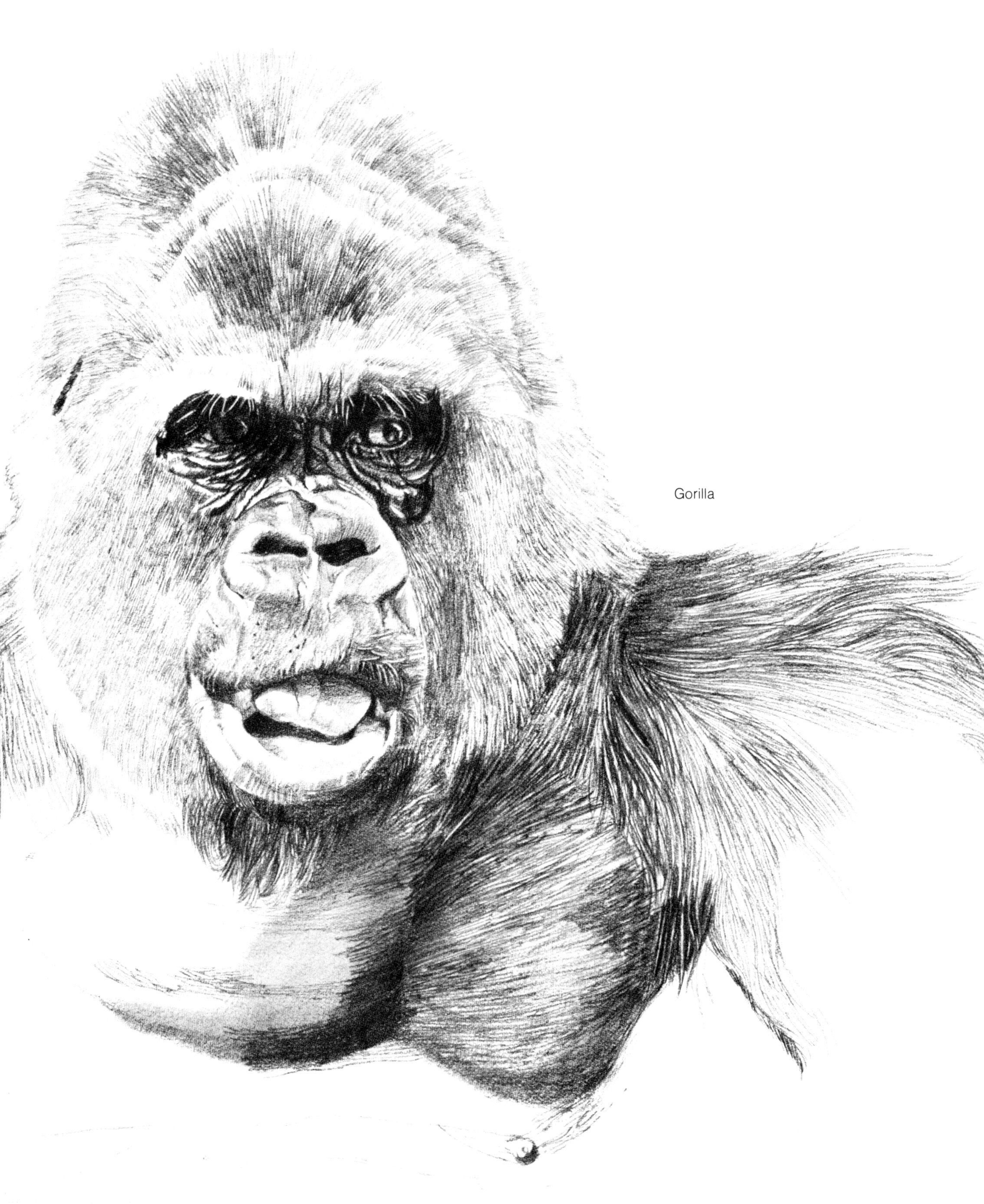

Gorilla

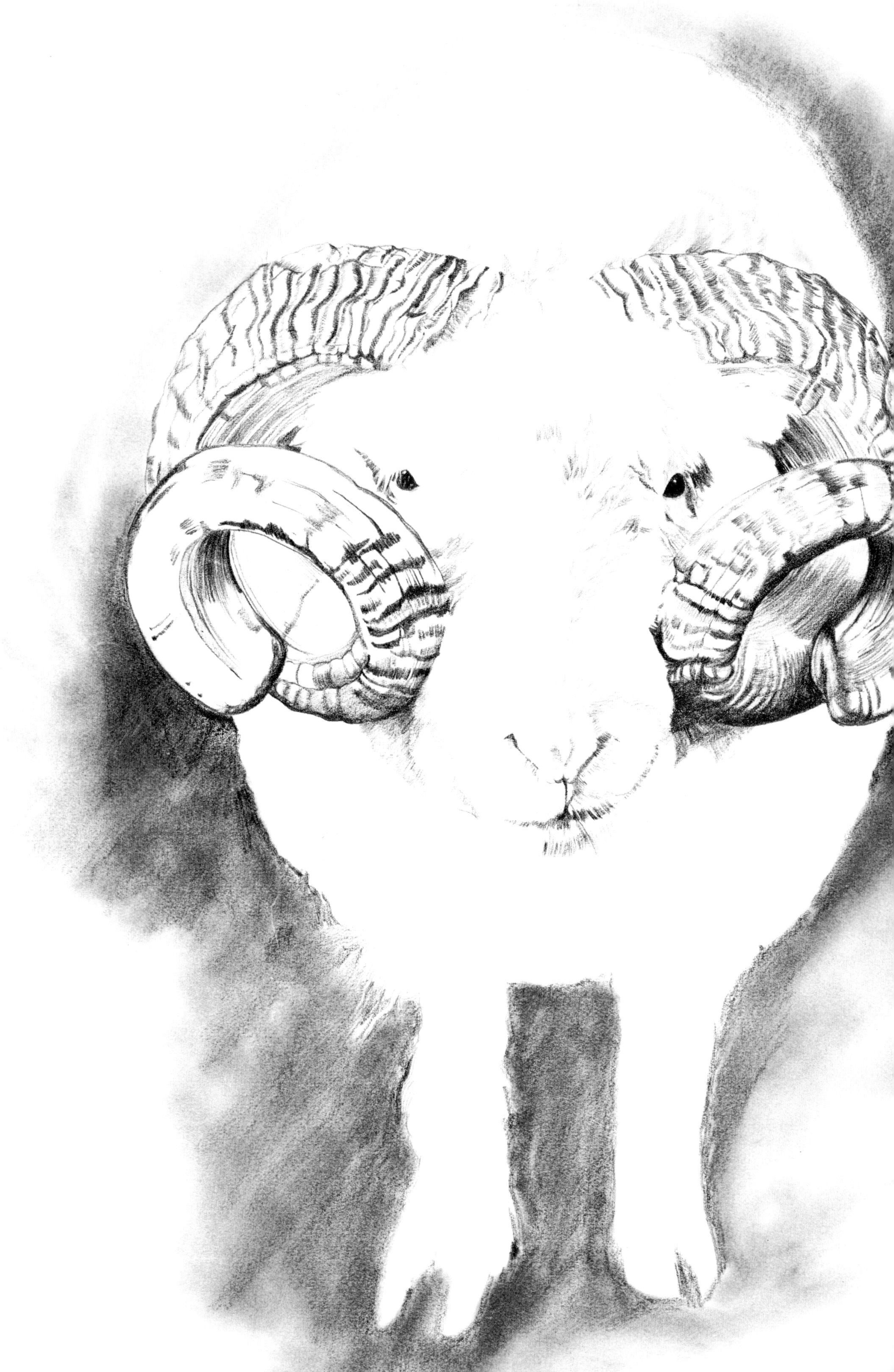

Part Three

Looking at Animals

THIS NEXT SECTION describes how to draw and paint the character-defining parts of various animals—eyes, horns, feet, noses, etc. When painting animals, it is wise to recognize that certain parts of the animal reveal the essence of that particular species. The eyes of a mature predator, for example, are harder and more crisply defined than, say, those of a hunted animal or of a very young or old animal. Horns are also differently constructed in an evolutionary sense according to the way the animal uses them and therefore vary considerably in shape as well as texture. Feet can almost symbolize an animal (as in the case of polar bears, mountain goats, or a cheetah), and painting them properly can make or break a picture. Most of the time, when using a photograph, it's difficult to really study the organic construction of an animal part, unless the photograph is extremely clear.

When you work from photographs, you must be aware that they flatten and take away three-dimensional form. Therefore, to understand the animal better, you must try to observe the living, moving animal—at zoos or in the wild—noting details of specific parts as well as observing the animal as a whole. Also try to get a hold of animal parts, such as a set of horns or a mounted head, and study them closely. Every bit of knowledge will go back into your painting and make you a better animal artist.

Eyes Give Life

Eyes are like water in a still lake—they reflect the colors of the sky or the vegetation. But because they are curved, they distort the shapes of the reflections in the same way that a photographer's fish-eye lens does. Mysteriously, they also reflect and express emotion, so that the eye of, say, a snarling cheetah will contain some indefinable quality that is quite different from the eye expression when the animal is calmly gazing into the distance. To the wildlife artist, the eyes are all-important. They can breathe life into a painting, if properly expressed.

The following pages of my sketchbook are devoted to eyes and how to draw and paint them. Even though the eyes are separated from surrounding features, you can see quite clearly whether the animal is calm or angry, whether the animal is a predator or a hunted species, and even whether it has great intelligence or not.

Cat Eyes

These eyes belong to a cheetah that is gazing, but here the sun is directly overhead so large, dark shadows from the lid and the brow darken half of the eyes.

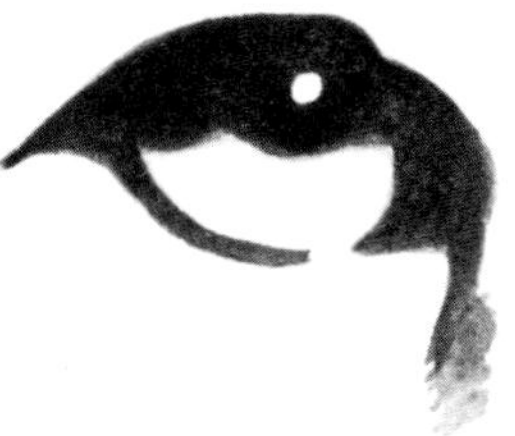

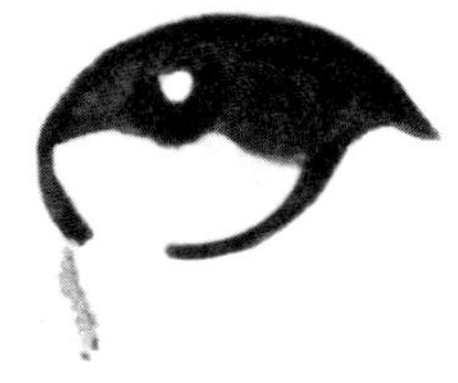

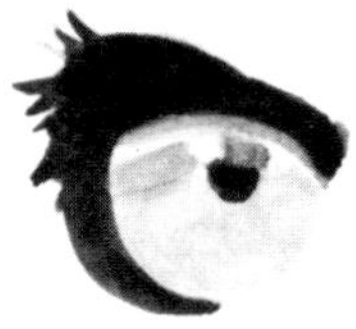

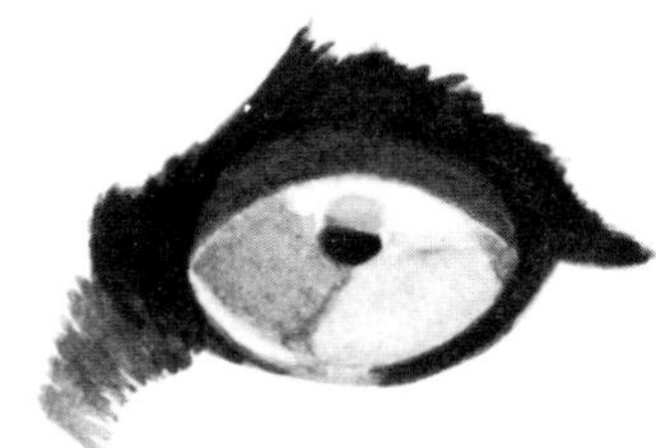

Here the cheetah has lifted its head so that the light throws a reflection across the center of the eye while the brow and lids continue to darken the top half with their shadow.

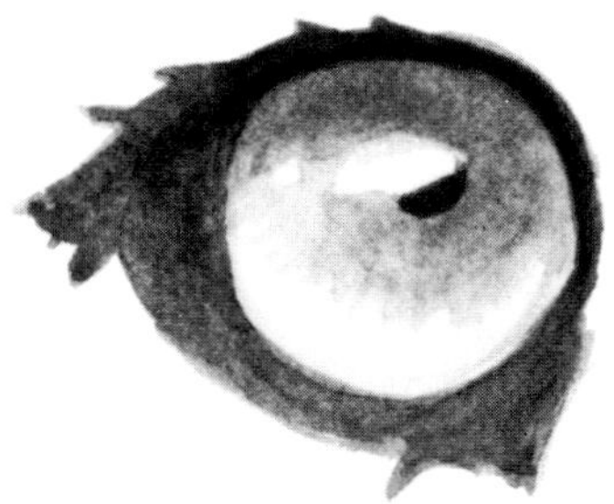

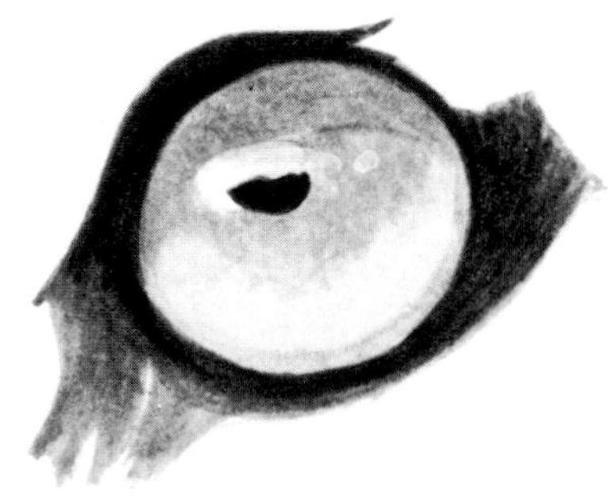

These eyes belong to a lioness staring intently on a moving object in middle distance.

Drawing the Eyes of a Lioness

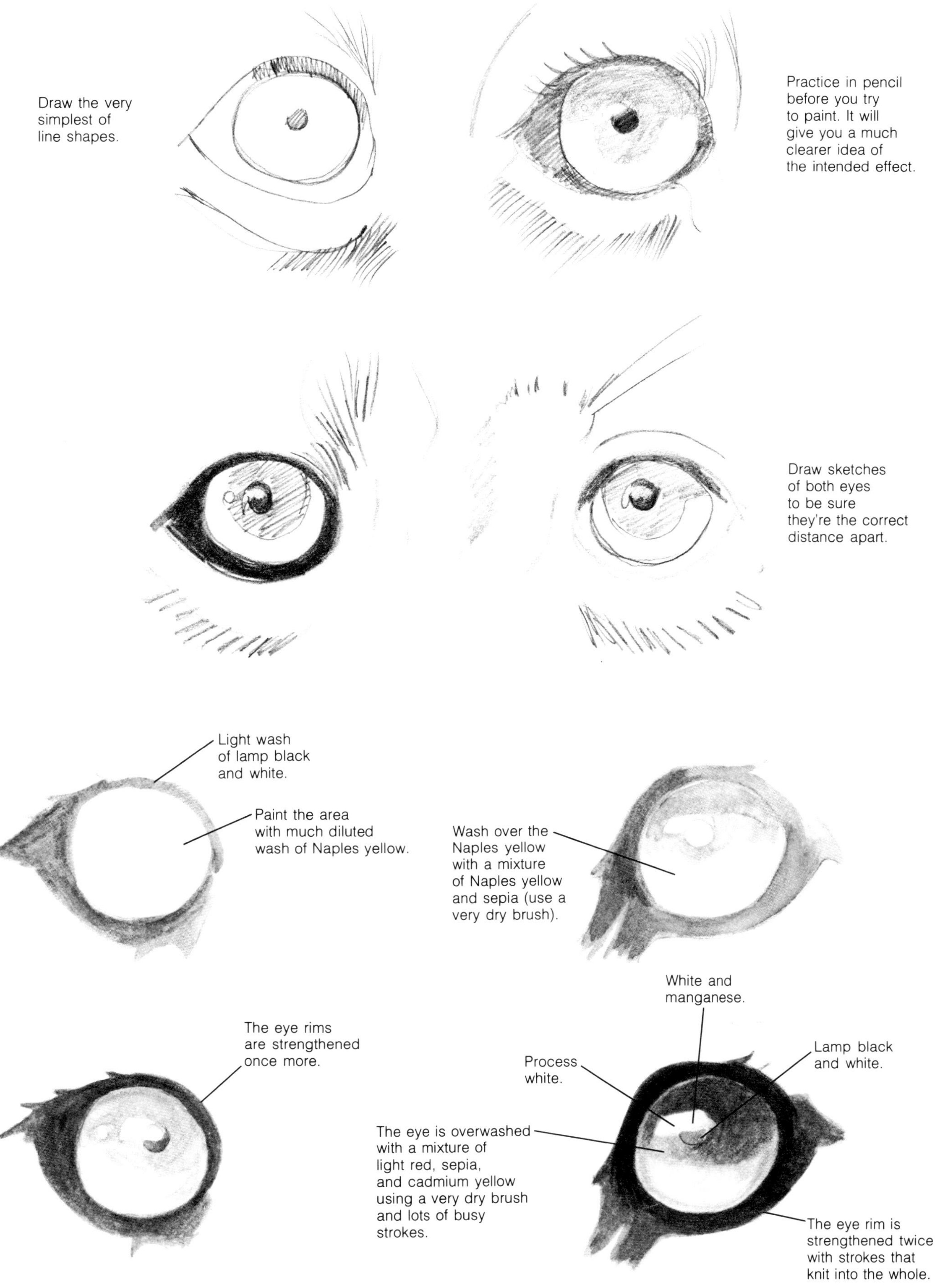

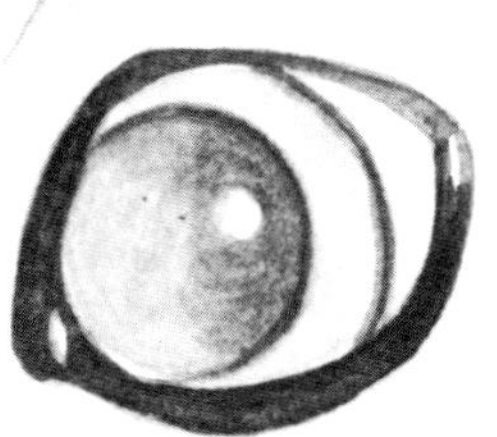

The hare's eye shows the alarm and the wide-awake alertness of the continually hunted.

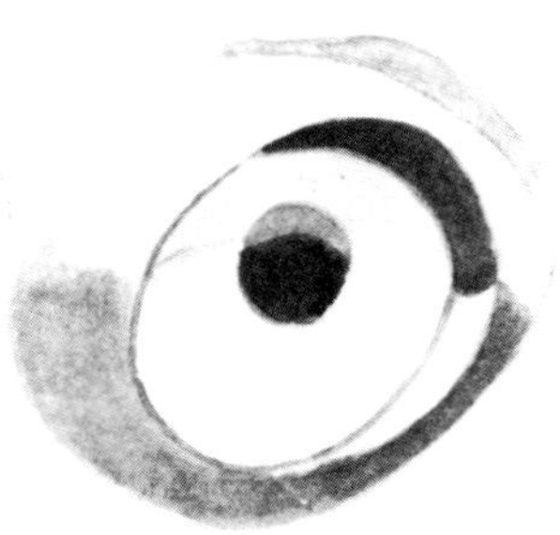

The crested crane (which is a zoo specimen) has an eye with a blank, almost enigmatic quality.

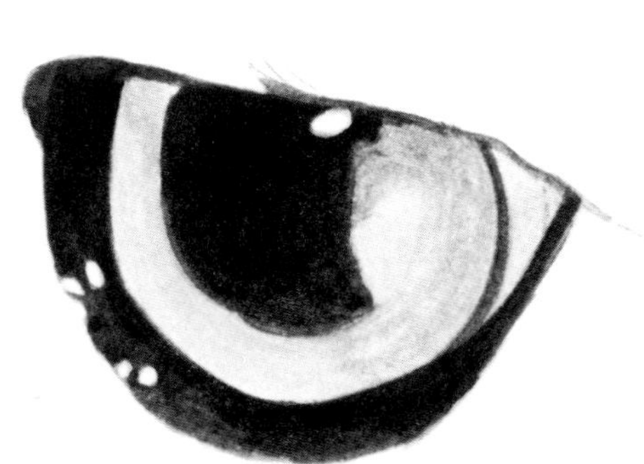

The fox is confident and does not even recognize fear as a possibility. Its expression is bold and unfaltering.

Drawing Hare Eyes

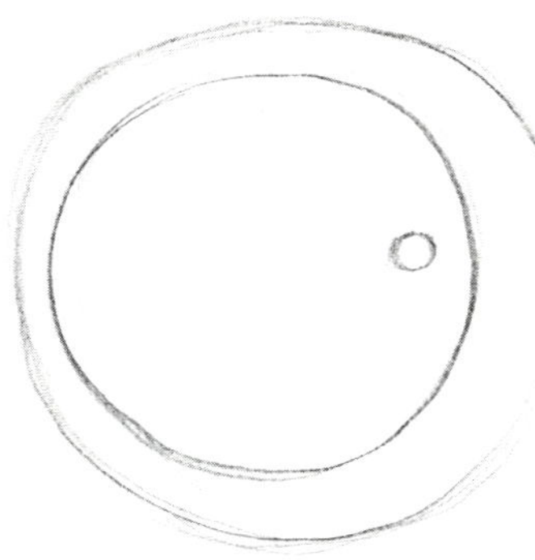

It's easier to start with the inner circles of the eye and then add the outer rim when the circles themselves are correct. Don't be tempted into drawing around a coin, as this will look far too rigid.

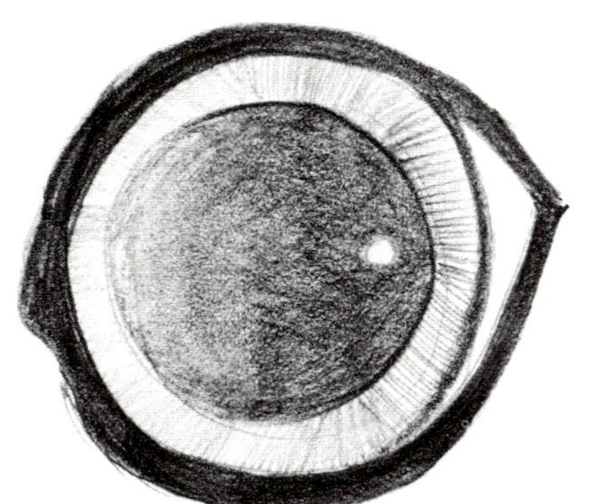

Shade with a 2B pencil.

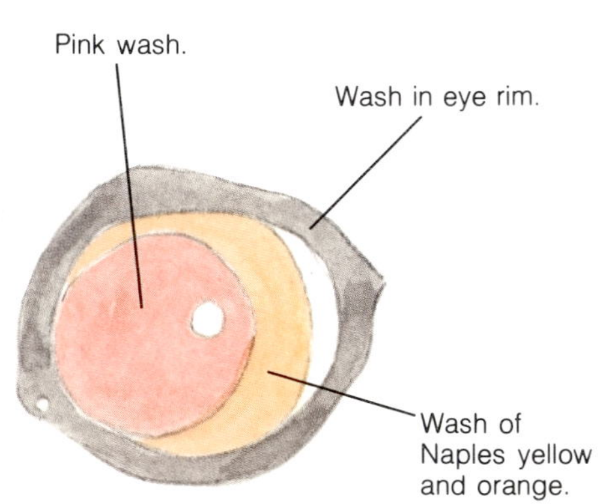

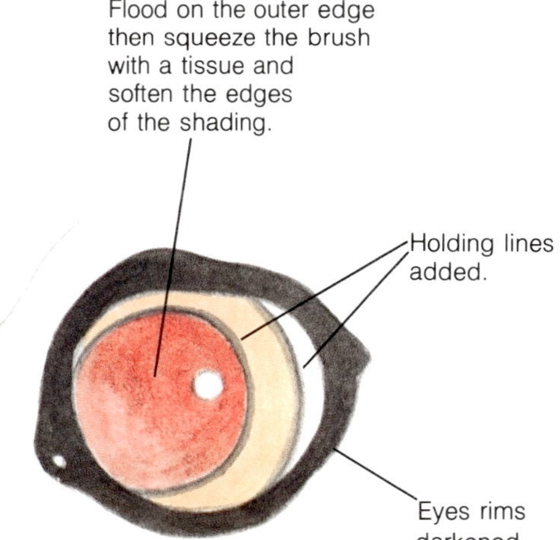

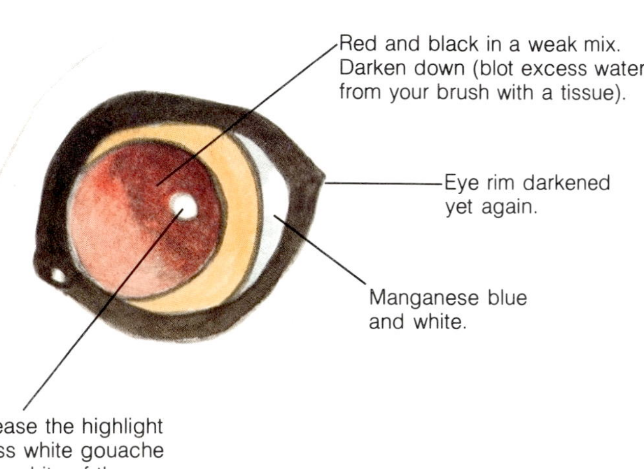

Eyes Express Personality

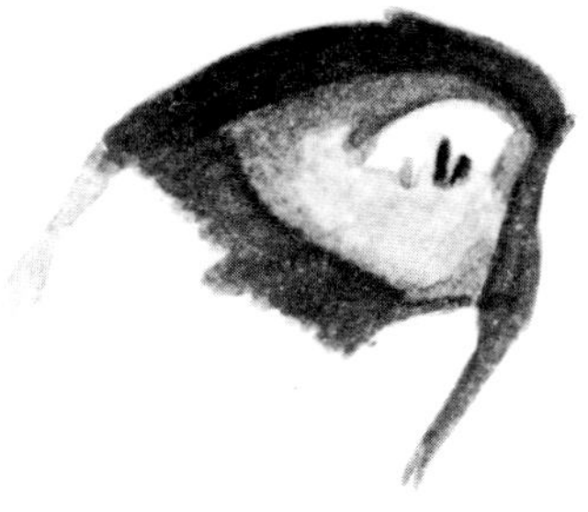

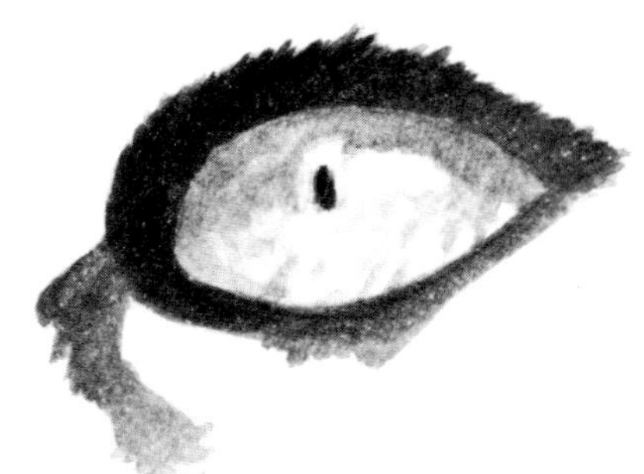

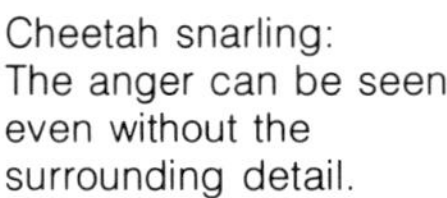

Cheetah snarling:
The anger can be seen even without the surrounding detail.

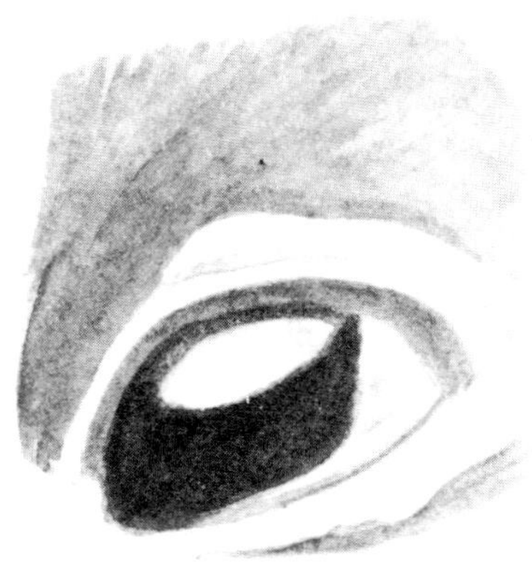

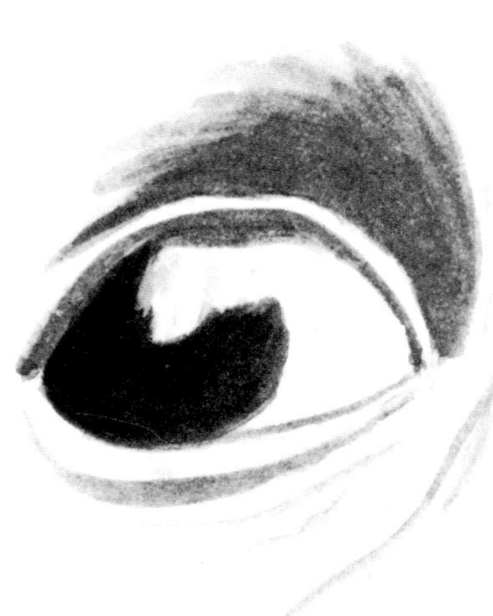

Baby gorilla:
Intelligence, vulnerability, and youth are all evident.

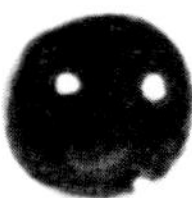

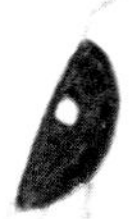

English dormouse:
Small, beady, ever-alert eyes.

Drawing Gorilla Eyes

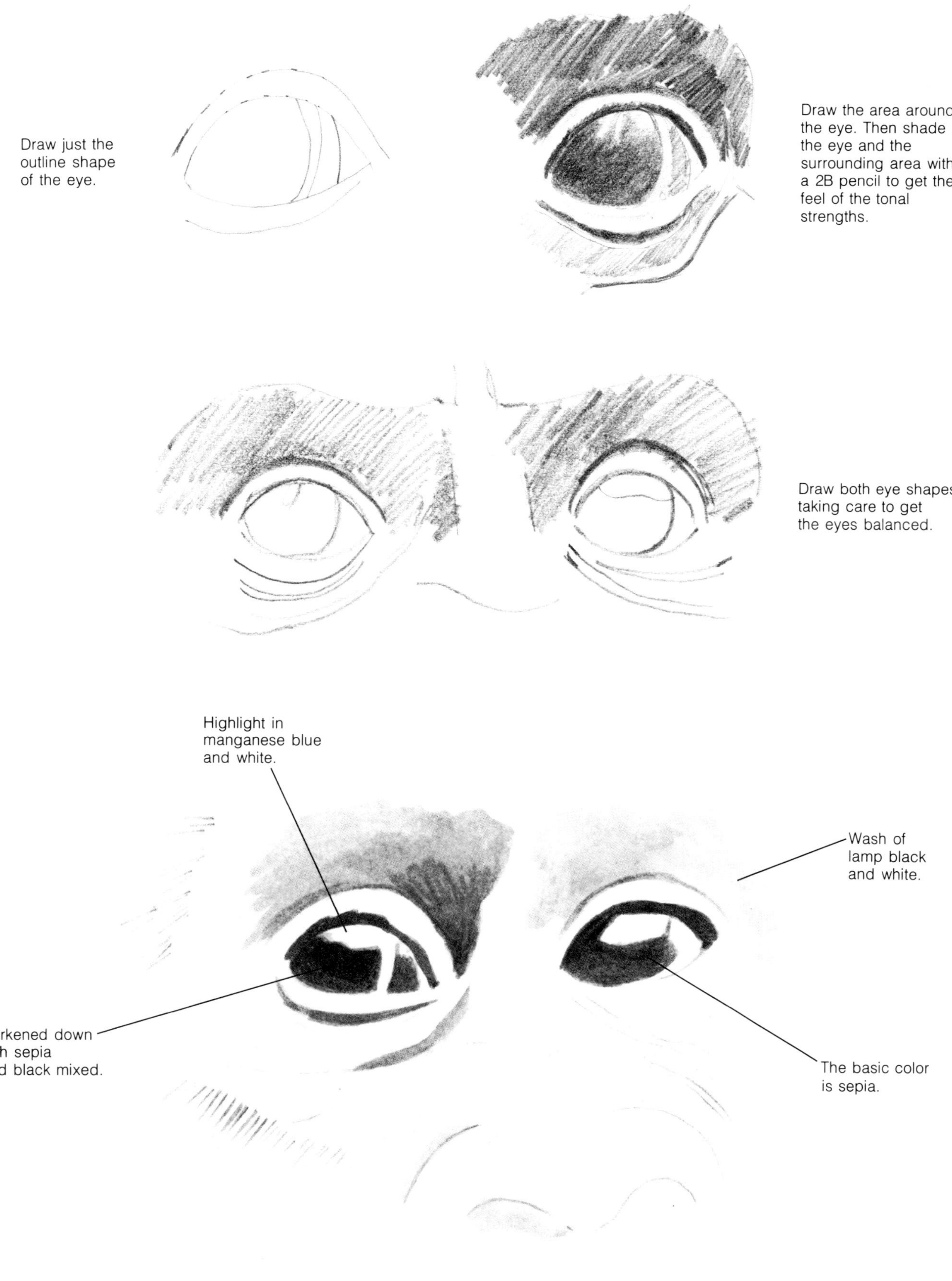

I have kept the painting simple so that the colors and technique are clear. Aim to achieve your effect through many light washes of color rather than with one heavy paint application.

Young and Old Eyes

Here is an absolutely key lesson. We can go on painting eyes forever (and I hope that we all do), but the effort in achieving good technique often obscures some of the most important observations. What is it that gives one animal's eyes the ruthless decisiveness of an intent killer, another the haunted, concerned look of the hunted, and another the vulnerability of youth?

It's easy to assume that is not the eye itself but the immediate surrounding area that creates the expression, but this is not entirely true, as my drawings over the last few pages prove. Let's examine just what it is that gives an eye a particular mood that is recognizable as an emotion and a statement of the animal's age and demeanor.

The large eyes are those of an adult snowy owl. The smaller pair belong to a snowy owl chick, young enough to still be nest-bound and down-covered.

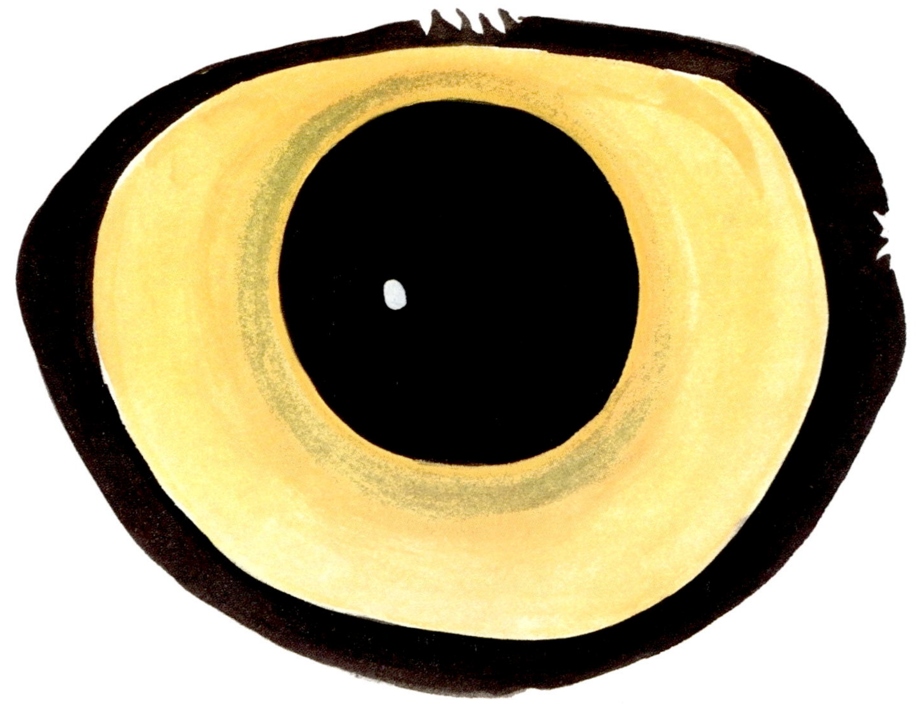

Snowy Owl: Chick

These young eyes have been executed with a completely different technique. The colors are soft, there is more light in the eye, and definition is nowhere near as firm. The smudgy technique makes the eyes look soft and uncertain.

The laws of nature hold true. The firm, crisp line and strong colors of the adult eyes denote a decisive mood and provide an image that reflects a firm, strong, and crisp condition, while pale colors and barely defined lines produce a soft image.

Snowy Owl: Adult

The absolute lack of fear and the merciless expression show a mature hunter. Imagine being a rodent! In terms of art, the call-out points on the sketch show the technique needed to capture what is needed.

The lines of the adult (the rims of the eyes and the pupils) are strong, crisp, and sure. The pigment is darker and the colors more uncompromising. Placement of the small, diamond-hard glint of light in the center of the pupil seems to give the eye its expression of intent as well as the direction of its stare. The pupil itself is almost jet black.

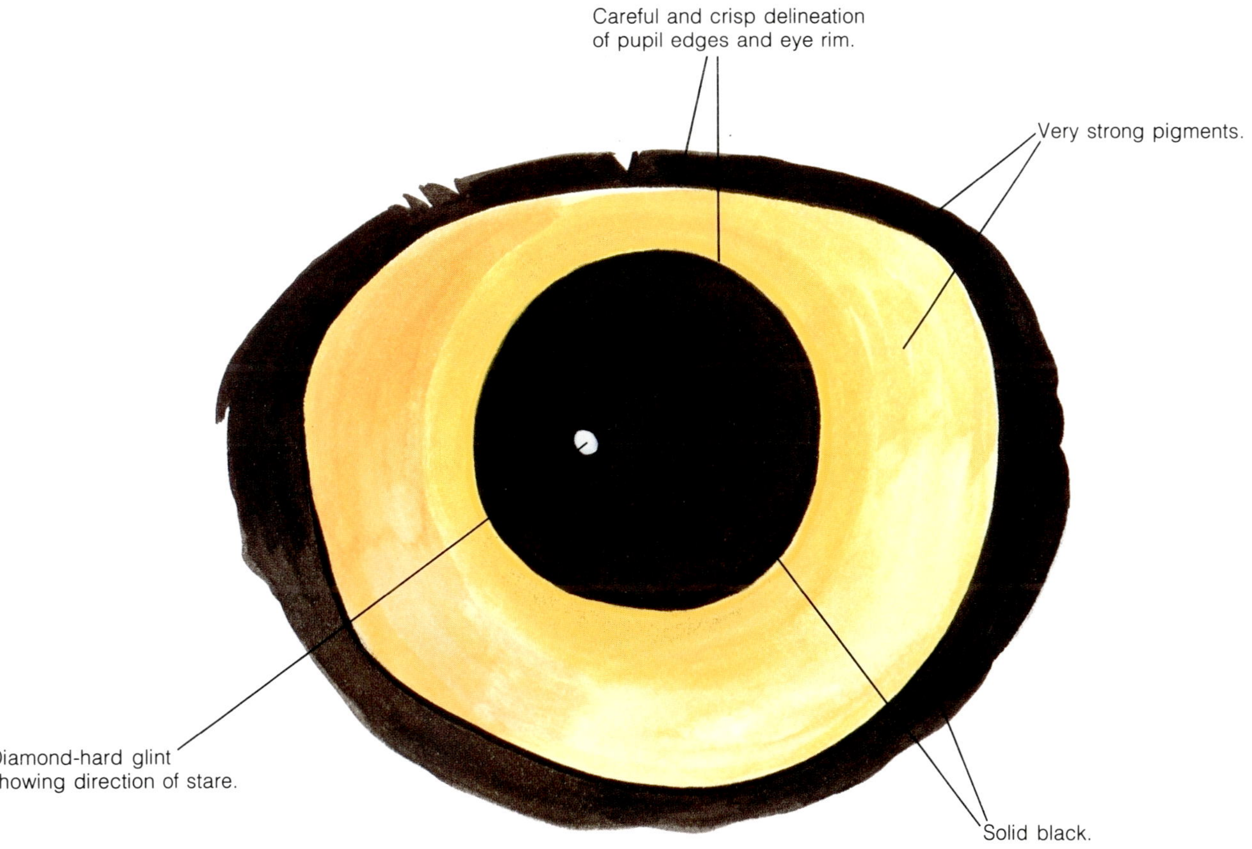

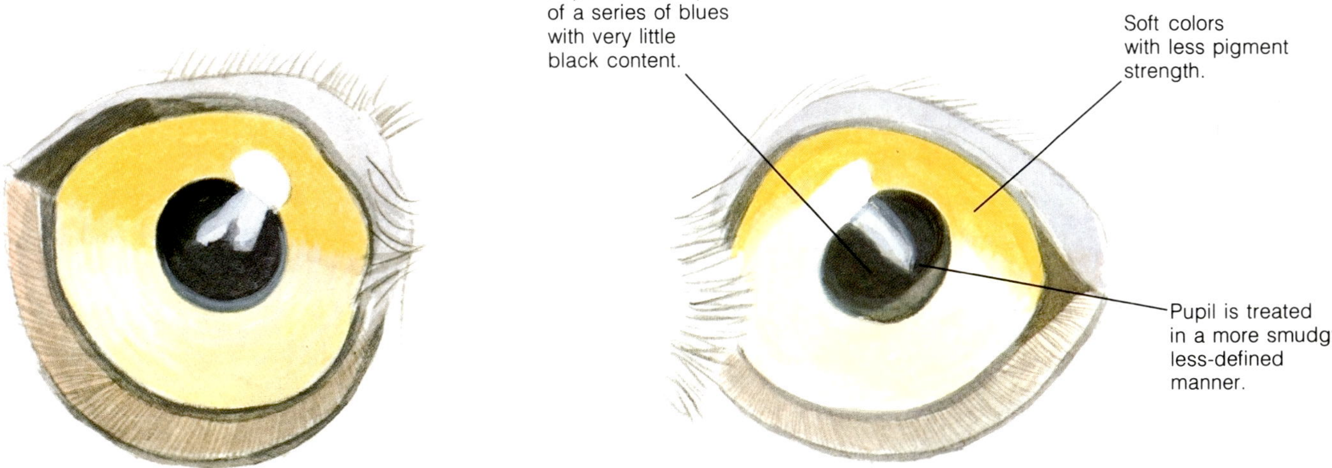

Hair: Direction, Texture, and Pattern

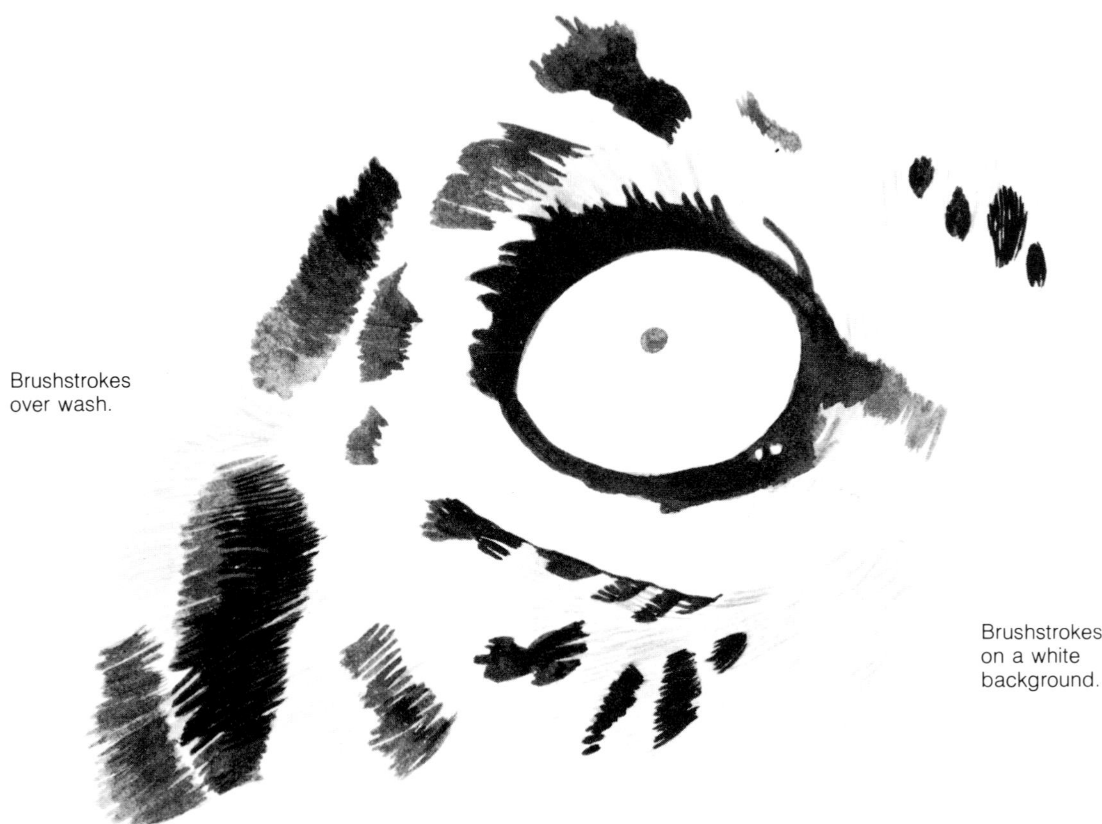

Practice hair strokes so that you become adroit at painting fine or coarse and long or short hairs without effort. Experiment with paint thickness and brush type to see what suits you best.

Paint Application

I have used a section of the head of a leopard as an example, since its hair direction is fairly typical of all of the shorter-haired cats. I've also kept my brushstrokes coarse so that you can clearly see the technique. First I drew a blueprint in pencil, then with a no. 4 brush and a mixture of light red and pale yellow in a dryish mix, I drew the lines of the fur straight onto the white board. This method, of course, can vary depending on the effect you want to achieve.

Some of the hairs were painted over a wash of Naples yellow, while other hairs are on a white background. Again, choose the method you prefer. A wash with overlaid strokes will give solidity and is ideal where the animal is partly in shadow and form and shape are important. On the other hand, hairs painted straight onto the white board give a cleaner and more dramatic effect.

Hair Direction

I have sketched the head of a leopard to show the absolute importance of drawing the correct hair direction. Hairs bend around shapes (that goes for spots, stripes, and patterns, too). They differ in length and vary in thickness, depending on their location on the body or head. Practice drawing a curve and bending the hairs around it. In order to fully understand the principle, which is an absolutely key one, look closely at the drawing.

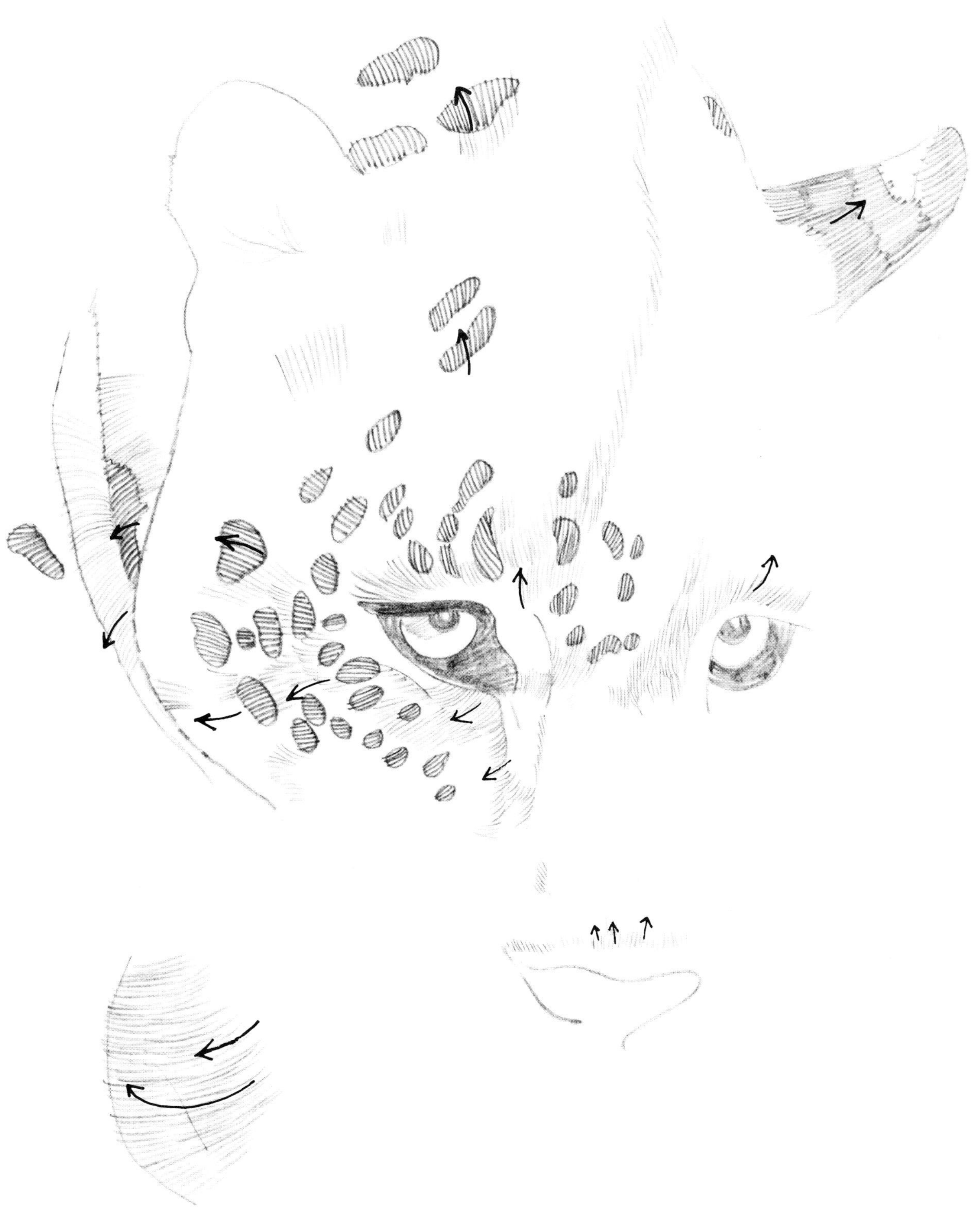

Layering Hair

Painting one wash over another works beautifully on some animals, especially those depicted in middle distance or those possessing a velvety, soft coat—any animal, in fact, whose coat is shown in a precise and detailed fashion. I also find this technique perfect for animals who are basically one color, with shades of the same color within their coats, as it allows light and movement into the picture. Lots of painters find that they work better in a linear style than a washy style. It takes more patience, but better results are more certain.

The fox is a good subject for this technique. The hairs on its muzzle are short, defined, and directional and lighter color shows through the gaps between some of the dark hairs. Remember that any technique is good only if followed with some license. The band of gradating color should help you to decipher just what has happened here.

On both the fox and the puma, I applied a wash with a 3/8″ (8mm) flat brush. After the wash had dried I used a blunt, no. 00 brush to tick in light hairs, and then changed to a well-pointed brush and slowly built up the detail. I finished by cutting out lighter hairs with gouache process white, either used alone or mixed with the lighter colors in the painting. Everyone has a patience limit, so make sure you're not working too large. The pictures here were painted same size.

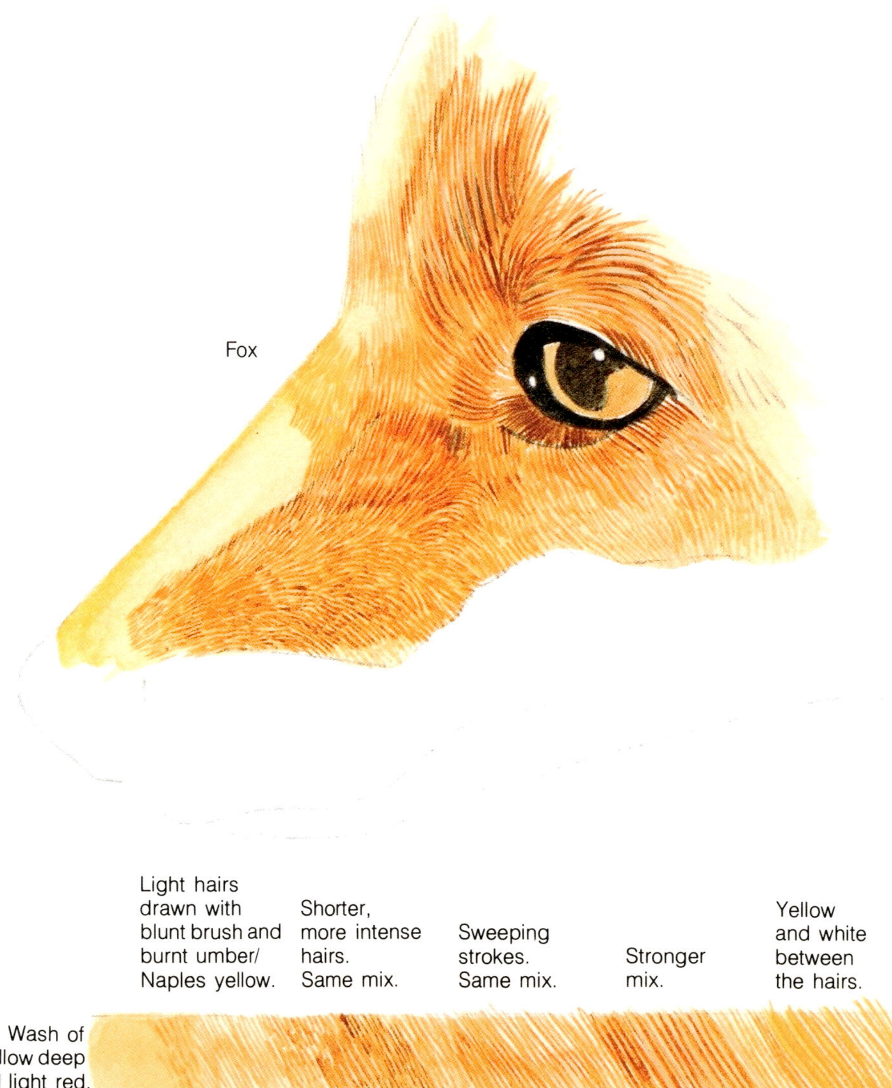

Fox

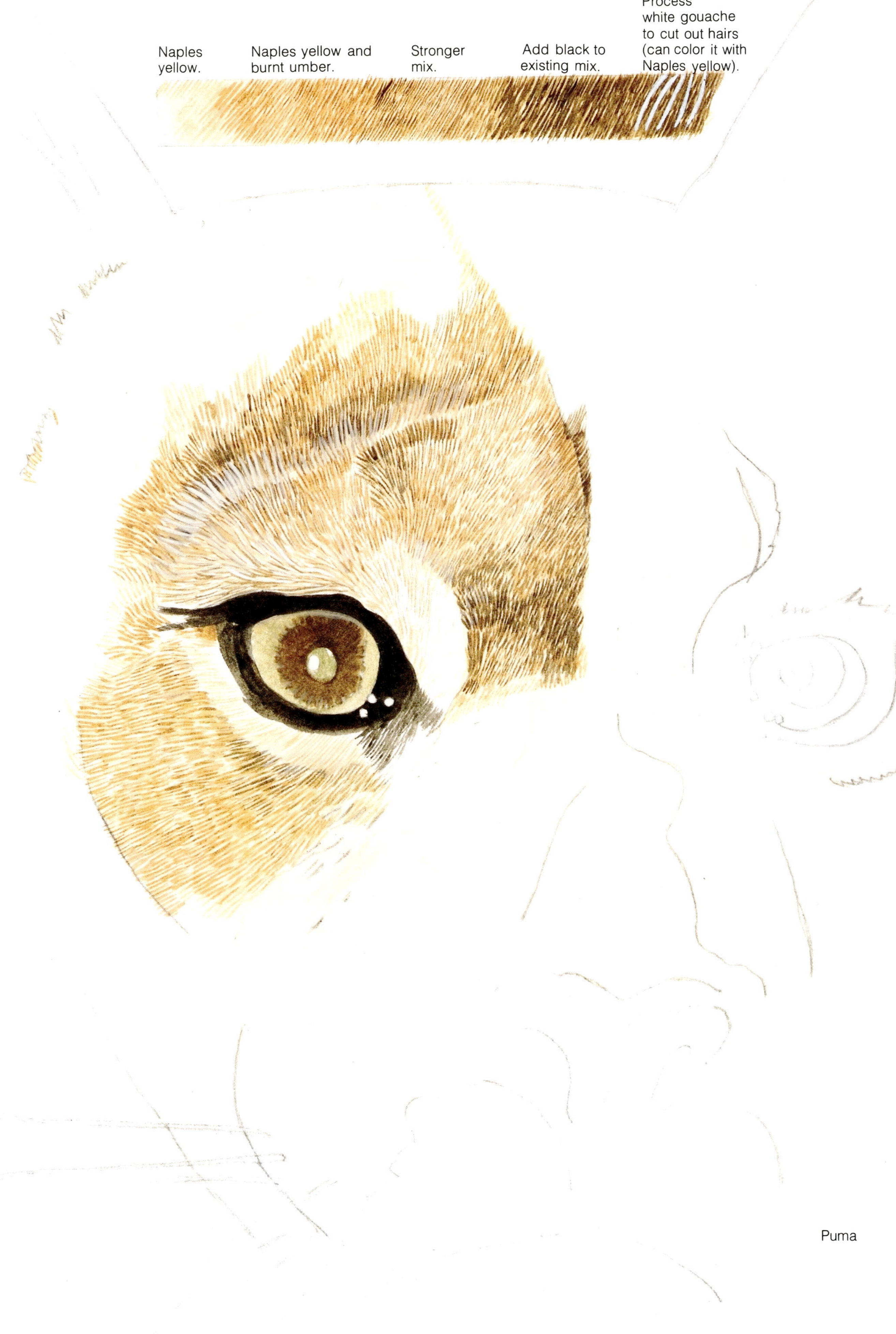
Naples
yellow.
Naples yellow and
burnt umber.
Stronger
mix.
Add black to
existing mix.
Process
white gouache
to cut out hairs
(can color it with
Naples yellow).

Puma

Painting Tiger Fur

The small squares are arranged in the order that the various colors, brushes, and techniques are used in this sketch:

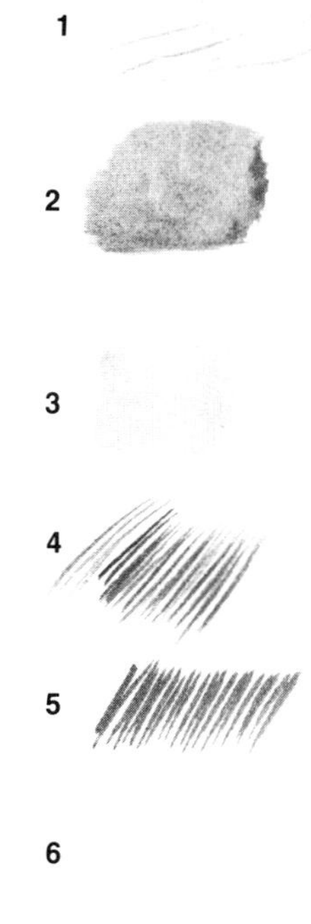

1. I sketched in a blueprint drawing of outlines using an HB pencil, making sure that those lines to be covered by shadow would still be visible.

2. With a 3/8″ (8mm)-wide flat brush and a very dry mixture of burnt sienna and raw umber, I flatly painted the shadowed areas of the tiger's face.

3. Using a fairly well-pointed no. 4 round brush, I washed in the tiger's black stripes, leaving gaps where white hairs would cross the black.

4. With a stronger mixture of burnt sienna and raw umber and a finer brush, I overpainted the hairs in shadow.

5. Using the same brush, I ticked in the black of the stripes more firmly, this time noting the hair direction. With a finer brush and a weaker black, I ticked in dark hairs among the brown ones already painted.

6. Using a wash of black and white, I painted an area that would eventually be in darker shadow. (Don't forget that the white parts of the tiger go through graduated shadow changes, too.)

7. Using a weak mixture of light red and pale yellow and a very blunt no. 0 brush, I ticked in part of the sunlit area of the coat. (*Note:* The hairs on the nose and cheeks of a tiger, and on most cats, is short. This, combined with the obliterating effect of strong sunlight, means that fine detail is not necessary. Hence, a blunt brush and dabbing technique is enough.)

8. I finished painting the bleached area with dabs of thick process white. The sun is capable of removing all color when it strikes the subject in certain ways, which is why a brightly colored big cat like the tiger can camouflage itself in a host of different habitats so successfully. Light bleaches or fades color, shadow deepens it, and trees or shrubs break up the lines of the tiger, so it's impossible to say with accuracy and assurance that a Siberian tiger is painted in this color and a Sumatran tiger is painted in that one. The same goes for all other cats, though it's not quite as dramatic as with the tiger.

Besides the opportunities provided by light and shadow, license can be taken to dramatize detail. For example, the area behind whiskers can be darkened more than it actually appears so the whiskers stand out.

Hair: Dark and Light

Most student painters take too little account of light and shade because they believe it too complicated to describe. The result is that many opportunities to turn a flat picture into one with drama are lost.

This Siberian tiger was sitting in strong winter sunlight. The sun was on the right and slightly behind it. Three-quarters of its face was in dark shadow, while the right-hand quarter was so bleached by the strong sunlight that all detail, wherever the sun struck, was obliterated.

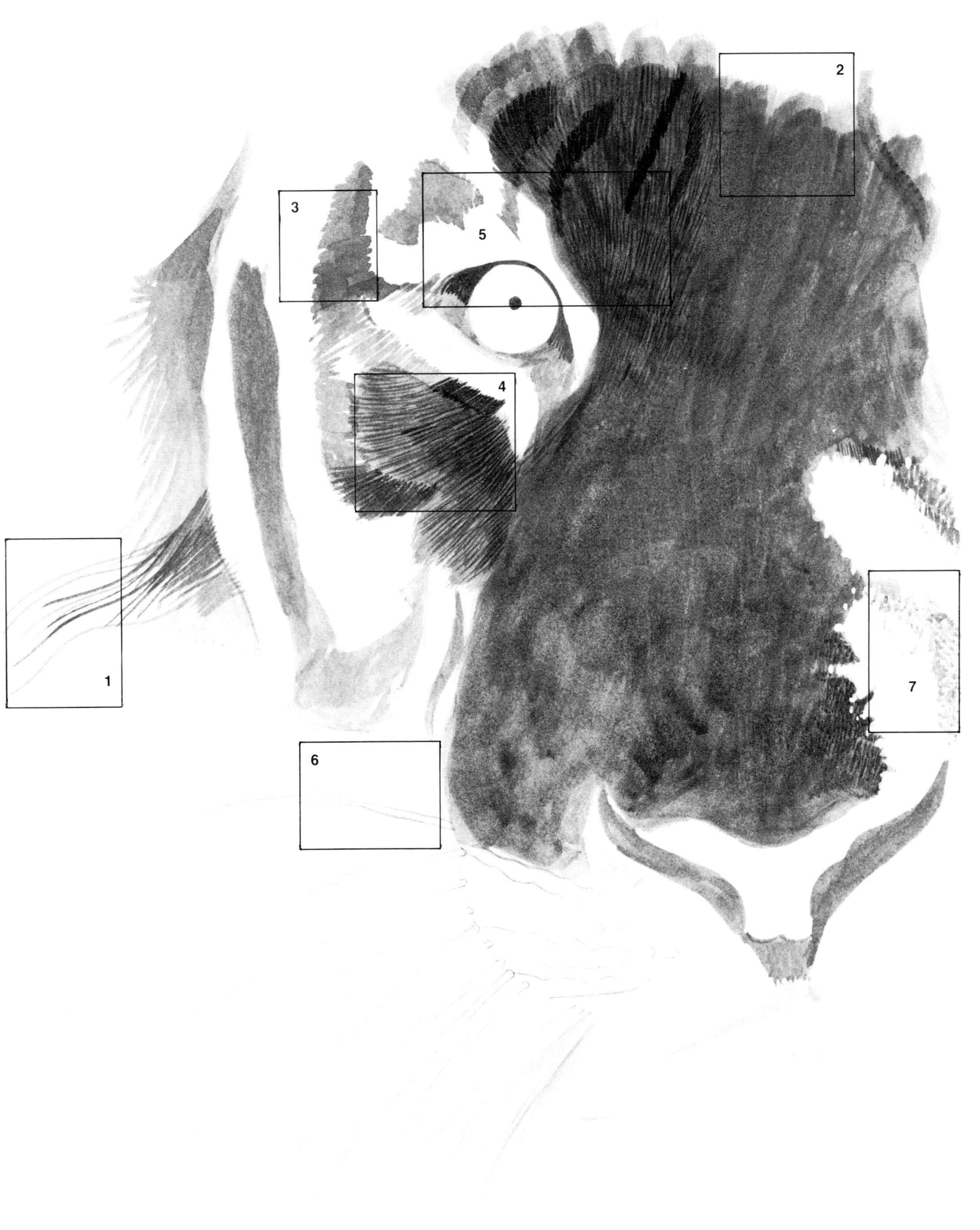
2
3
5
4
1
7
6

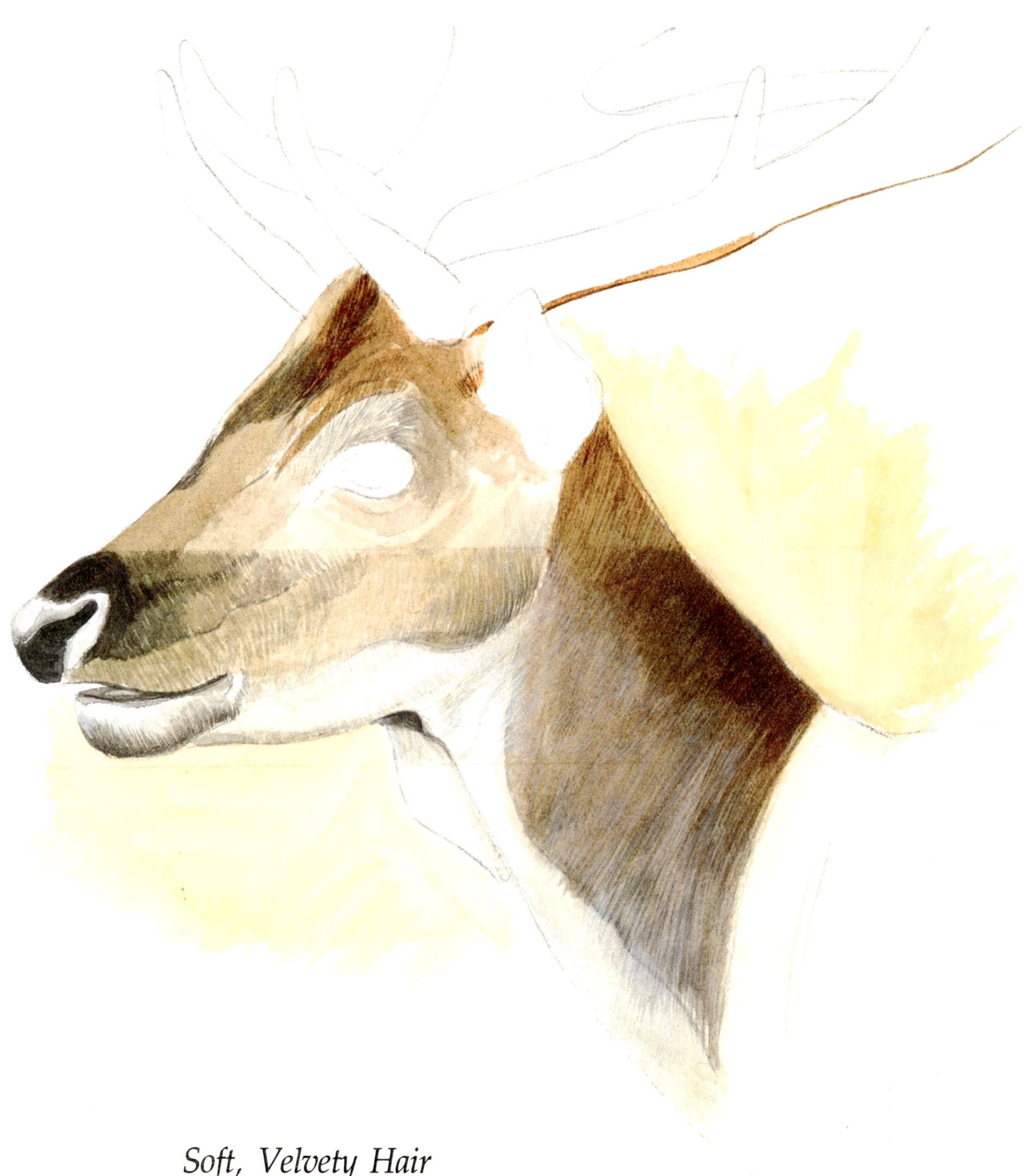

Soft, Velvety Hair

This English fallow deer presents a great problem. Its coat is short, sleek, and velvety and there is a subtle gradation from one color to another, made even more difficult to see because it is standing in a hazy, misty light. If you over-accentuated the hair direction and detail, it would make the image too crisp and hard.

To paint this texture, I changed to a rougher surface and changed my technique, too. The painting was started with a series of very watery washes and then progressed with very short strokes of a fine-haired brush. I kept the colors very understated and watery throughout the entire sketch. The narrow band through the head shows the technique I used after the washes were applied.

Painting a Velvety Hide

This fallow deer is also standing in a brighter light, but it is farther away. Although distance softens the detail on the animal, its colors seem more intense under the stronger light. I have progressed the painting through sections so that the stages are clear:

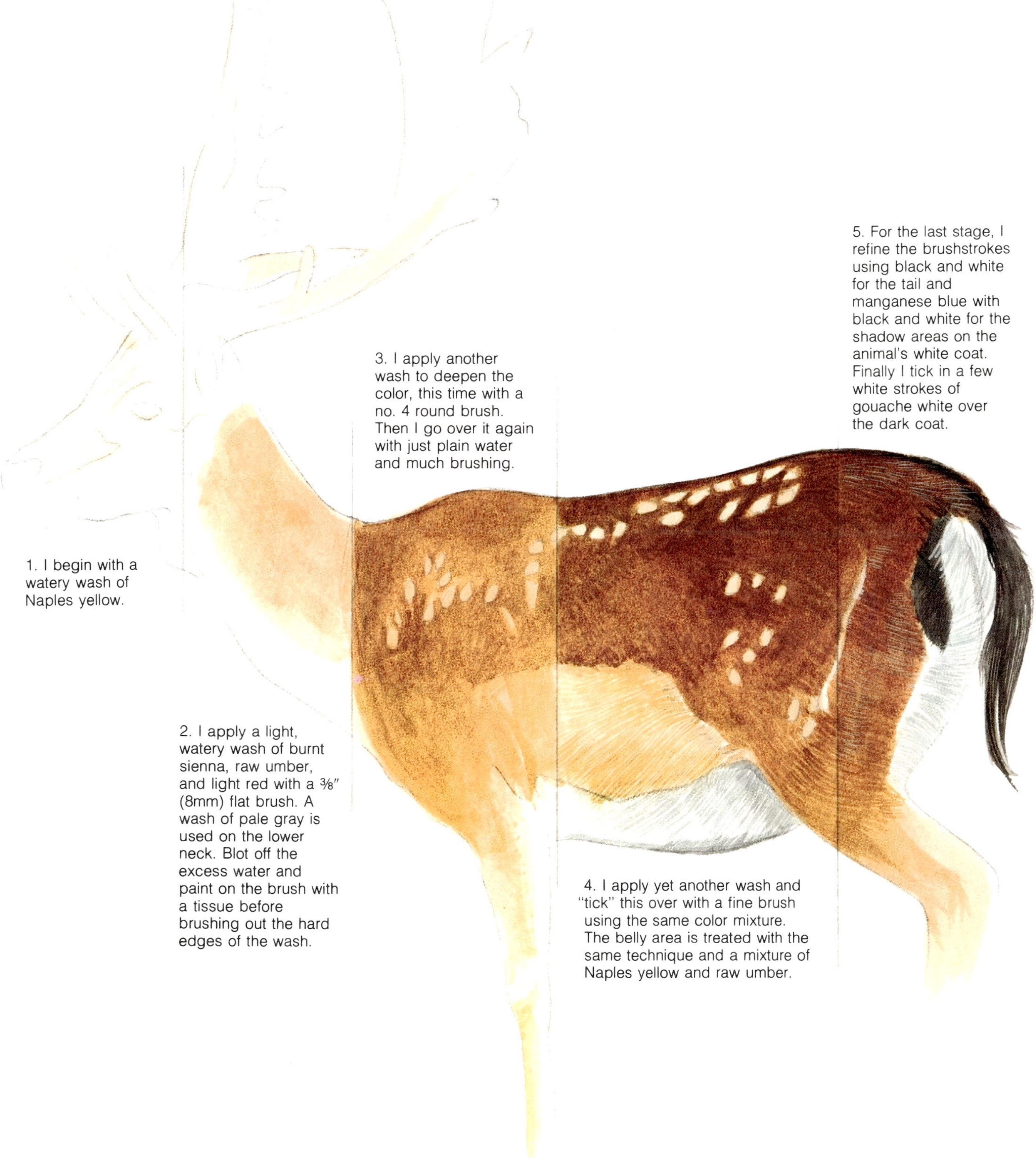

1. I begin with a watery wash of Naples yellow.

2. I apply a light, watery wash of burnt sienna, raw umber, and light red with a ⅜" (8mm) flat brush. A wash of pale gray is used on the lower neck. Blot off the excess water and paint on the brush with a tissue before brushing out the hard edges of the wash.

3. I apply another wash to deepen the color, this time with a no. 4 round brush. Then I go over it again with just plain water and much brushing.

4. I apply yet another wash and "tick" this over with a fine brush using the same color mixture. The belly area is treated with the same technique and a mixture of Naples yellow and raw umber.

5. For the last stage, I refine the brushstrokes using black and white for the tail and manganese blue with black and white for the shadow areas on the animal's white coat. Finally I tick in a few white strokes of gouache white over the dark coat.

Horns and Antlers

Just as familiarity with drawing animals is beginning to make you feel easier about the whole thing, along come horns and antlers to confound you. It isn't just the linear nature of horns that poses a problem, but the greatly differing finish and texture that gives totally different effects with every change of light and species. But if you take a good close look, you'll see that formulas can be found here too—and then painting the horn becomes a challenge to be enjoyed.

Horns do need to be very carefully drawn and the initial draftsmanship is all-important. If the animal is portrayed close up, the texture of the horn needs to be detailed, too. On the left-hand page, I started a drawing of blackbuck horns using a stuffed head borrowed from a local antique shop.

If you're drawing and painting a close-up view of a creature with horns, a very detailed reference will be needed. There is no way that, at close range, any kind of fudging can take place, especially given the "crowning glory" nature a fine pair of well-painted horns can give.

The moment that you move the animal back further into the picture, on the other hand, you need a softer and less-detailed approach. My small watercolor sketch shows the decrease of horn detail on a blackbuck that has moved fifteen feet or so away. At that point, the general shape becomes even more important than the detail of ridges. The horn changes color and even appearance of shape as different light causes different strengths and angles of tone between the ridges. So if you're painting a horn close up, treat the ridges like hair detail and paint (or at least give the impression of painting) every line. Paint horns at a distance with a bigger brush and a looser wash style.

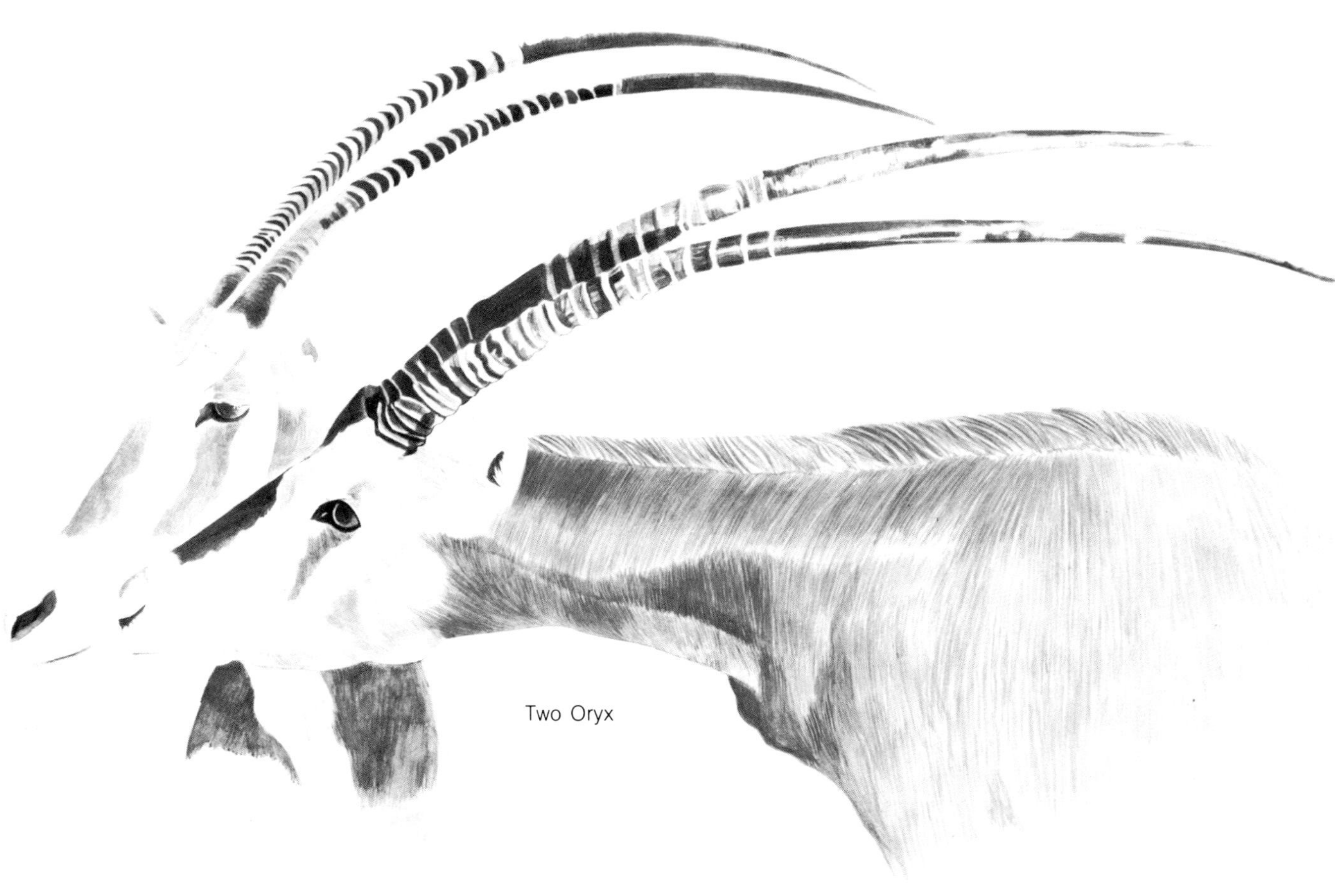

Two Oryx

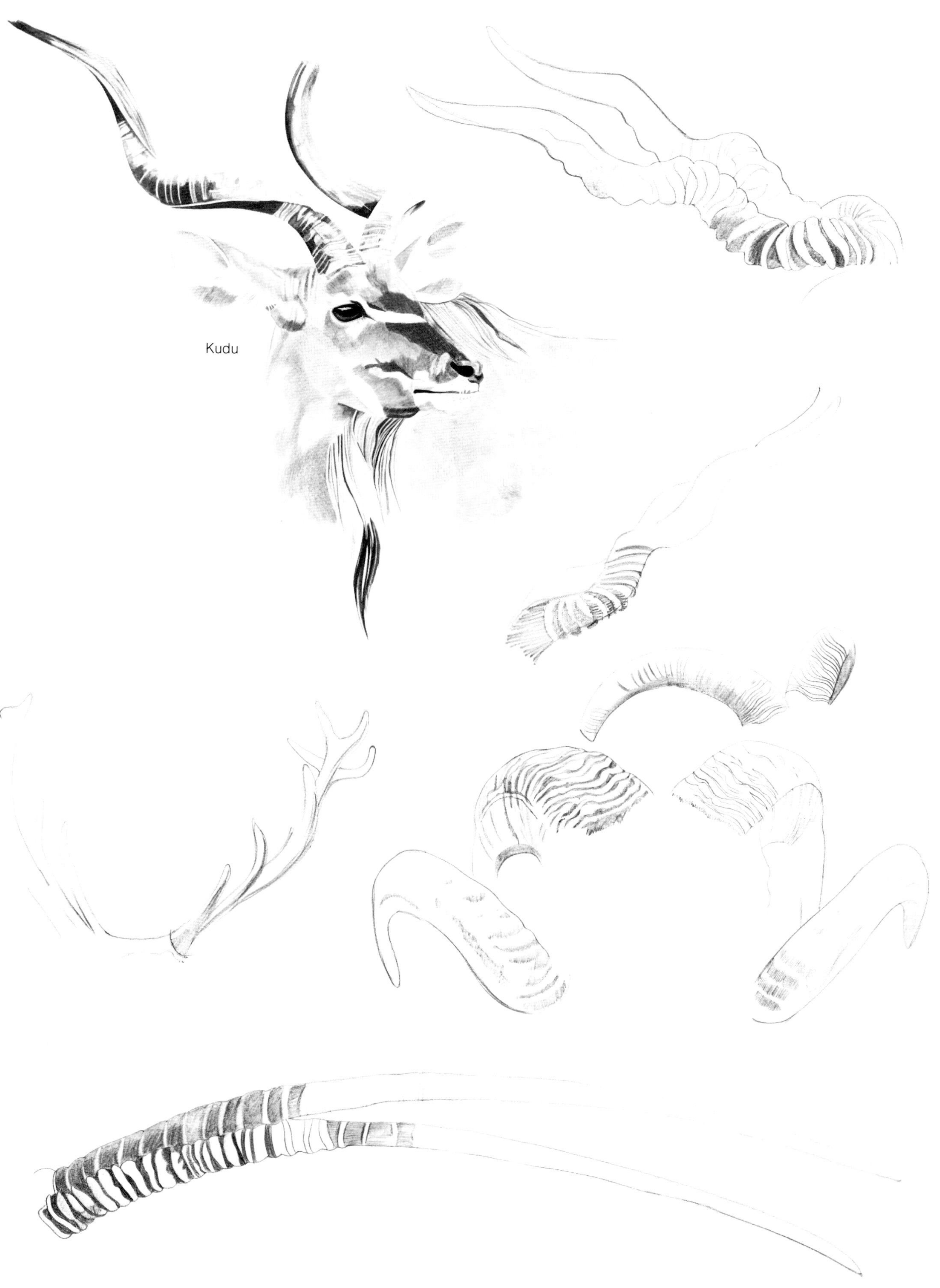
Kudu

Drawing Blackbuck Horns

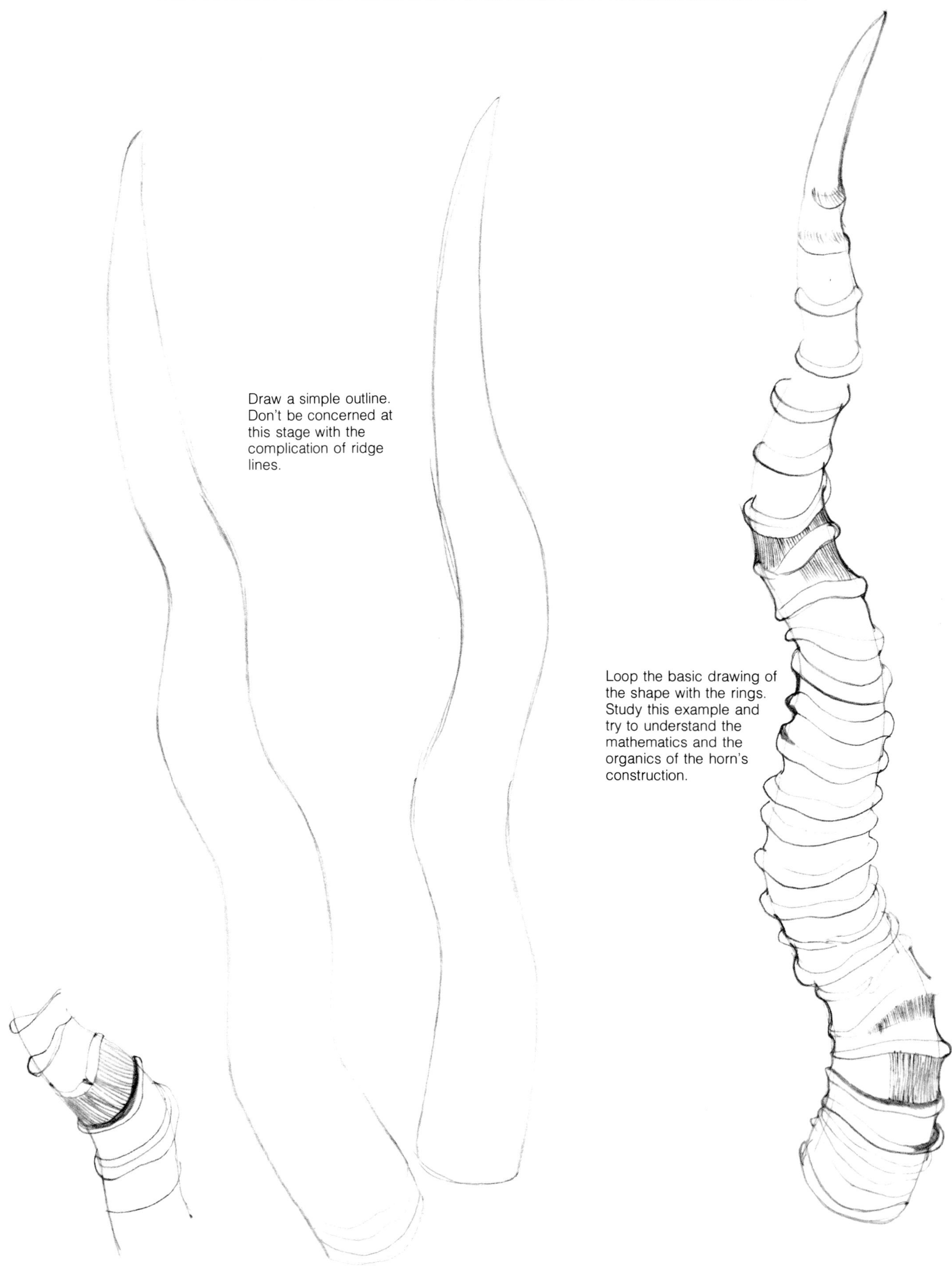

Draw a simple outline. Don't be concerned at this stage with the complication of ridge lines.

Loop the basic drawing of the shape with the rings. Study this example and try to understand the mathematics and the organics of the horn's construction.

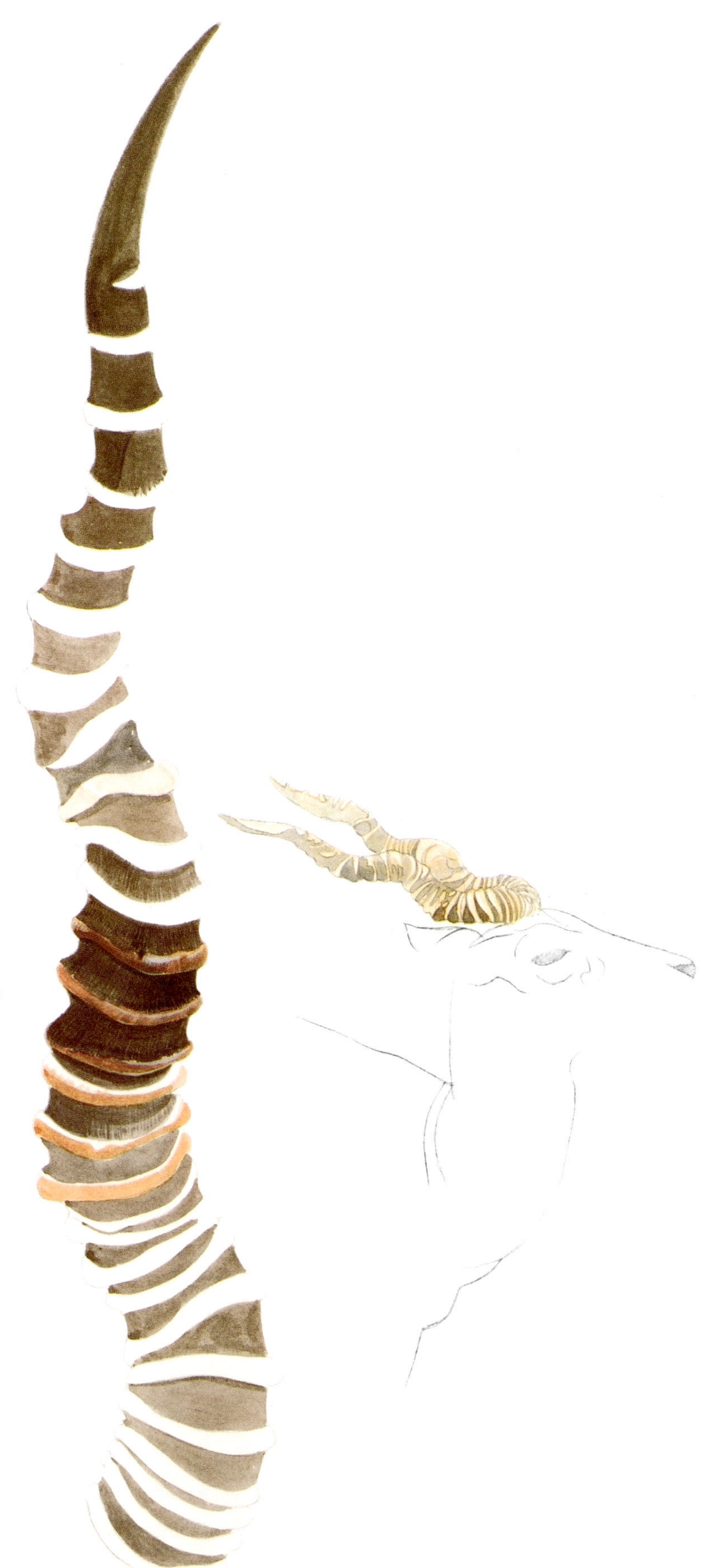

Three of the rings are finished. Notice the way the lines in the actual fabric of the horn follow its shape. The ridges become less pronounced at the tip of the horns. They are closer together at the base. Horns, like eyes, reflect light conditions so color formulas will change with the environment.

Drawing Scimitar-Horned Oryx Horns

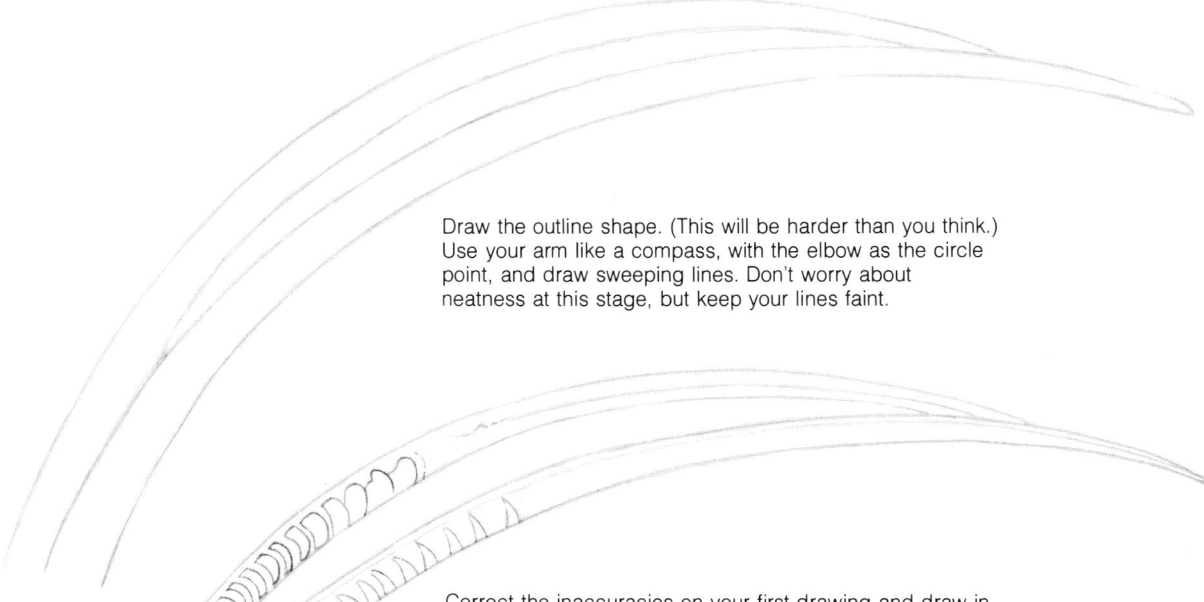

Draw the outline shape. (This will be harder than you think.) Use your arm like a compass, with the elbow as the circle point, and draw sweeping lines. Don't worry about neatness at this stage, but keep your lines faint.

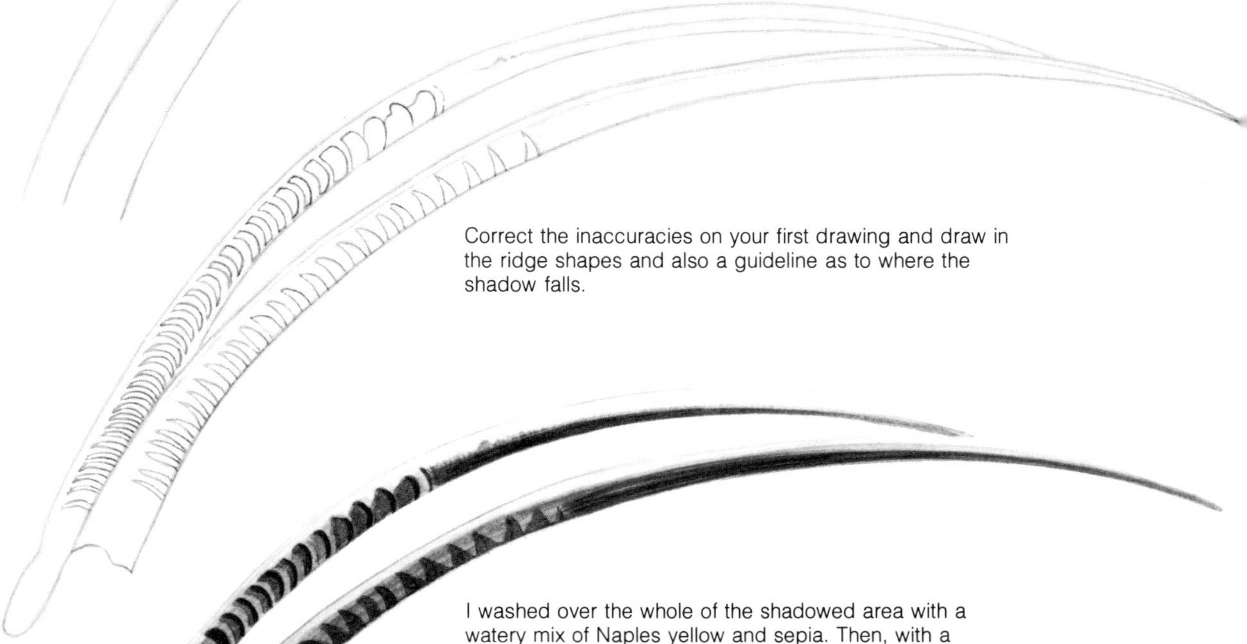

Correct the inaccuracies on your first drawing and draw in the ridge shapes and also a guideline as to where the shadow falls.

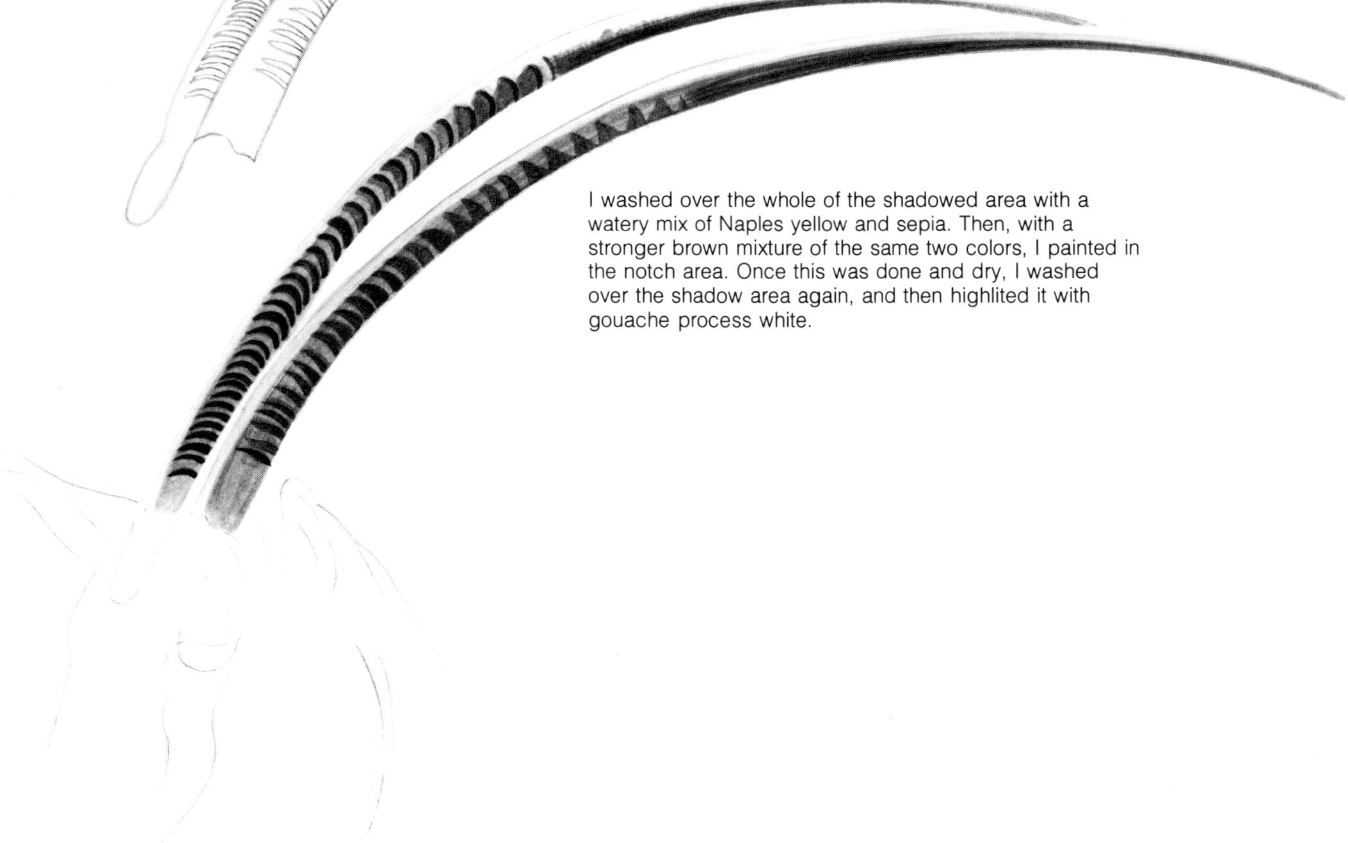

I washed over the whole of the shadowed area with a watery mix of Naples yellow and sepia. Then, with a stronger brown mixture of the same two colors, I painted in the notch area. Once this was done and dry, I washed over the shadow area again, and then highlited it with gouache process white.

Drawing Ram Horns

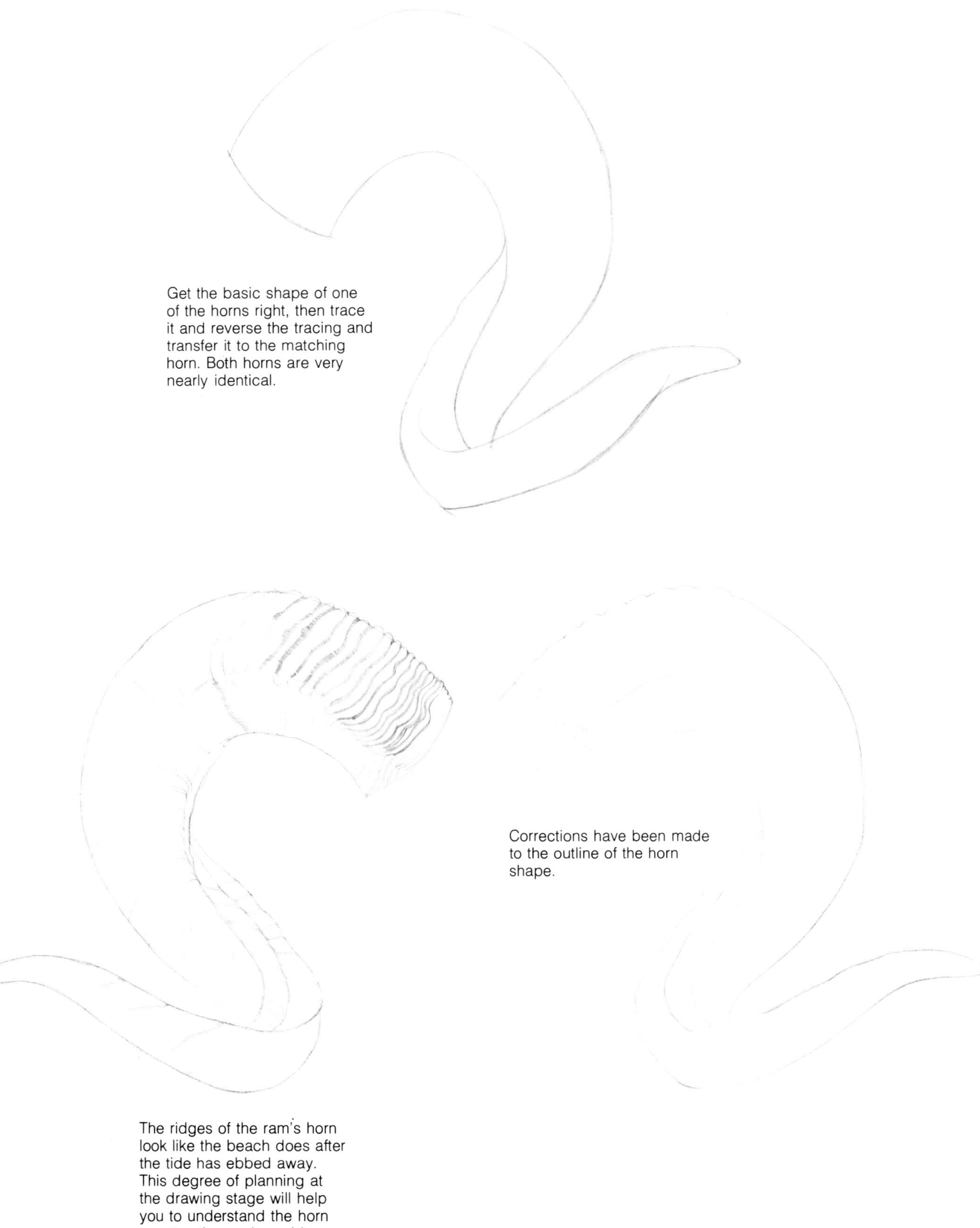

Get the basic shape of one of the horns right, then trace it and reverse the tracing and transfer it to the matching horn. Both horns are very nearly identical.

Corrections have been made to the outline of the horn shape.

The ridges of the ram's horn look like the beach does after the tide has ebbed away. This degree of planning at the drawing stage will help you to understand the horn construction and provide a method for painting it.

Noses and Mouths

There are so many different kinds of noses and mouths that I could not hope to cover a fair selection. But although shapes change, the material that makes up both has a lot in common and the technique needed remains the same. To paint noses and mouths, you need flatter brushes, more watery colors, and a technique more akin to portrait painting than wildlife painting.

Noses

Noses are usually either a bluish-black or a pinkish-orange. They are either pimpled (as in a dog's nose) or smooth in the case of most carnivores and herbivores. They should appear rubbery and mobile. I have sketched the noses of a tiger, lion, pudu, kudu, and horse, leaving the pencil lines and brushstrokes so that the method is clear.

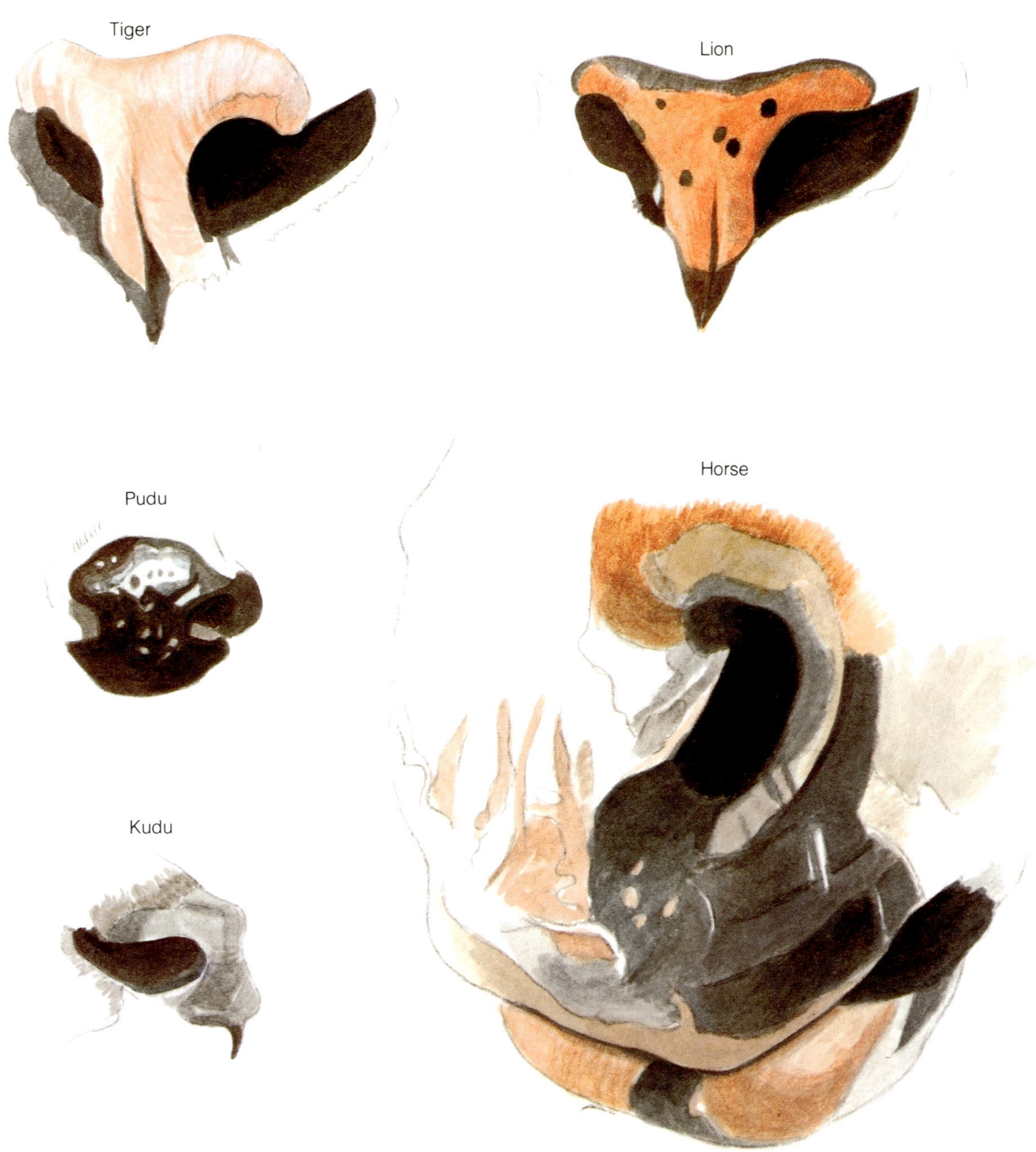

Mouths

Mouths change dramatically in shape but in a painting technique sense they are very similar. This mouth is progressed through three stages and shows the colors used on each stage. Think of each subject organically. For instance, the horse has a soft, velvety muzzle with rubbery lips. Imitate this feeling as you paint. On noses and mouths, you need a slow build-up of color through the stages using pale pigment in very watery washes, with much blotting of the excess water and color on your brush to avoid hard edges and give you the desired result. In the end, though, practice will improve the result.

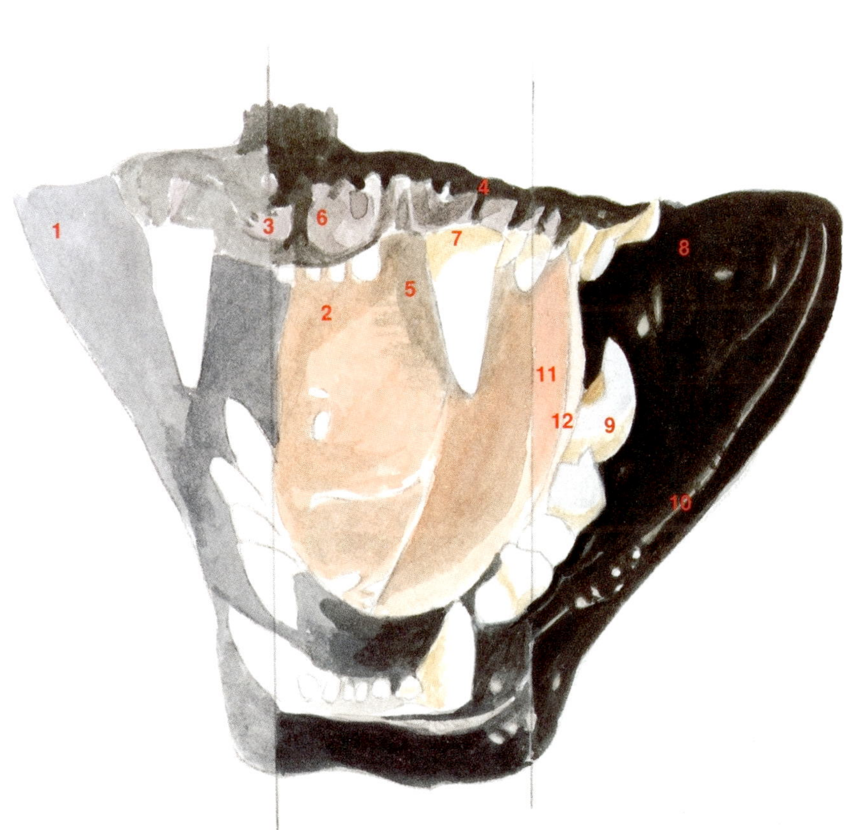

1

2

3

4

5

6

7

8

9

10

11

12

With a no. 4 round brush and a bluish-black wash, I painted the dark areas of the inside of the mouth, taking care to crisply cut out the teeth and tongue shape—blue first because I want blue areas to shine out of the finished black.

Next, with a weak wash of chrome orange, Chinese white, and bright red, I washed in the tongue, cutting out the crease and shine areas to allow the white paper to show through.

I used a lamp black with a touch of blue to wash in the extra intensity of dark parts of the mouth, then tissued off the surplus color to achieve the softer tones on the tongue and areas on the top gums.

The mixture of red, white, and blue darkens areas of the tongue. A light gray wash softens the central gum area. It was painted over the areas that would eventually become shiny. Naples yellow and white provide the basic shadow color of the teeth.

The lines and colors of preceding stages are strengthened and defined in the last stage.

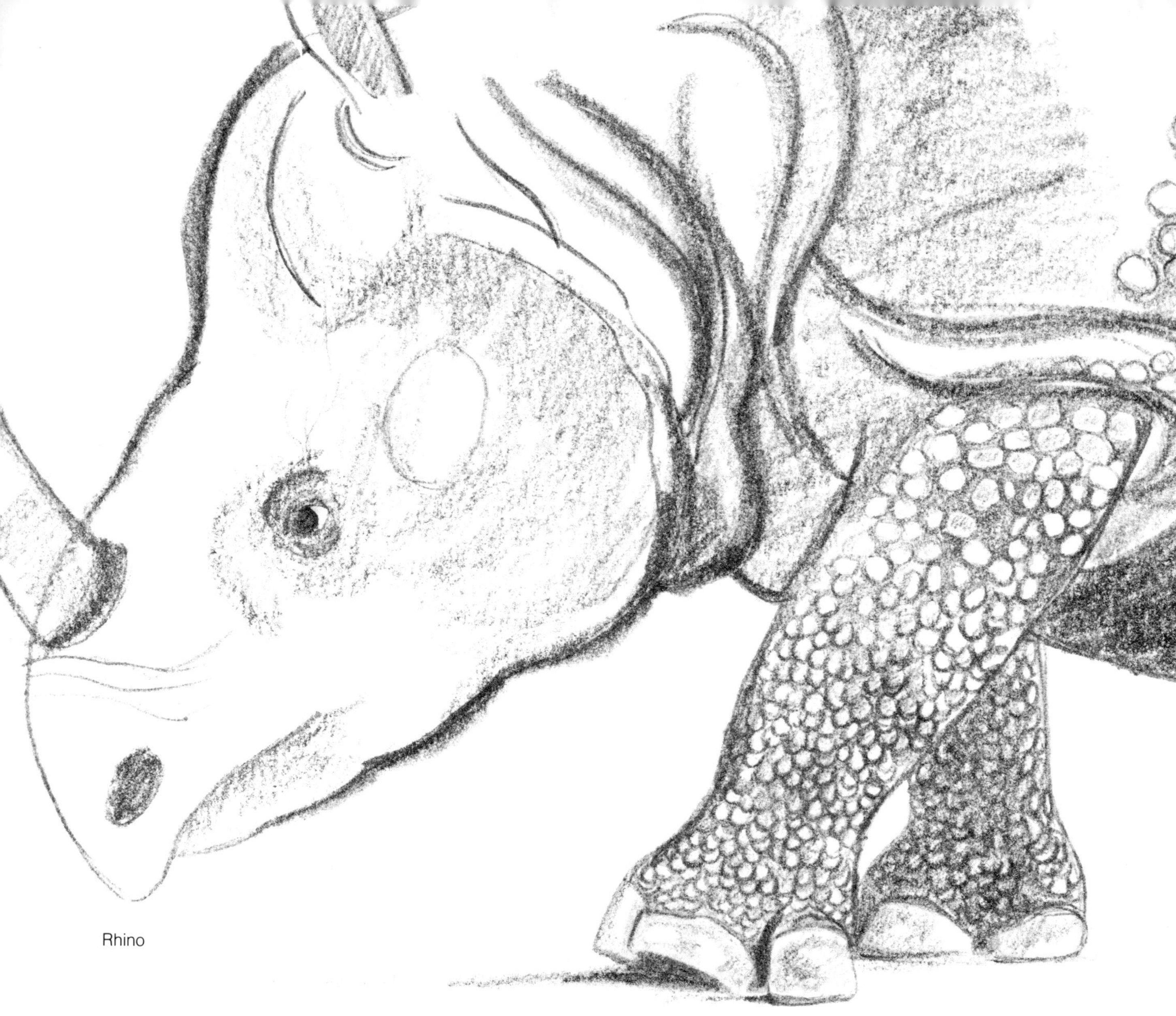

Rhino

I was tempted to smother these pages with drawings of feet until I thought carefully about what they meant to the painter and to the painting. For much of the time in wildlife photography, and therefore in drawing and painting animals, feet are obscured by grass or undergrowth. But where they do show, they are faithful to the character of the animal. The massiveness of a rhino or elephant or the prowl of a tiger is summarized and brought to its essence in the feet and the legs. A zebra's skittishness is likewise shown in the feet. I used to be a boxer, and my trainer taught me to watch my opponent's feet, pointing out that it was here that any movement of the body would start. In other words, a punch couldn't be thrown without the feet setting themselves up for it. For the painter, drama, power, and movement can be achieved by mastering the anatomy of the foot. But you will have to practice, for drawing feet is not easy.

These sketches of zoo animals, though extremely untidy, do show how the feet of a *rhino* are massively built to support its vast weight, and how the graceful, yet strong legs of the *zebra* give it speed and maneuverability. There is a compositional lesson here, too. Show the feet, and your picture will gain in excitement.

Hooves, Paws, Hands, and Feet

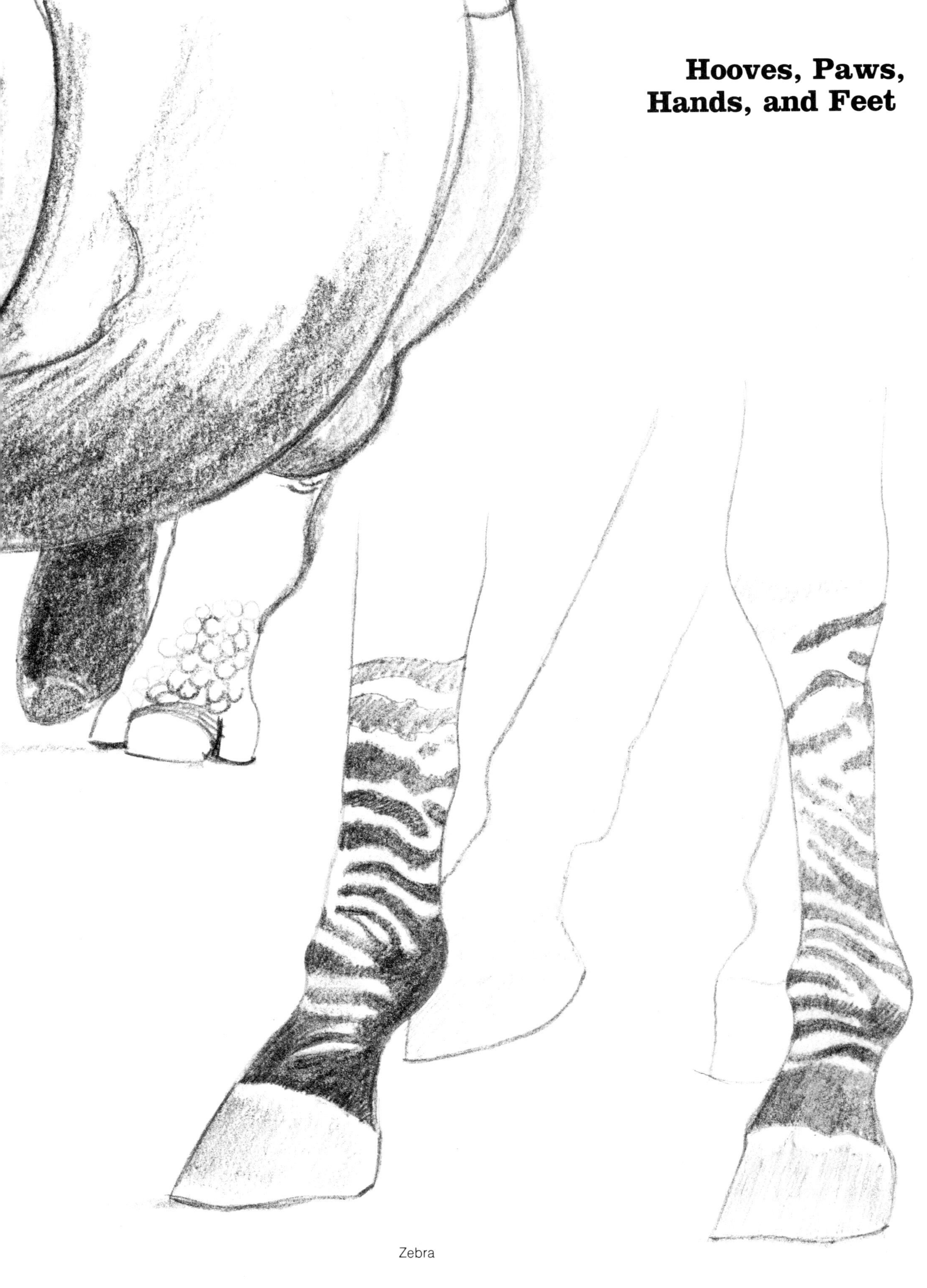

Zebra

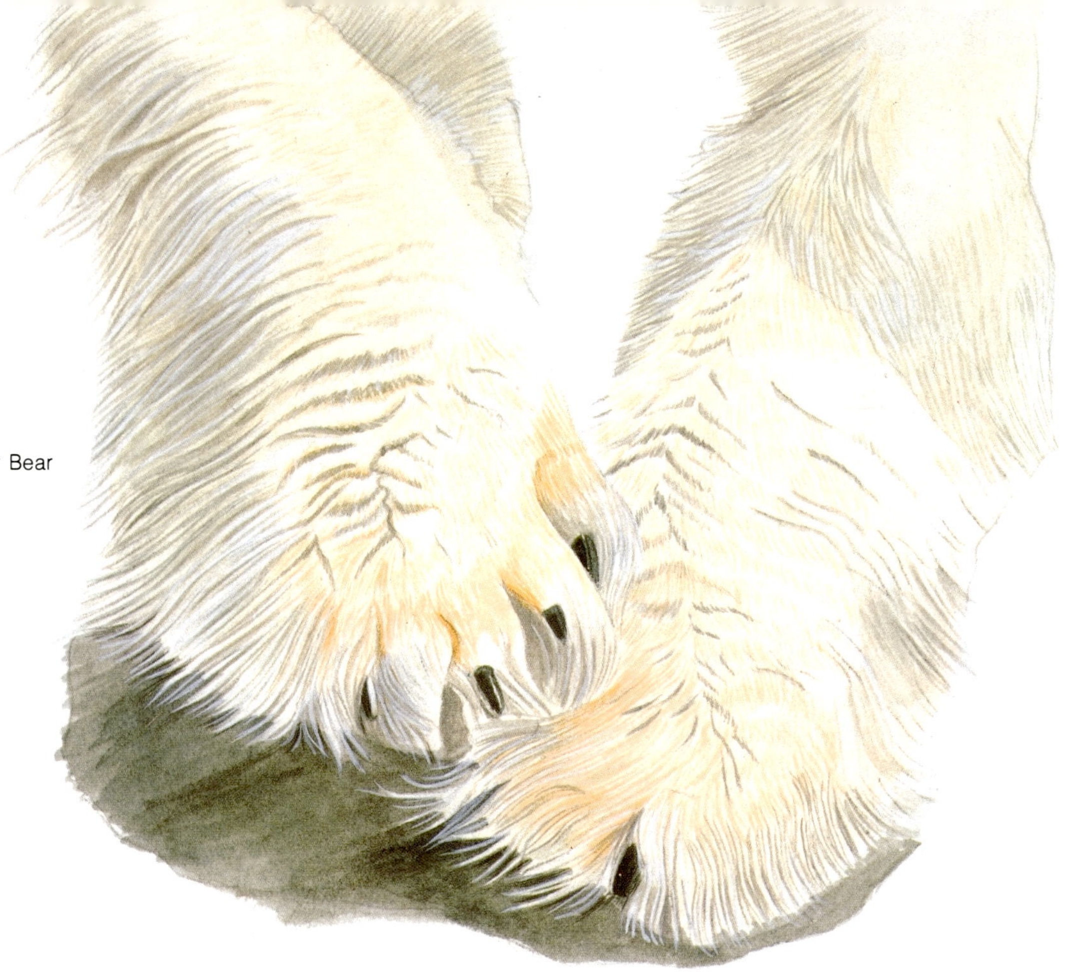

Polar Bear

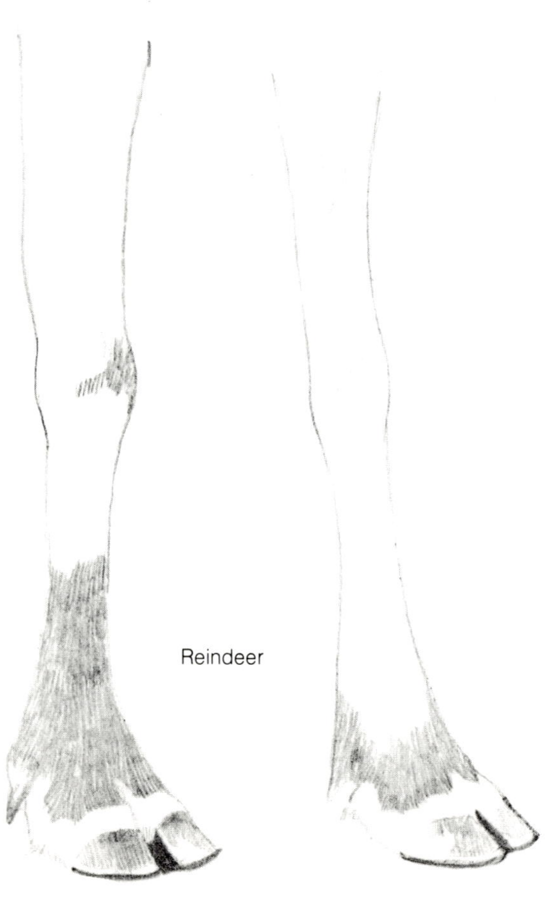

Reindeer

The usual mistake in painting a white animal like the *polar bear* is in not recognizing, right at the start, that by the time light and shade have done their work, the paw is not, in fact, white. Most students heap thicker and thicker white on top of white. But that won't work. To show you what to do, I have sketched the front paws of a polar bear. They're big and flat to give the animal a grip in ice and snow. Notice that I painted the shadows between the hairs and added yellow tones, and only at the very end did I carefully paint just a few white hairs with process gouache white paint. I have placed most of the bear against a white background except for the shadow under the paws themselves, which give emphasis to the key point—the animal's hairs and weight.

With the *reindeer,* again function is the thing to remember. Go through the function drill every time you start and restart a painting. The feet and every other part of an animal's body are designed to function in particular environments and situations. When you clearly understand this, you'll be well on your way to painting wildlife successfully. The reindeer is a fleet animal, and its hooves are split or cloven and opened well out to provide a wide platform for grip on ice and snow. Everything in nature is designed for a purpose.

Look at the graceful, almost human hands of the *ring-tailed lemur.* The long, elegant fingers with their spatulate ends are functional holding and gripping hands. Try to draw the shape accurately and remember that the fingers are round, so paint some dimension and form into its shape.

The foot of the *chimpanzee* makes a good exercise. Its skin texture is just like our own, but the shape is designed for gripping. I used a series of very wet washes, and then re-defined the foot with a very fine brush. Your drawing needs to be precise or the feet will look like bunches of bananas.

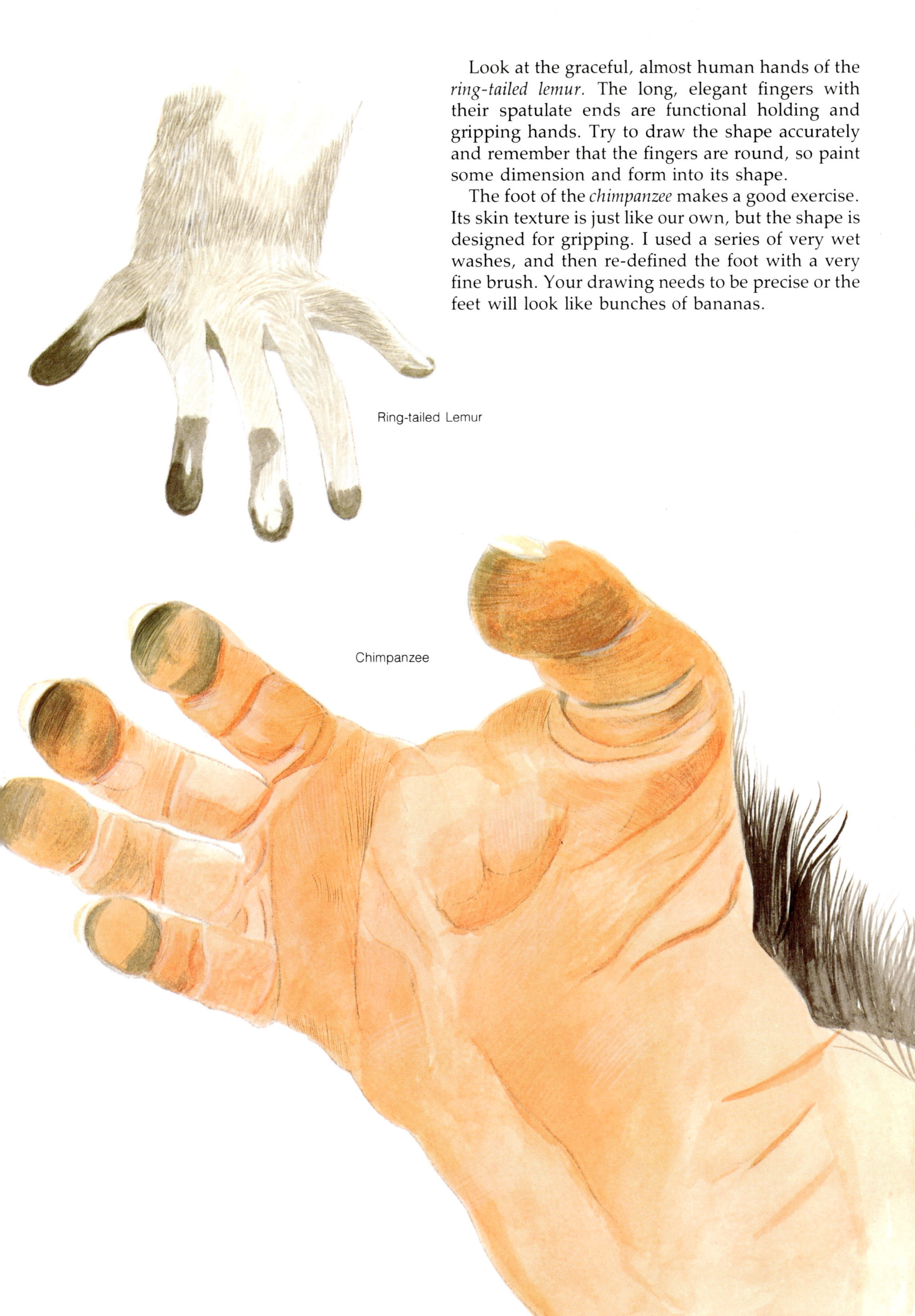

Ring-tailed Lemur

Chimpanzee

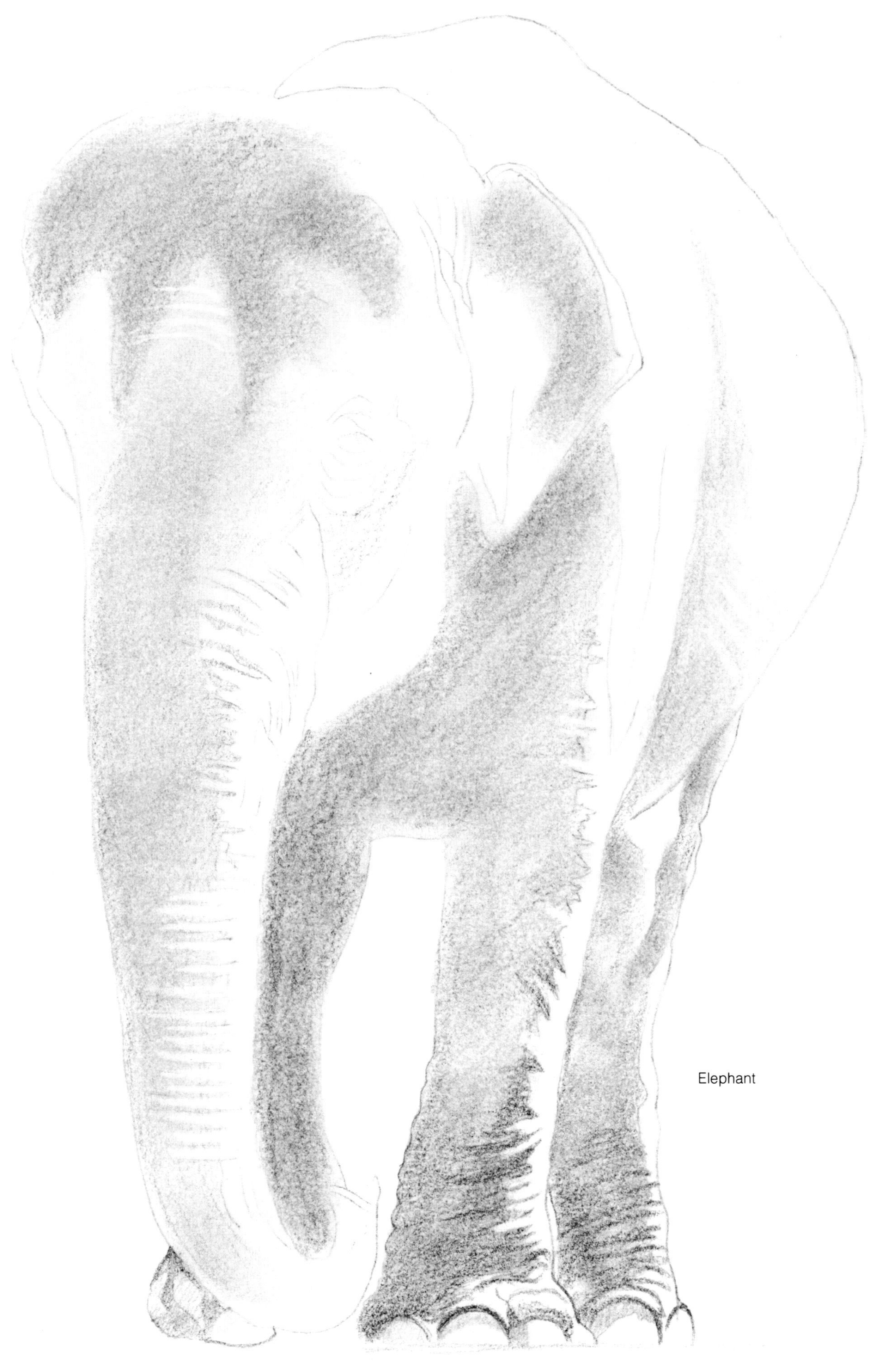
Elephant

Whenever you start to draw hooves and paws—or any other part of the body—think first of its function. That is, make sure you understand just what role the underpinnings have to perform. For example, the *elephant* needs big strong, stable platforms to transport its vast bulk as well as its height. (Incidentally, the technique used on the elephant is 2B pencil, gently shaded, rubbed with a tissue, with the highlights lifted out with a soft piece of kneaded eraser.)

Look at the split hoof of the *mountain goat.* When it's climbing upward, it can dig its hooves into the scree and gain a grip. Coming down, it's hooves spread and offer enough resistance to gain a good footing.

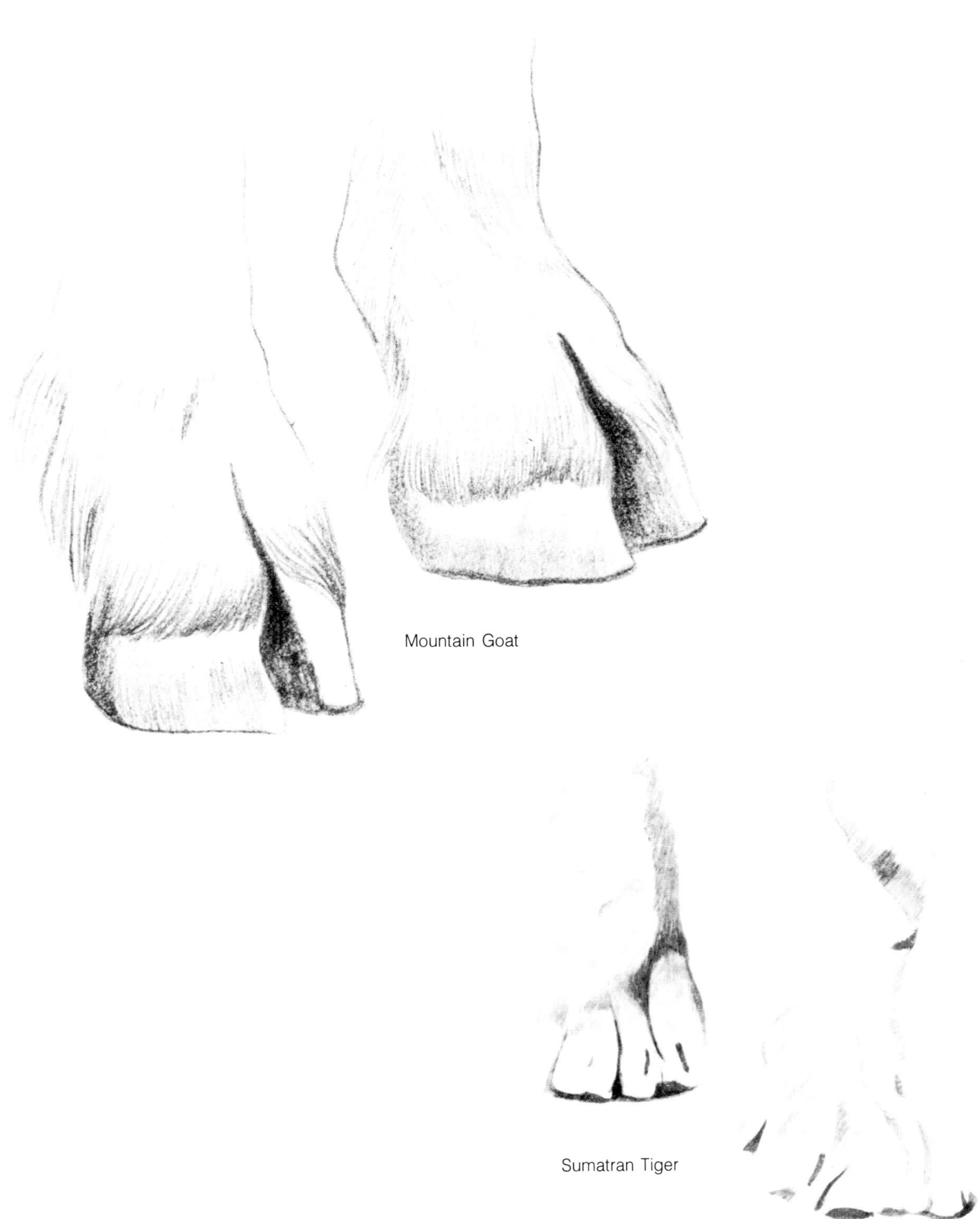

Mountain Goat

Sumatran Tiger

Differentiating Textures

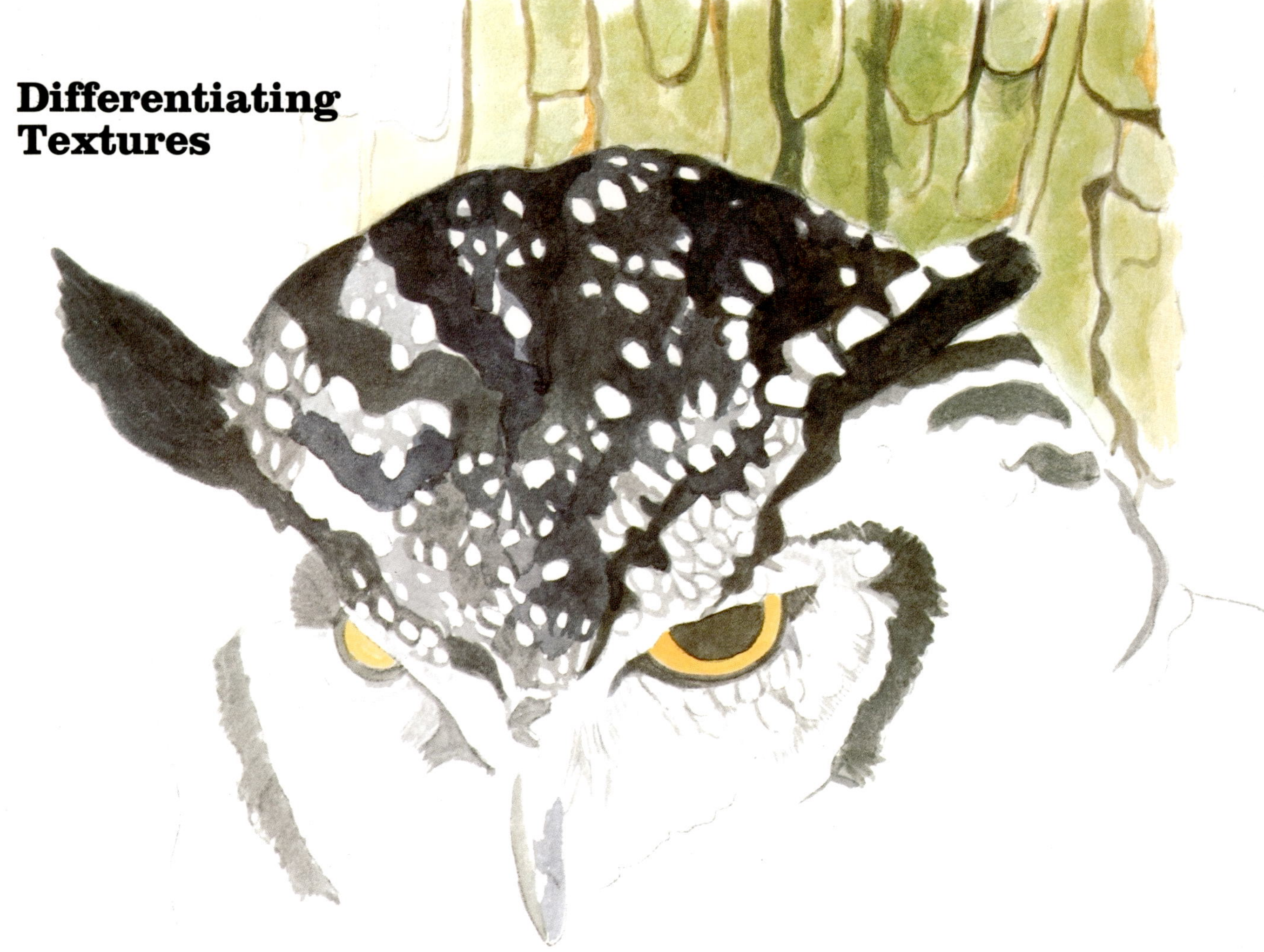

Complicated against Complicated

The European eagle owl shown against the bark of a pine tree represents a complicated texture set against a complicated background. Don't be tempted into a compulsion for detail or you'll end up producing a "chocolate box" or "too-good-to-be-true" image. Too many wildlife artists, in my opinion, forget that an animal merges into its background, whether that background is near or far away. God or evolution—or both—designed it that way, hence the camouflage.

I have kept my watercolor sketch fairly unfinished so you could follow it. I wanted the eagle owl to sit about 6″ (15cm) in front of the pine tree and have each object work comfortably and naturally with the other. The eye normally does not see every detail on each object unless it studies them all individually, so where complex textures meet, don't be afraid to do away with detail. A good painting is not judged by the proportion of work that goes into it. The owl stands out enough from the pine tree because the pigment strengths and the techniques for painting foreground and background are different.

I painted the owl with a fairly strong but watery wash using a no. 4 round brush and floated in the colors through a series of glazes. On the bark, I used a ⅜″ (8mm) flat brush and the driest possible wash and laid faint colors over faint colors. The crevices between each scale or flake of bark have been painted in with a finer brush and slightly stronger color. If you want to increase the definition of the bark, do it an inch or so away from the owl's head. Don't let two equal pigment strengths or two equal detail areas meet each other.

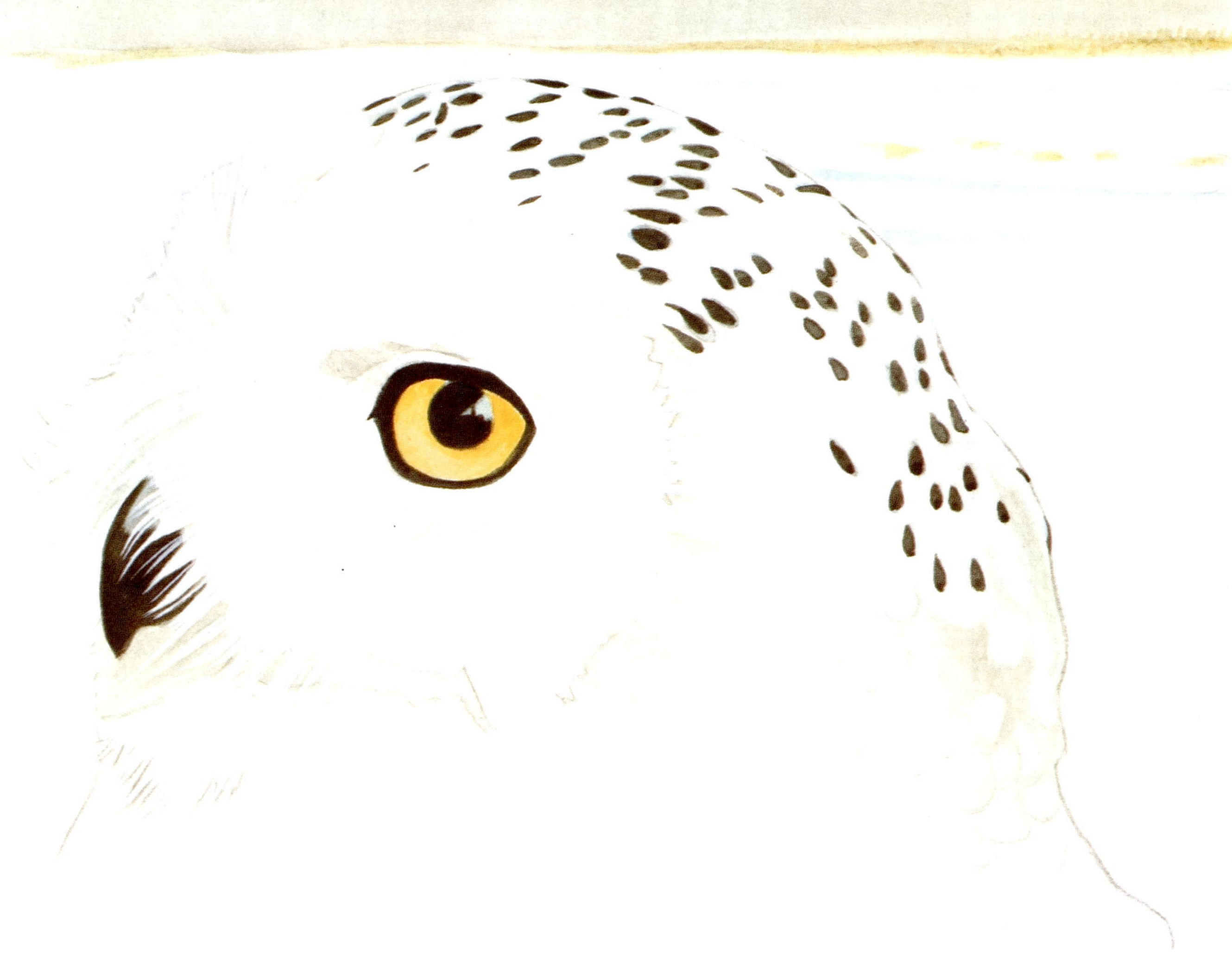

Bland against Bland

This white snowy owl sits against the white treeless and flat landscape of the tundra—bland against bland. This apparently difficult example is, in fact, nowhere near as hard to paint as it would appear, providing that you judiciously use the few advantages available. For example, license can be taken with the landscape—after all, snow isn't pure white all over—and even the flattest landscape has some point of focus.

The owl is as near to white as it can get, but there are a few colors and shapes that can be exploited. Painting its very brightly colored eye will firmly fix the image of the owl against the same color background. Its spots also can be moved around slightly to lend emphasis. (I placed some spots that weren't on the original owl at the edge of the outline of the head to give some delineation between head and snow.) The sky color was deepened to provide both coldness and contrast. Just remember as you add these things that the snowy owl was designed to be able to lose itself in its background, so there's no need to overdo the contrast. Just work gradually toward the finished result and put in only what is needed as you proceed. The real separation here between subject and background has been achieved by subtle colors, with one understated color glazed over another. Process white gouache has been applied thickly but sparingly to highlight and separate areas.

This particular species of owl is very fluffy, so I underpainted the feathers with a very wet and understated wash to suggest a three-dimensional shape and to provide shadow between the fluffy hairlike feathers around the beak.

Evidence

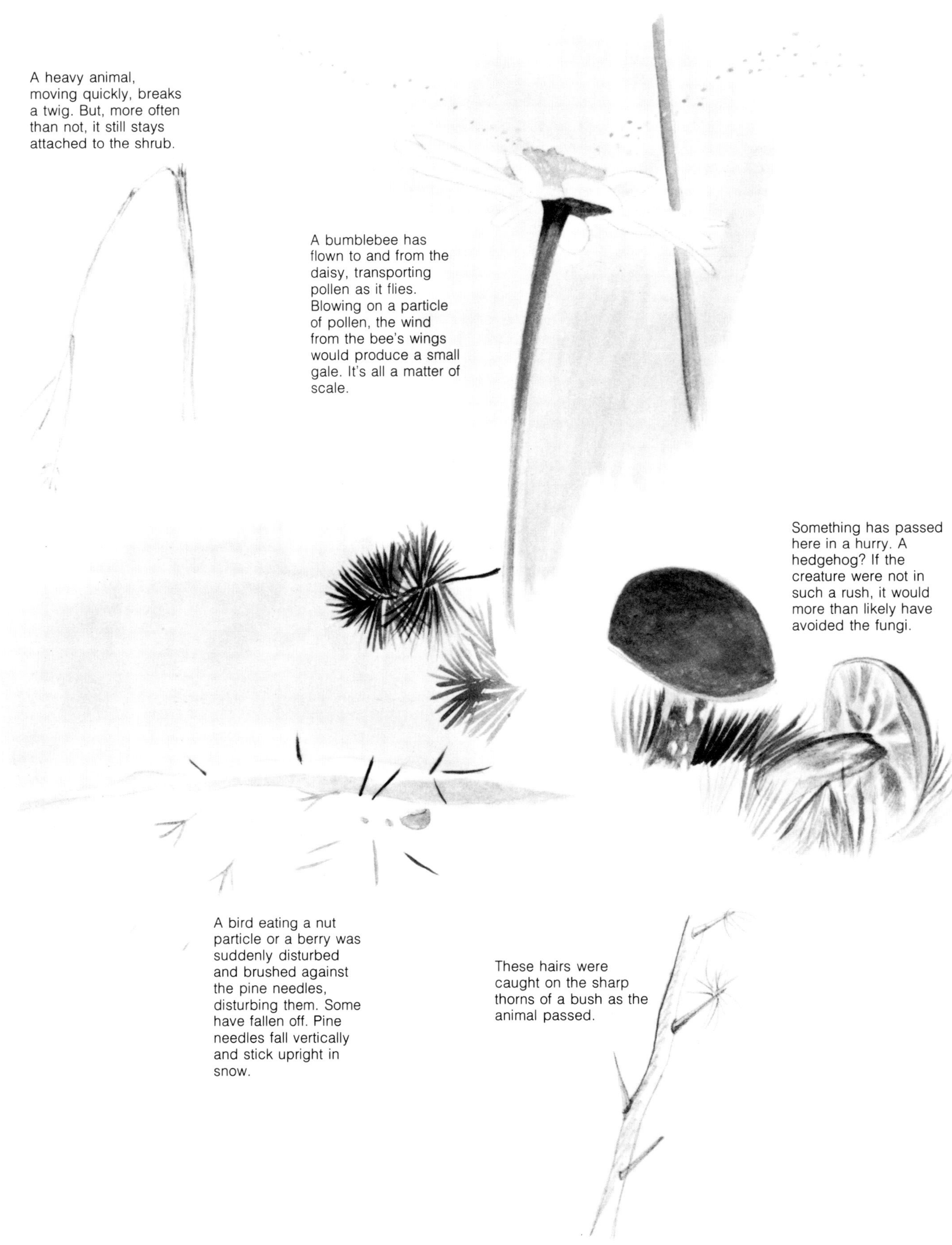
A heavy animal, moving quickly, breaks a twig. But, more often than not, it still stays attached to the shrub.
A bumblebee has flown to and from the daisy, transporting pollen as it flies. Blowing on a particle of pollen, the wind from the bee's wings would produce a small gale. It's all a matter of scale.
Something has passed here in a hurry. A hedgehog? If the creature were not in such a rush, it would more than likely have avoided the fungi.
A bird eating a nut particle or a berry was suddenly disturbed and brushed against the pine needles, disturbing them. Some have fallen off. Pine needles fall vertically and stick upright in snow.
These hairs were caught on the sharp thorns of a bush as the animal passed.

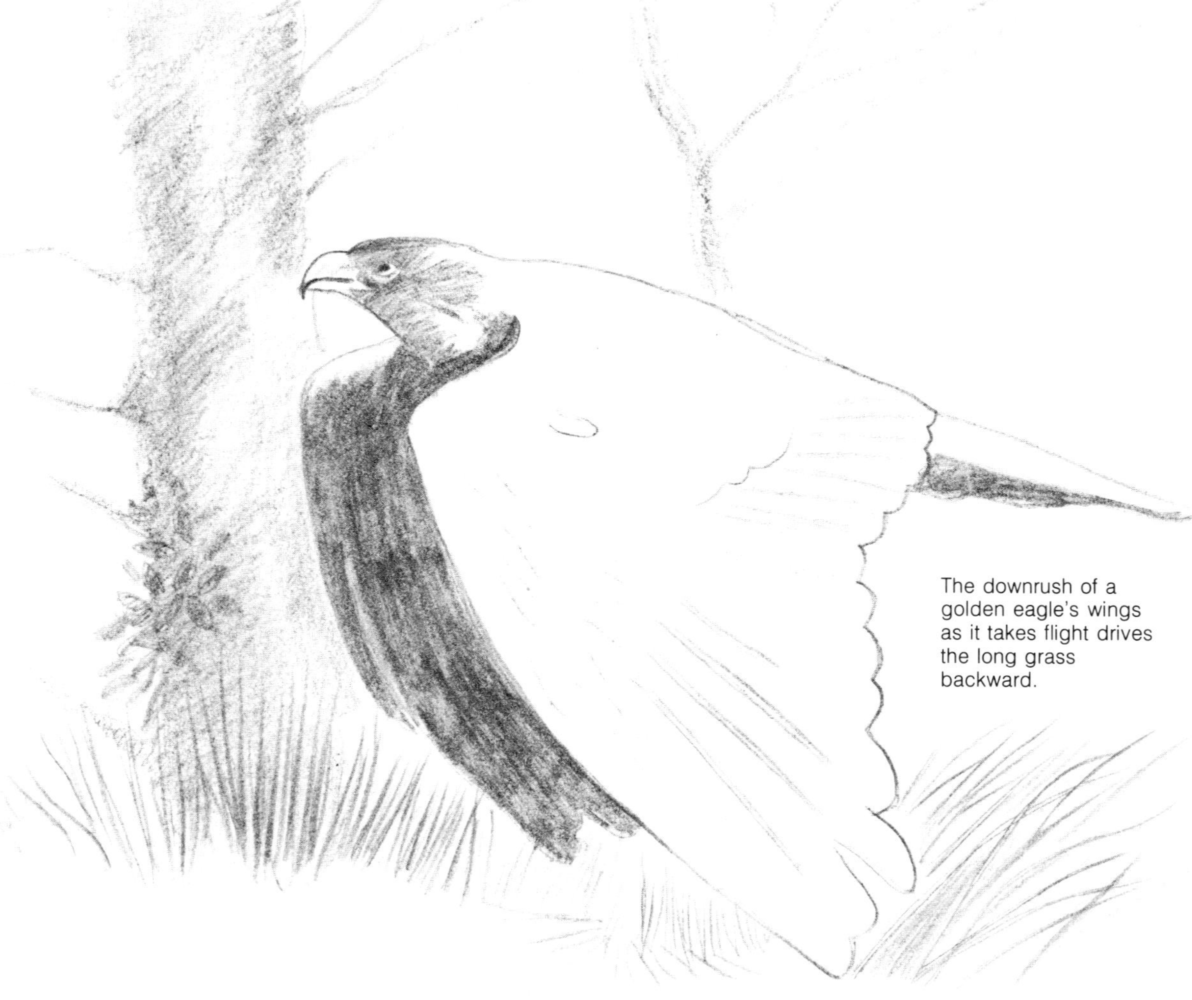

The downrush of a golden eagle's wings as it takes flight drives the long grass backward.

The wings also flatten the grass directly below it.

Most students are so intent on finishing the central subject of their painting that they forget to put in those little touches that give the picture authenticity and narrative power. So often you'll see a painting of an animal on snow or some other receptive surface with no footprints on the snow or other evidence of how it got there.

Whenever an animal is moving about, it is always manifested in some form of evidence. Animals don't merely pose in the middle of pristine grassland. Obviously the signs of animal presence are just small, subtle details and therefore not of overwhelming importance, but used with discretion, they can help to make a picture convincing.

There are countless clues—evidence—you can use both in the background and on the central subject itself. Here are some examples:

1. It would be unusual for a lion to reach maturity without having a lot of fights, so there should be scars, particularly on its muzzle, and its ears will have pieces torn out of them.
2. A squirrel is likely to eat nuts in a regular place, so the debris there should be considerable.
3. When heavy animals pass, they break things like twigs and branches.

Just keep your eyes open and consider these things. Don't get carried away to the extent that you just paint anecdotes. The subject is still the subject, but a little additional detail can help give your painting authenticity.

Where Different Textures Meet

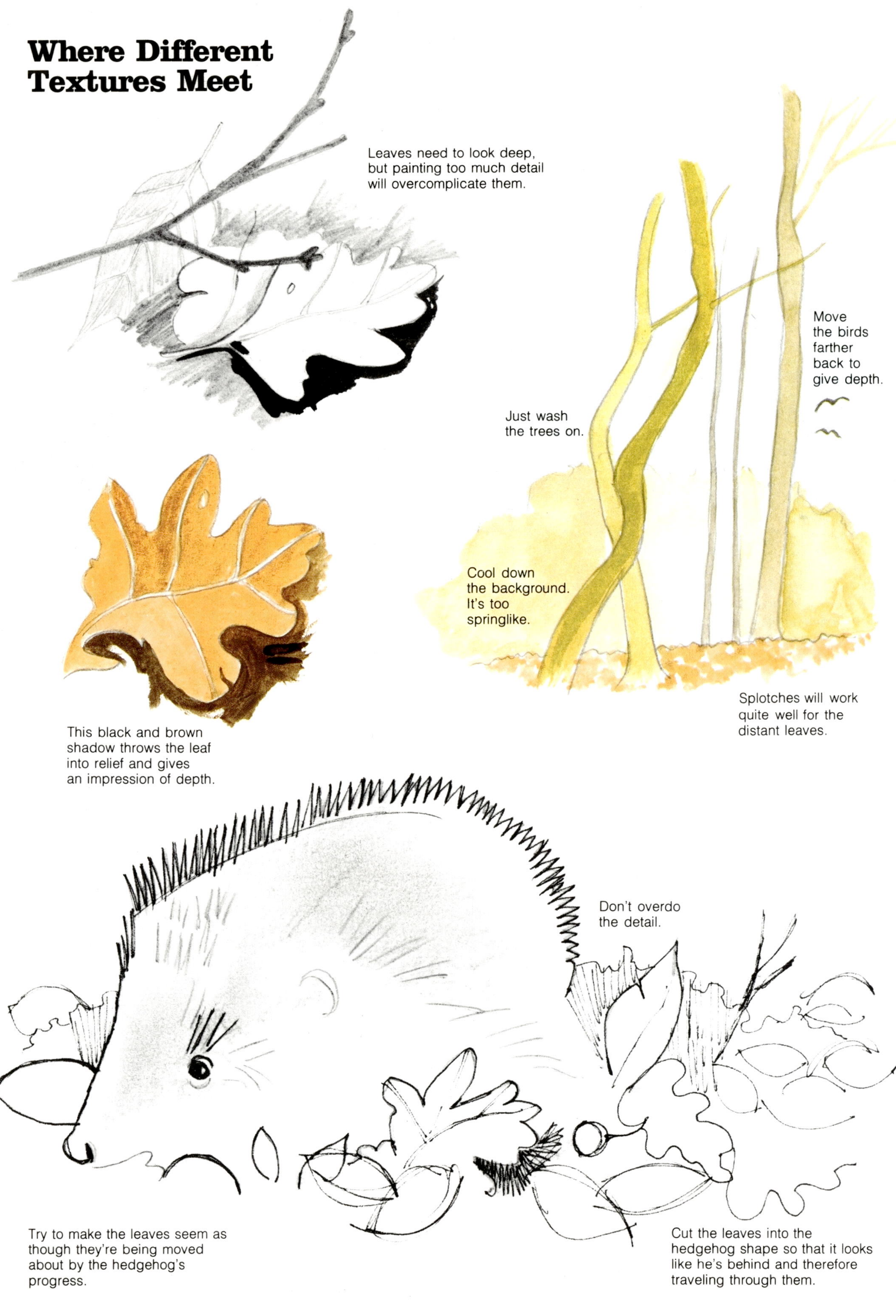

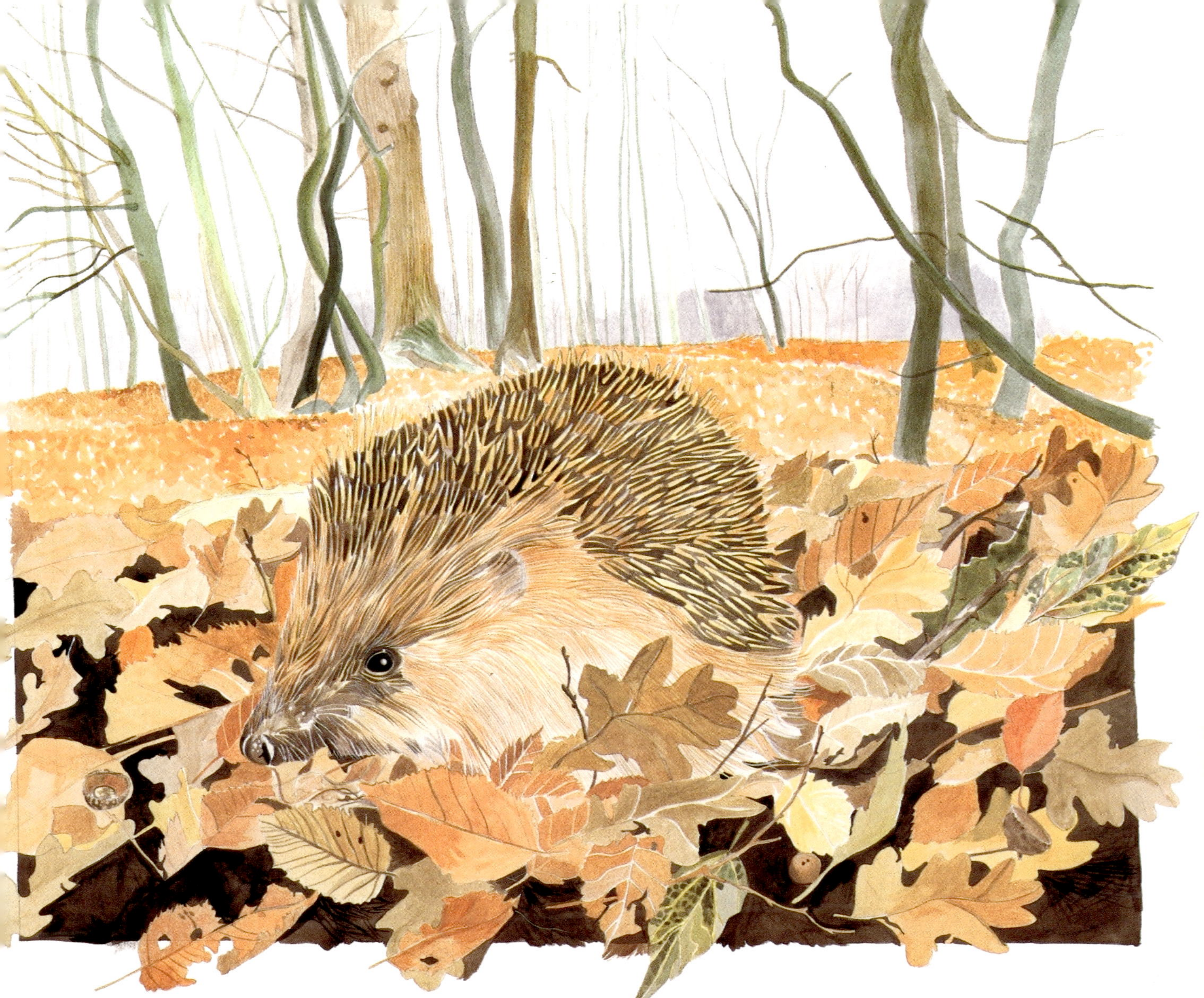

Hedgehog and Details

This hedgehog is one of the illustrations from a children's book I wrote. I have included it because it sums up what happens when different, yet similar, color textures meet. I still have some of the preparatory sketches I made, with my observations noted alongside, and these have also been included to show how I worked.

The problem I faced was that the hedgehog, which was covered with detail, had to sit among leaves that were also detailed. I had a perfect photograph of a hedgehog, a good series of sketches of the woodland that it was to travel through, and a box full of leaves and twigs. But somehow the whole lot had to be knitted together to provide a natural and believable painting.

I solved the problem in a series of preparatory doodles: The leaves in the foreground have firm outlines but very little surface detail, and they're washed in. The leaves in the middle and background are literally splotched on, and the detail on the hedgehog is limited, but firmly painted. The leaves were made to look deeply layered by painting the spaces between them sepia and black.

I think the several textures here meet well to provide a picture that looks as though it could have been painted out in the wild but, in fact, was patched together from several different sources.

Part Four

Exercises and Demonstrations

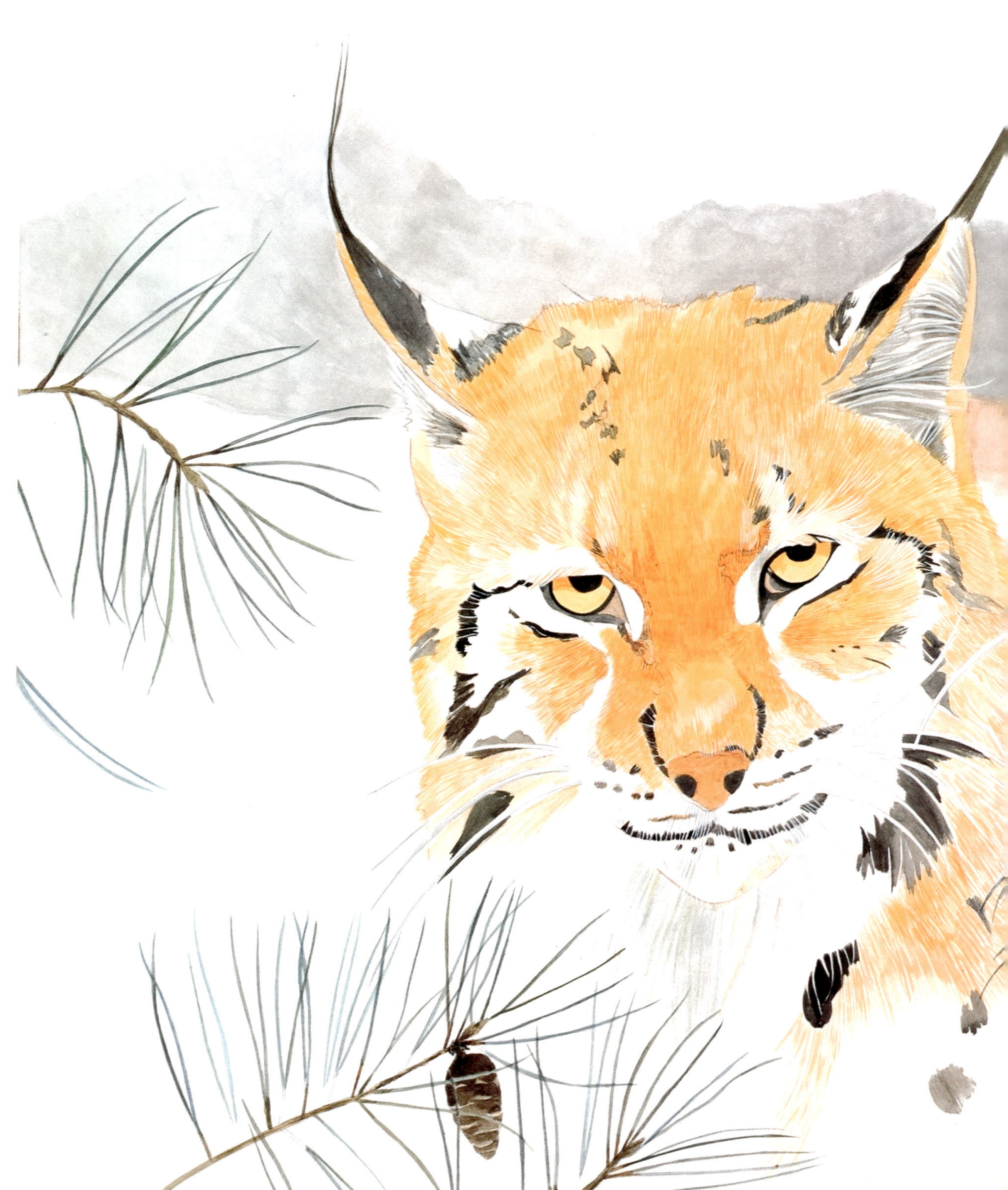

BEFORE ATTEMPTING the complicated, let's practice the straightforward. We will begin with four simple exercises in line, tone, and form, using insects as the subject. These exercises are designed as starters and will help you gain brush control, give you drawing practice, and provide you with the all-important feel of color mixing and watercolor handling. The exercises will also help you gain confidence and demonstrate an almost-systematic way of using watercolor, in preparation for the more complex demonstrations and exercises that follow.

When you understand the procedure, turn to the next exercise, on the stages in making a painting. Notice how the painting progresses in a series of layers. The third subject involves the painting of the original "identikit" lions (the ones we placed on the illustration board in the first section of the book). Now that they've been see how these animals are painted. Finally, there are seven more demonstrations—another Siberian tiger (this time, a portrait), tropical fish, mandrill, Canada goose, penguin, ducks, and a peacock. Follow along with me as I work—we will paint them together. Incidentally, don't hesitate to return to earlier chapters for specific details, to check on anything you don't understand. Here we will paint them together; later you will have twenty more projects to tackle on your own.

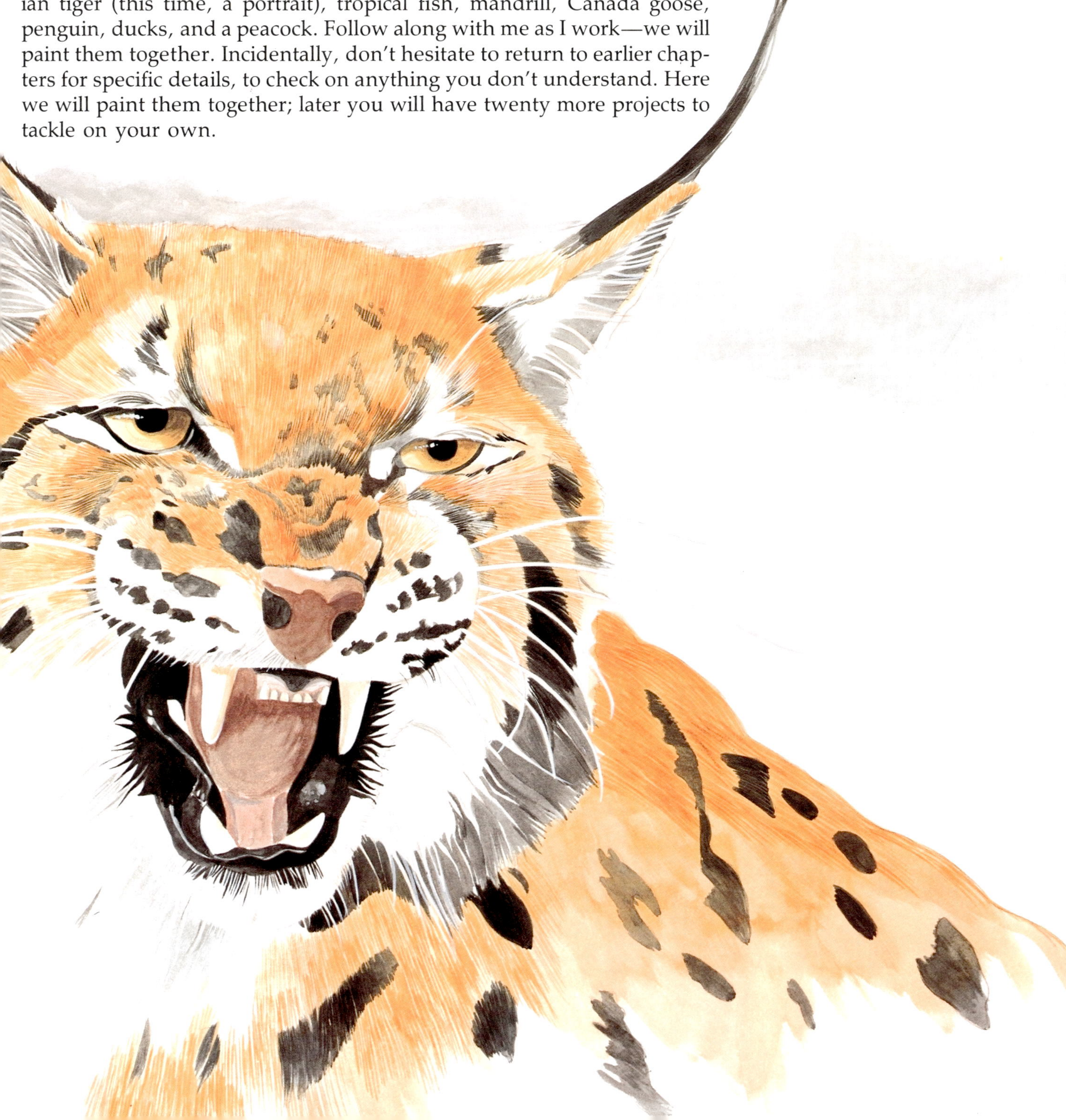

Four Simple Exercises

Bumblebee

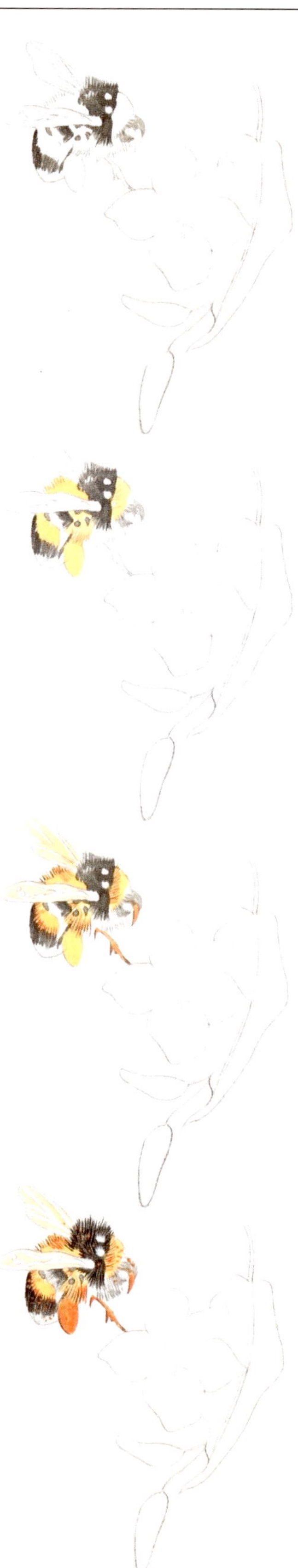

1. The first exercise is a bumblebee, a study in contrasting tones. This creature has a very simple shape, requires just a few colors, and just a little work to capture its heavy, hairy shape. Use a fine no. 0 brush and a mixture of lamp black and Chinese white and paint in, hair by hair, the sections that I have completed. Unload your brush in the center of the shape and use a drier brush for the fine hairs that make up the outline of the body. (If you use too much water, use a dry brush to mop up the surplus.)

2. A watery wash of cadmium yellow provides the solid areas of the bumblebee that alternate with the black. Use a no. 2 round brush and a fairly broad stroke. Don't worry too much about detail yet or about going over the edges.

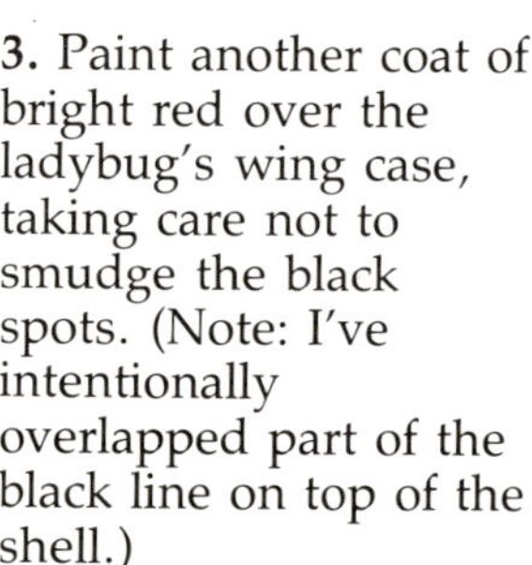

3. Use a fine no. 0 round brush for the whole of this stage. With a very watery mix of Naples yellow and a touch of light red, paint in the flat areas of the wings, leaving the ridges clear. Then with light red and cadmium lemon, carefully "tick" in just a few lines to show the fluffy darker hairs of the bumblebee's overcoat.

4. Use a no. 000 brush for the whole of this stage. Enliven the bee's color with pure chrome orange. Then with a fairly thick (but still fluid) solution of process white gouache, reinforce the ribs of the wings and refine the fur with lamp black. Mix lamp black and Chinese white for the gray, and a few dots of thick cadmium yellow pale form the sprinkled pollen that the bumblebee is seldom seen without.

Ladybug

1. This is an exercise in line and solid colors. Use a fine no. 0 brush and a fairly watery, but not uncontrollable solution of lamp black, and paint the ladybug's spots. You will have to go over the spots several times to get them solid and neat. With a slightly drier mix, paint the legs and head.

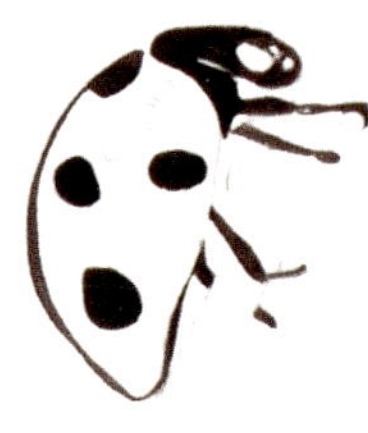

2. With a no. 2 brush, mix a watery solution of bright red and paint over the wing case of the ladybug, making sure you paint around rather than over the black spots.

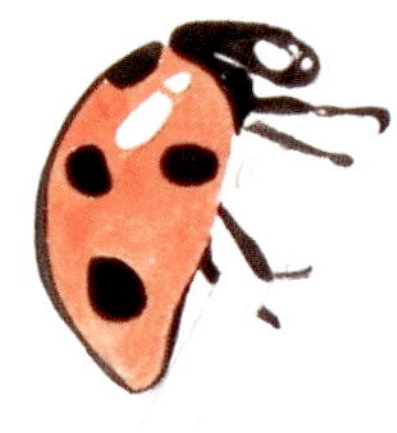

3. Paint another coat of bright red over the ladybug's wing case, taking care not to smudge the black spots. (Note: I've intentionally overlapped part of the black line on top of the shell.)

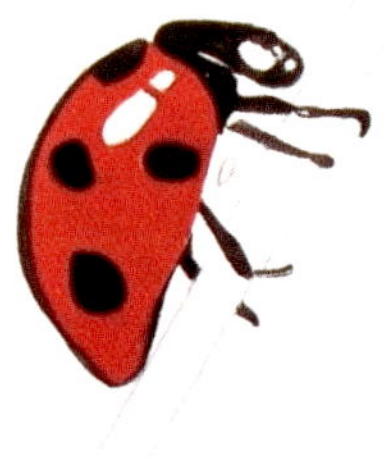

4. Carefully redefine all the black areas with lamp black and then, with process white, add the shine to the small white spot. Add cerulean blue to the process white for the larger, duller shine.

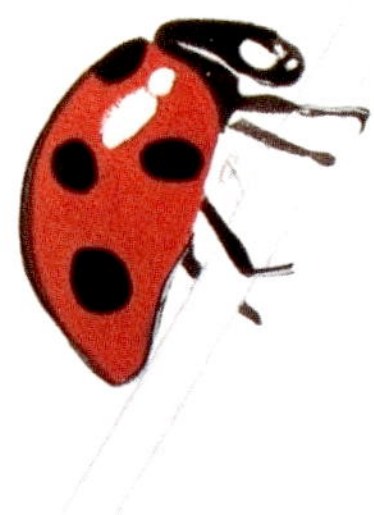

Blister Beetle

1. Start with a watery mix of lamp black and Chinese white. Load a no. 2 brush with enough paint to enable you to float the color on. (Practice on a spare piece of board.) Keep it simple and try longer, more definite, sweeping strokes.

2. With a no. 2 brush, float a wash of Naples yellow on the wing cases. With a wash of Winsor red, paint in the two stripes on the beetle's body and the two areas of the wing case.

3. Paint the antennae with chrome orange and cadmium lemon and use a mixture of light red and cadmium yellow pale to paint in the reinforcing ribs of the wings.

4. With a no. 000 brush and lamp black, darken and redefine areas of the wing cases, body, and head. Use sepia for the lighter areas of the body and legs. With cadmium lemon and Naples yellow, indicate the ridges on the wing cases and then use Chinese white and cadmium lemon to highlight the antennae and flick in a hint of wing color. Cerulean blue and Chinese white provide the shiny effect, and touches of bright red enliven the duller red sections.

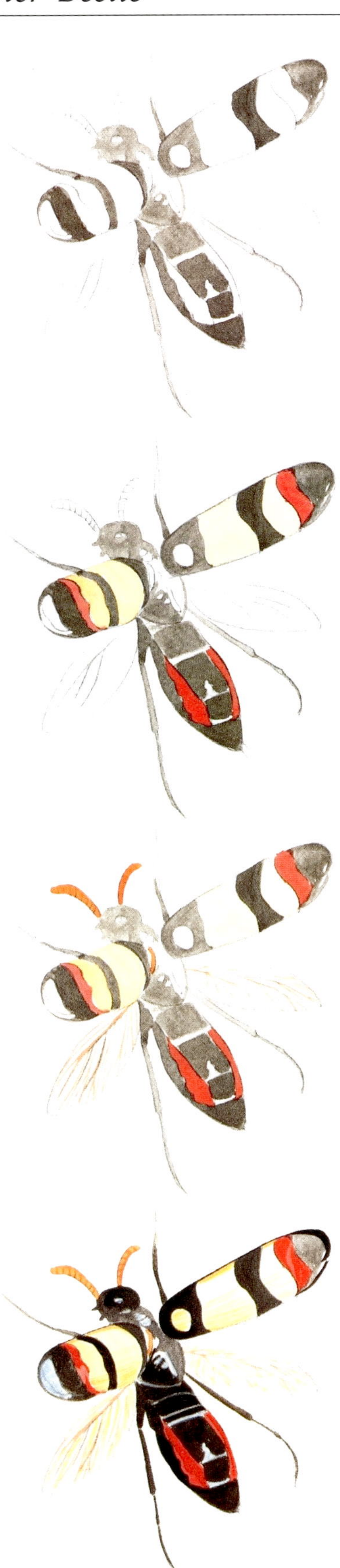

Butterfly

1. This is an exercise in line and tone to make a pattern. The butterfly is slightly more complex than the ladybug, blister beetle, or bumblebee and is an excellent exercise for gaining brush control. With black sketch part of the pattern area.

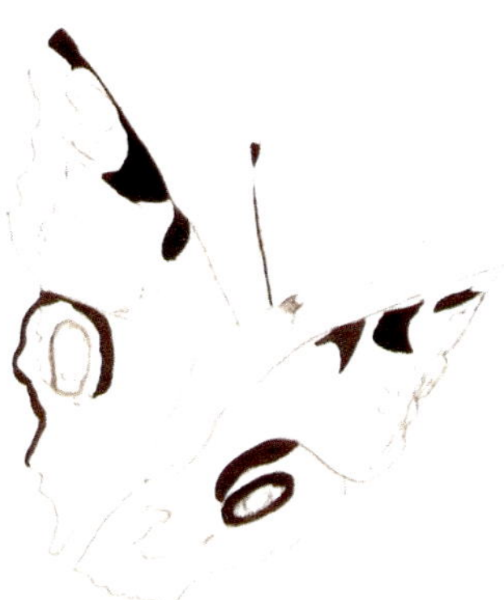

2. With a wash of chrome orange, paint the carefully delineated areas of the wings. Use the tip of a no. 1 round brush and don't let the mixture get too watery or you'll lose control.

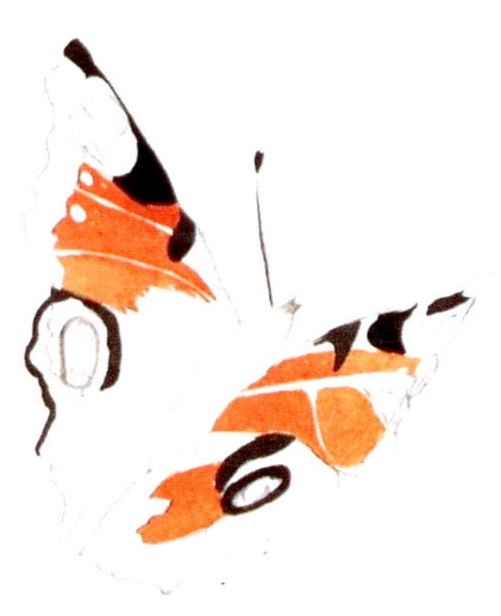

3. With sepia and cadmium yellow deep, paint a section of the wing, and then, with the same mix, tick in the fine hairs of the body. With cobalt blue and Chinese white, paint more of the pattern, overlapping some of the black areas with this mix.

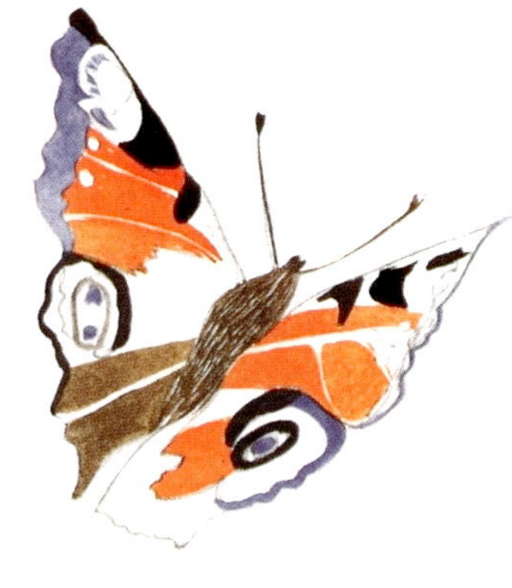

4. You can use a no. 000 brush throughout this final stage. Darken some of the blue areas with cobalt blue and some of the wing areas with a mixture of bright red and cadmium yellow deep. Sepia and cadmium yellow deep are used for the body and antennae. Redefine the black areas and "speckle" on gray with Chinese white and lamp black, and then finish with process gouache white.

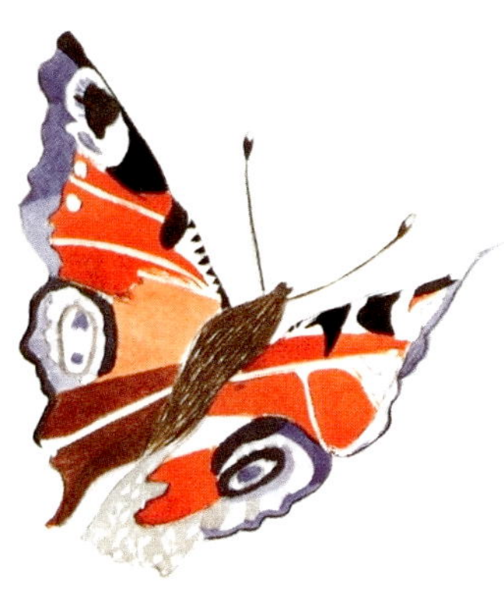

Stages in Making a Painting

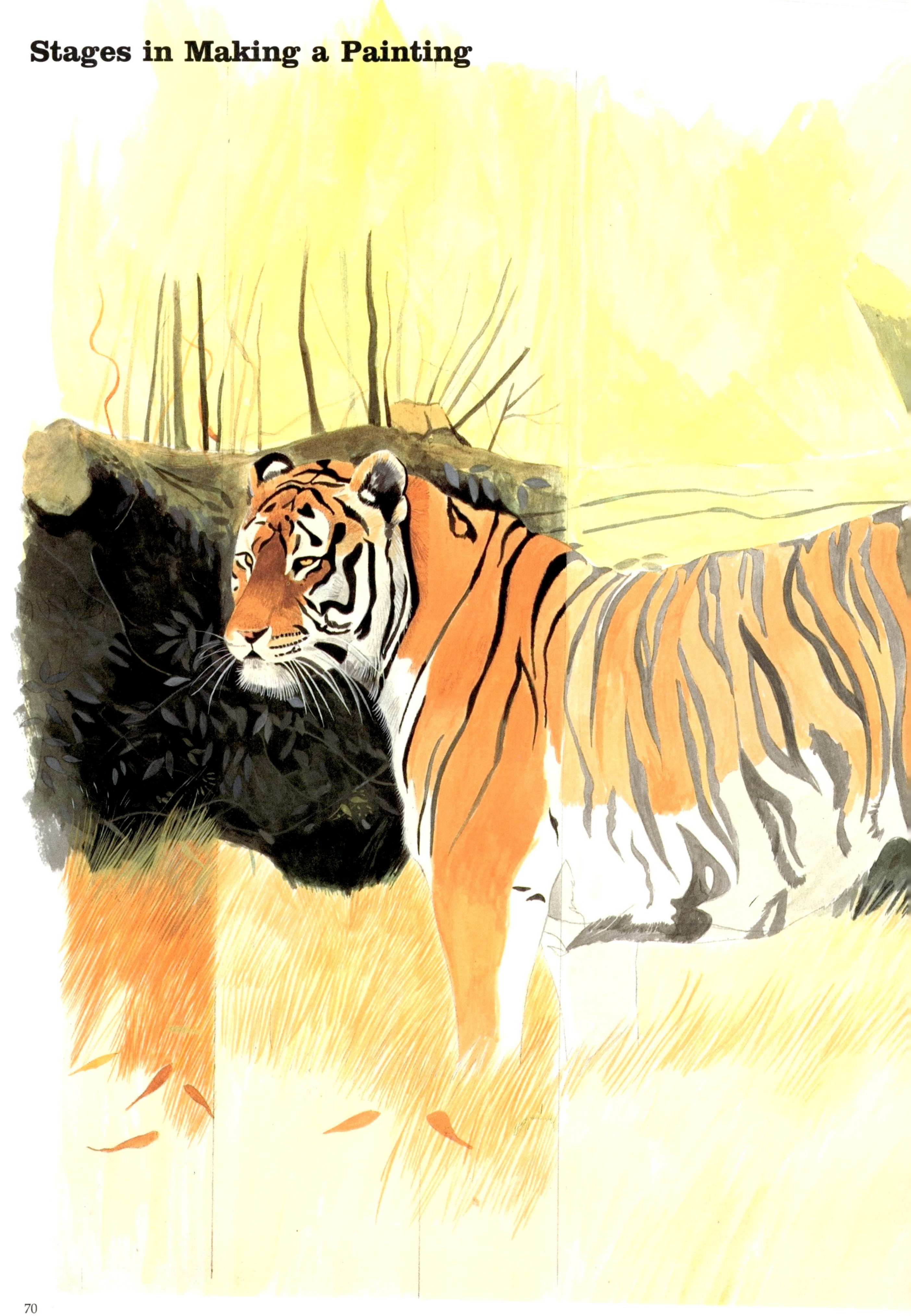

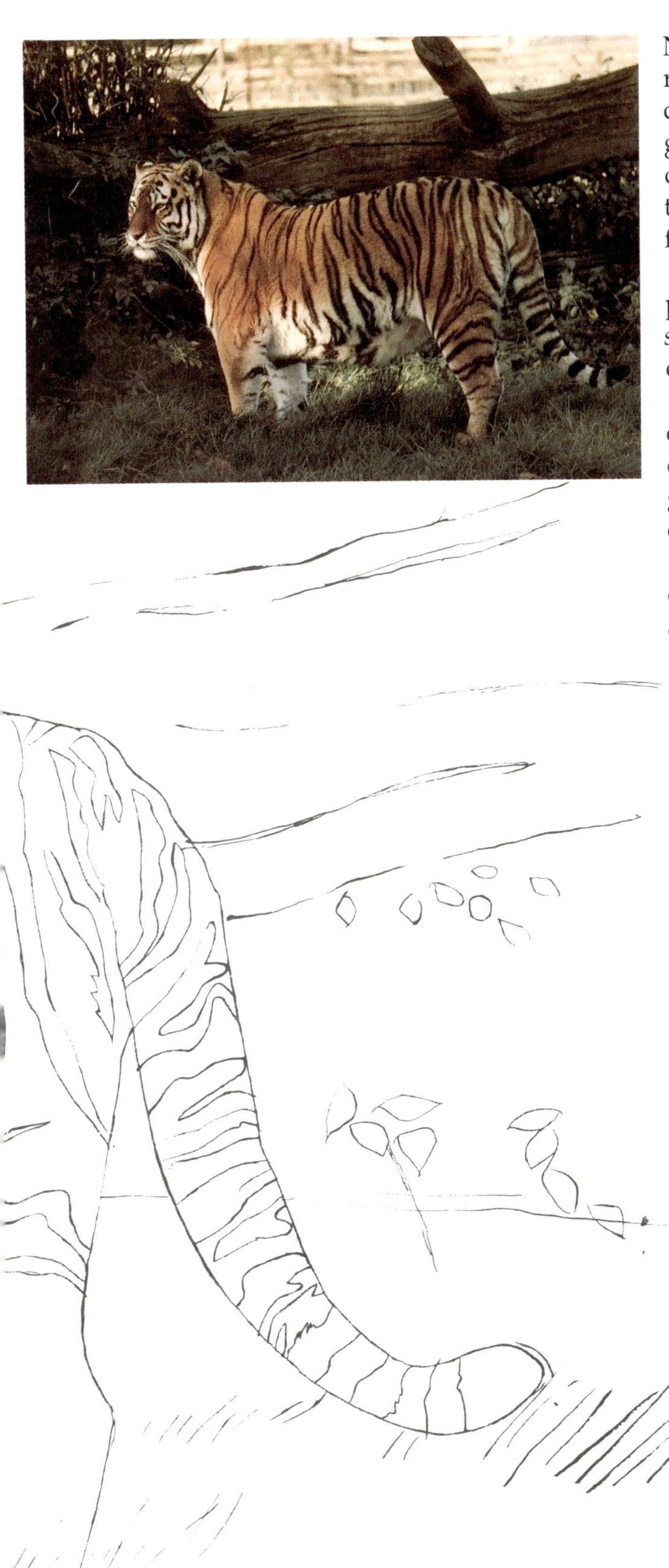

Now let's look at a more complex subject—a Siberian tiger—and see how a painting is made. As you can see from the photo, the tiger is standing in long grass against a background of a fallen tree and undergrowth, giving the picture compositional and tonal opportunities. The original print is taken from one of my own 35mm shots.

You can clearly see the build up of the stages as I progress from the tiger's tail to his head. *The first stage* shows the careful drawing of the basic shapes of the picture with a 2B pencil.

The second stage shows the washing in of the base colors: orange in the coat and gray/black for the darker stripes, with a yellowish wash for the background, plus the beginnings of some overpainting of grass and tree detail.

The third stage describes the deepening of the colors—the bolder definition of the tiger's stripes and an increase of color in the background, with leaf and branch shapes beginning to emerge.

The fourth stage includes the tiger's head and an almost completed background. I have concentrated here on painting in the detail of the head with a finely pointed brush and, for the first time, the contrast between the dark, shadowed background and the brightly colored tiger begins to give the picture depth and interest.

The final stage demonstrates a deepening of the background tone in order to make the subject really stand out. Obviously, painting this picture virtually in strips created an artificial situation that prevented the conclusion of a fully completed picture—because in these final stages, what makes a painting good are all the small touches that are added while looking at a fully painted, equally finished piece of work. But this painting is still useful because, apart from demonstrating the progress on a painting, it contains some good compositional and color contrast lessons. For example, the continuing line and dark background of the fallen log will dramatize and clearly thrust the shape and solidity of the huge tiger forward, and the three depth stages—foreground, middle, and back ground—shows how realistic recession adds a three-dimensional feeling.

The "Identikit" Lion

Earlier in the book we arranged two lions into a composition by overlaying several tracings. Now we'll paint these lions, using photos, tracings, and the Identikit method.

Stage One

When the final image is transferred onto the board, look over the picture several times to make sure it's complete, then carefully remove the masking tape. Save your identikit tracing just in case you make a mistake while painting. (I always roll up my tracings and file them. They are useful as a record and tool for future work.)

Wash your hands thoroughly, for in the process of tracing down, they will have become almost black. To protect the red drawing lines (the blueprint), apply an almost colorless wash immediately. Mix a little Chinese white and Naples yellow on the palette with a 3/8" (8mm) sable brush loaded with water, but apply the wash with a reasonably dry brush. Work the brush up and down in short strokes and do not worry about going over the edges of your picture as the wash is almost colorless and a little wandering will not spoil the painting. Take your time and lightly brush on short strokes, using your brush to outline the shapes. Resist all temptation to add more color—the purpose of this wash technique is to fix the red lines, not obscure them. Once the wash is complete, leave it for several hours. I always leave it overnight for two reasons: first, the surface must be dry before applying any detail, and second, the rest improves my technique and gives an objective view of the subject. Never paint or draw for too long without a break, as overwork dulls the mind and produces a stale painting. Remember to paint slowly to produce good results.

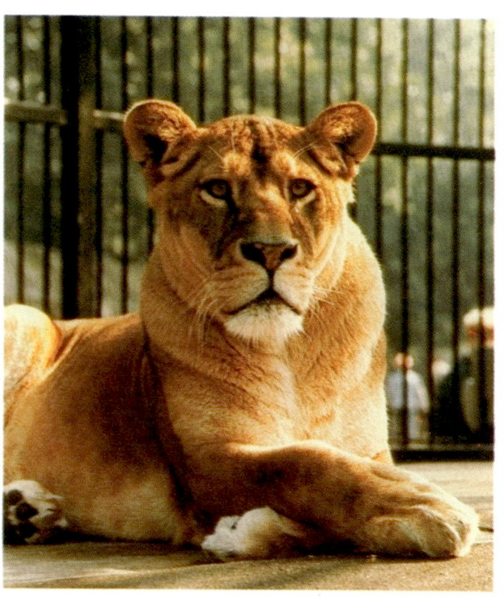

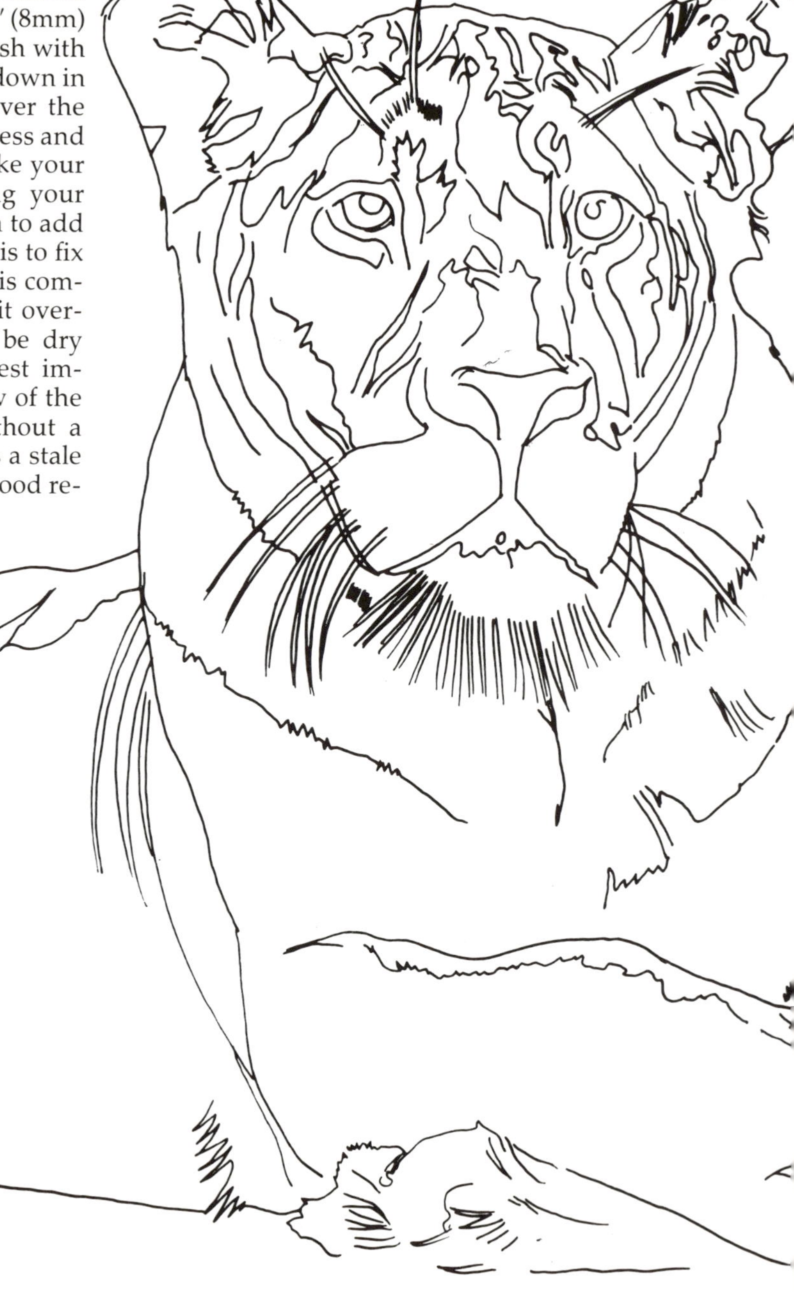

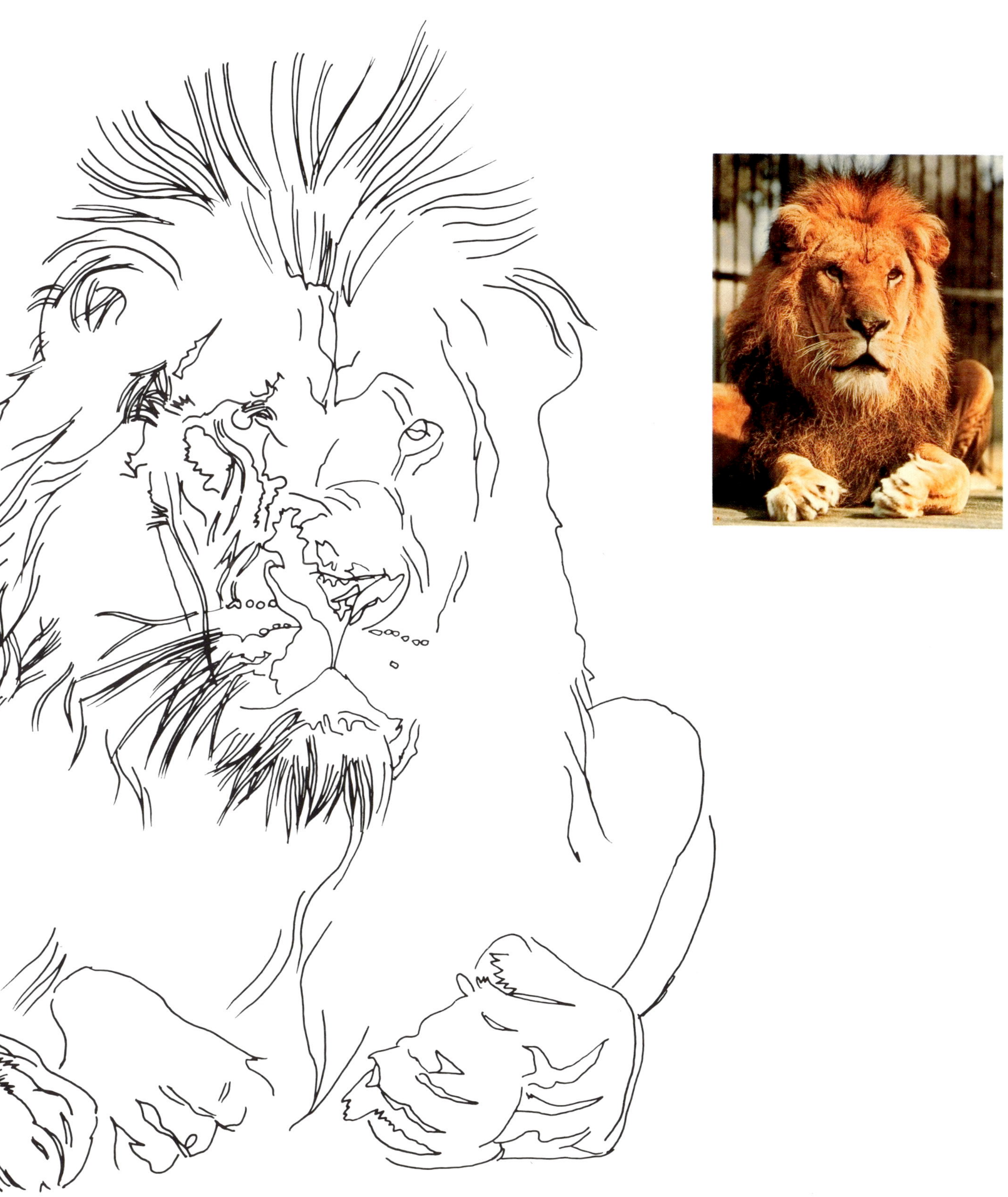

Stage Two

Now that the wash is dry, the serious painting begins. At this stage, I make sure everything is where I want it—the right brushes are ready and the palette is clean. It is most discouraging to make a mistake now, after all the effort so far. Avoid making mistakes by following two rules. Tape a piece of white bond writing paper above your painting and use this as a test area before applying paint to the picture. This is a safe way of testing pigment density, delicacy of brushstroke and the right consistency of wash. The second rule is that, up to stage 3, use understated colors. A mistake is permanent only when the pigment is too rich.

Begin by painting the dark areas that frame the main features. Use an understrength mixture of lamp black and Vandyke brown on a no. 1 round sable brush to paint the eye edges and the nose and mouth hollows. Once the outlines are dry, start on the inside of the eye. The eyes of an animal determine its expression and if you paint these well, the whole painting will have life and force. Look very carefully at the shapes within the eye and correct them with an HB pencil using the lightest of strokes. Wash in an understated mixture of cadmium yellow and light red, with cadmium yellow providing the dominant color in the mixture. Leave the pupil area and the white highlight areas unpainted. Undercoat the pupil area with a watered down (but not runny) lamp black, avoiding the highlight areas. (I use a round no. 1 sable brush for this delicate operation, but you may prefer to use a smaller no. 0 brush.) Once the basic eye pattern is set, float in the darker areas with a mixture of cadmium yellow and light red, with light red providing the more dominant color in the blend. Lions are a blend of these same two colors, with density and direction of fine detail lines providing tone and form. Nature has provided the ideal coloring for the lion to blend into its natural habitat.

Using a 3/8″ (8mm) brush and a weak solution of cadmium yellow (or Naples yellow), block in the large areas of tone where fine hair strokes of one color overlay areas of another. Deposit most of your excess mixed paint on the test paper before applying your brush to the painting. Remember, colors that are too rich at this early stage will make the essential overlaying of detail difficult later, so understate your color washes.

To put in the first fine details, I use a really clean no. 00 brush. Using a fairly dry mixture of Naples yellow, Vandyke brown, cadmium yellow, and light red, indicate the contours of the lioness's face. A no. 1 brush is most suitable for this part of the exercise. Use short, definite strokes that follow the hair direction, as in the reference photograph.

Concentrate on the lioness, starting with the eyes. The basic shape already exists, just add the finer details. The color is darker around the pupils and under the top of the eyes. Use a no. 1 round sable brush and mix a slightly darker brown with cadmium yellow, Vandyke brown, and light red, with Vandyke brown dominant. Float a fairly wet wash over the area around the pupils and under the eyelid, avoiding hard brown edges. If hard edges develop, soften them before they dry with a damp 1/8″ (3mm) flat brush. Once this is done, darken the outlines of the eye and the pupil with lamp black and Vandyke brown. Use process white tinged with just a touch of cerulean blue for the highlights of the eye. Using a no. 0 brush, paint a thin line of cadmium yellow pale around the bottom of the curve of the eye and put a strong brown/black line under the eyelid.

Repeat the same process for the lion's eye, but because the lion is stronger in color, the eye pigment must be stronger, too. The great advantage of watercolor is that effects can be built up gradually and safely. Throughout the process of painting, gradually modify the eyes to suit the density of the surrounding features. If each stage is understated, the eyes will evolve quite naturally. For the nose, wash in a weak pink of bright red, Chinese white, and the smallest speck of yellow. Once this is dry, add the freckles with a watery mixture of lamp black and cerulean blue. Above the noses of both lions is an area of blue/black—a combination of lamp black and cerulean blue, mixed with a little white to soften it. Add shape to the nose by increasing the density of the pink wash.

The secret of painting animals, using my method, is to paint every hair, or at least give the *impression* that every hair has been painted. Always make sure that the direction, density, and length of each stroke accurately describe the contours of the animal. Masses of lines can be built up and joined to each other to produce tone and form.

To bulk up the body areas, apply a dry wash with Vandyke brown, cadmium yellow deep, and light red. Drybrush the body areas of the lioness's back and front leg with this misture with a 3/8″ (8mm) flat brush. Use a thicker mixture of this color and a no. 2 round sable brush to paint the shadow section of the lion's mane.

Stage Three

Complete the hair with light and dark color combinations. For light-colored areas, use cadmium yellow with a touch of light red. For darker areas, use cadmium yellow with Vandyke brown and light red. Create the paw shadows with a combination of lamp black, cerulean blue, and Chinese white. The large areas of white are just clean paper. Complete the painting by adding whiskers with process white and increase the small area of light in the eyes with a speck of process white. To paint highlight areas on the fur, mix cadmium yellow with process white and add a few well-defined hairs. Process white is much thicker and more opaque than ordinary watercolor and so you can add small highlights on top of the watercolor.

I wanted the lions to be the central feature of this painting and did not want to clutter the effect with background landscape foliage, so I picked out a shadow at the bottom of the lion's feet with gray (cerulean blue, lamp black, and white), and rubbed an almost-matching pastel around their heads, just to lift them from the white of the background.

In the demonstrations that follow, I will show you how to paint a variety of animals.

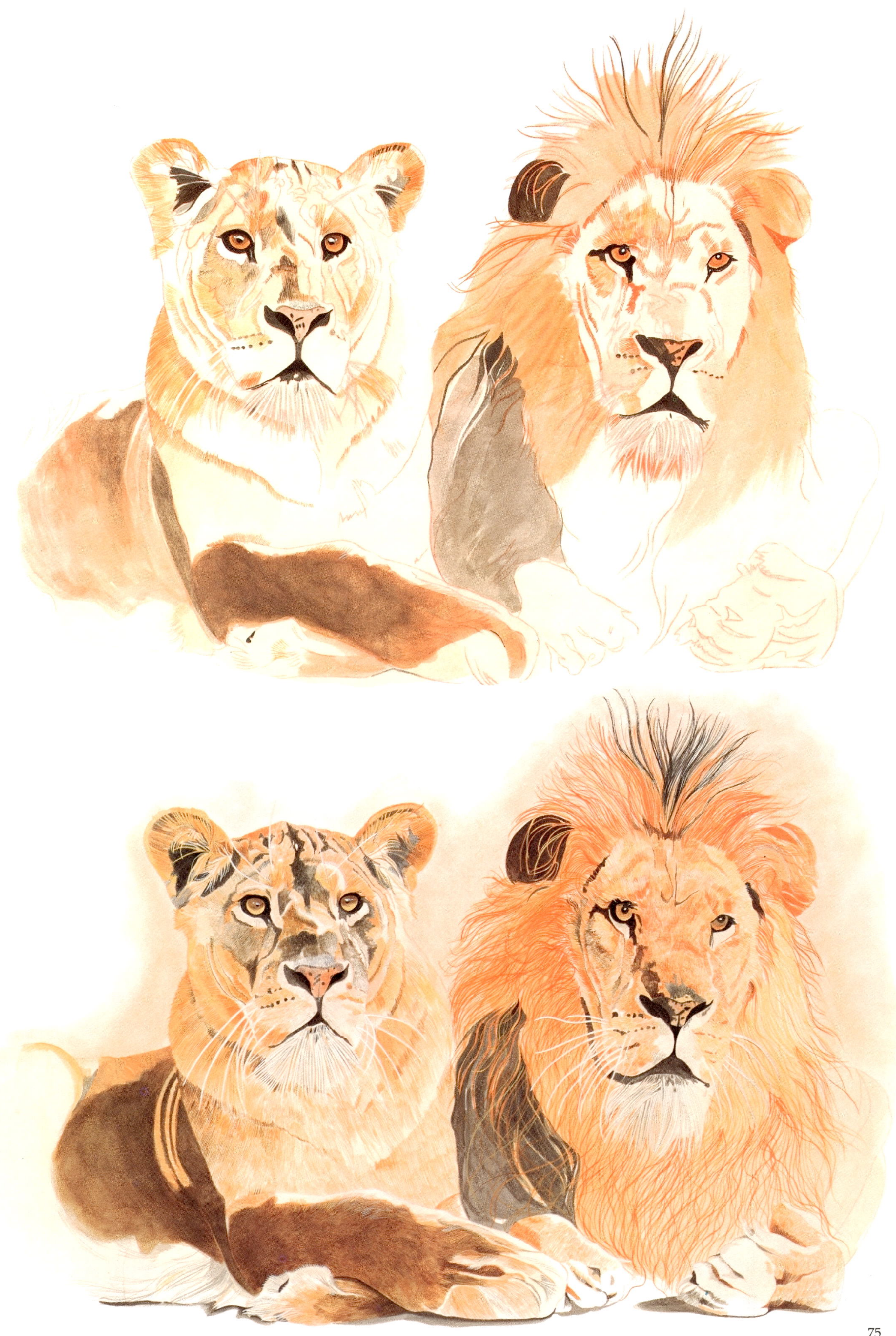

AFRICAN DUSK, 1977
Collection of my daughter Alison

I also based this painting on the photographs of the lions, with a change of background. This picture pleases me. It has mood and accuracy, and there is a real feeling of sunset, with both of the lions fully awake and alert for a night of hunting now that the heat of the sun has faded. I can remember working enormously hard on this picture and having an inspirational feeling about it before I had even started.

I spent months on the picture, applying stroke after careful stroke to the hair detail, and working with glaze after glaze to achieve compelling eyes. Because the colors of the grass, the sky, and the lions themselves are accurate, it was difficult to know how they would appear in the lighting of their natural habitat.

I think that, apart from the compositional merits of this painting, what actually makes it work are the different techniques used. The sky is washed in a series of layers with a large, flat housepainter's brush, with generous drying time allowed between each wash. The trees are only vaguely indicated, and the lions are almost overdone in a photographic and careful treatment to make them look ready to spring out of the background. With so many almost matching colors, contrast of painting treatment was essential. I painted the grass with very strong strokes, clearly defining the foreground blades to help the strong detail of the lions sit well in the ground cover. I also showed by the lean of the grass that a breeze is blowing. This contrasts with the upright stance of the lions and heightens our awareness of the cooler temperatures of African evenings.

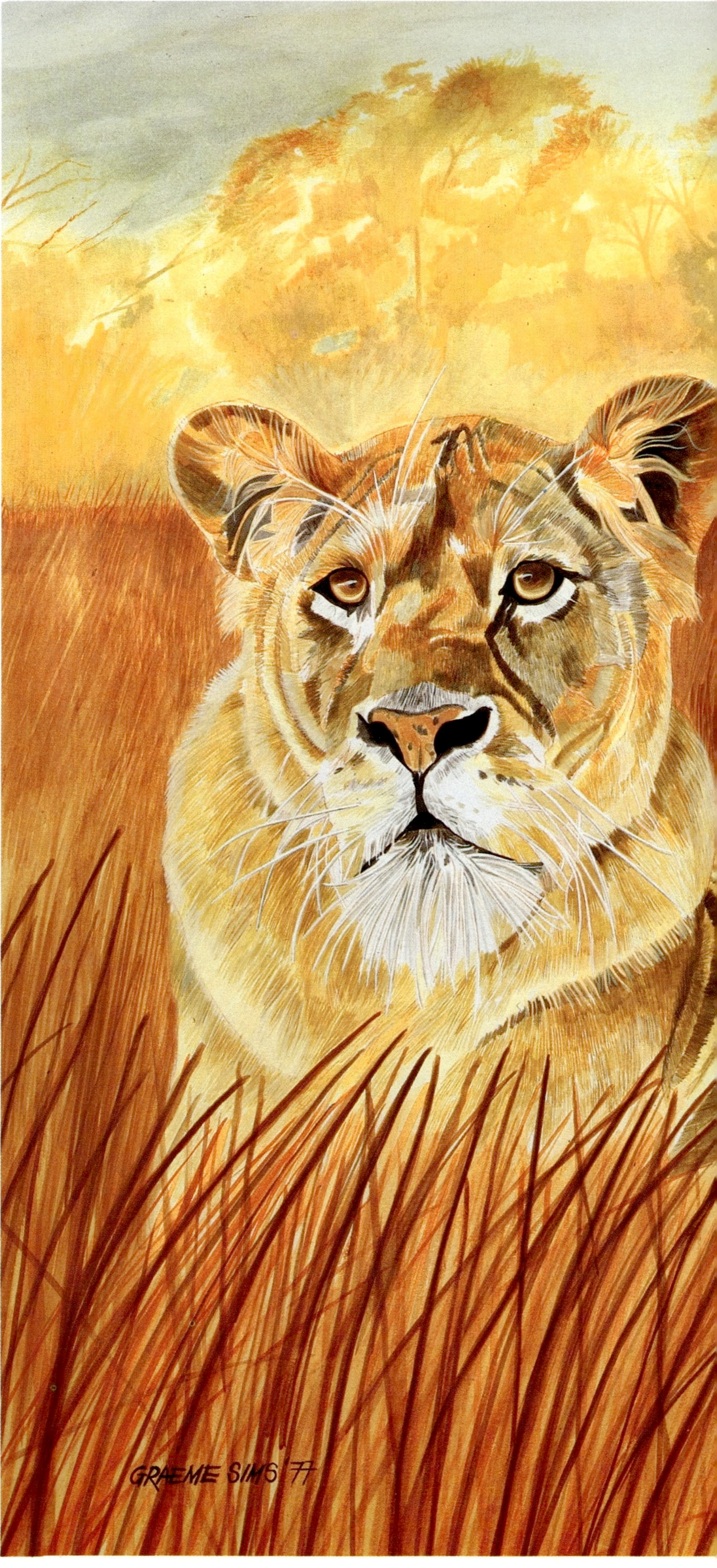

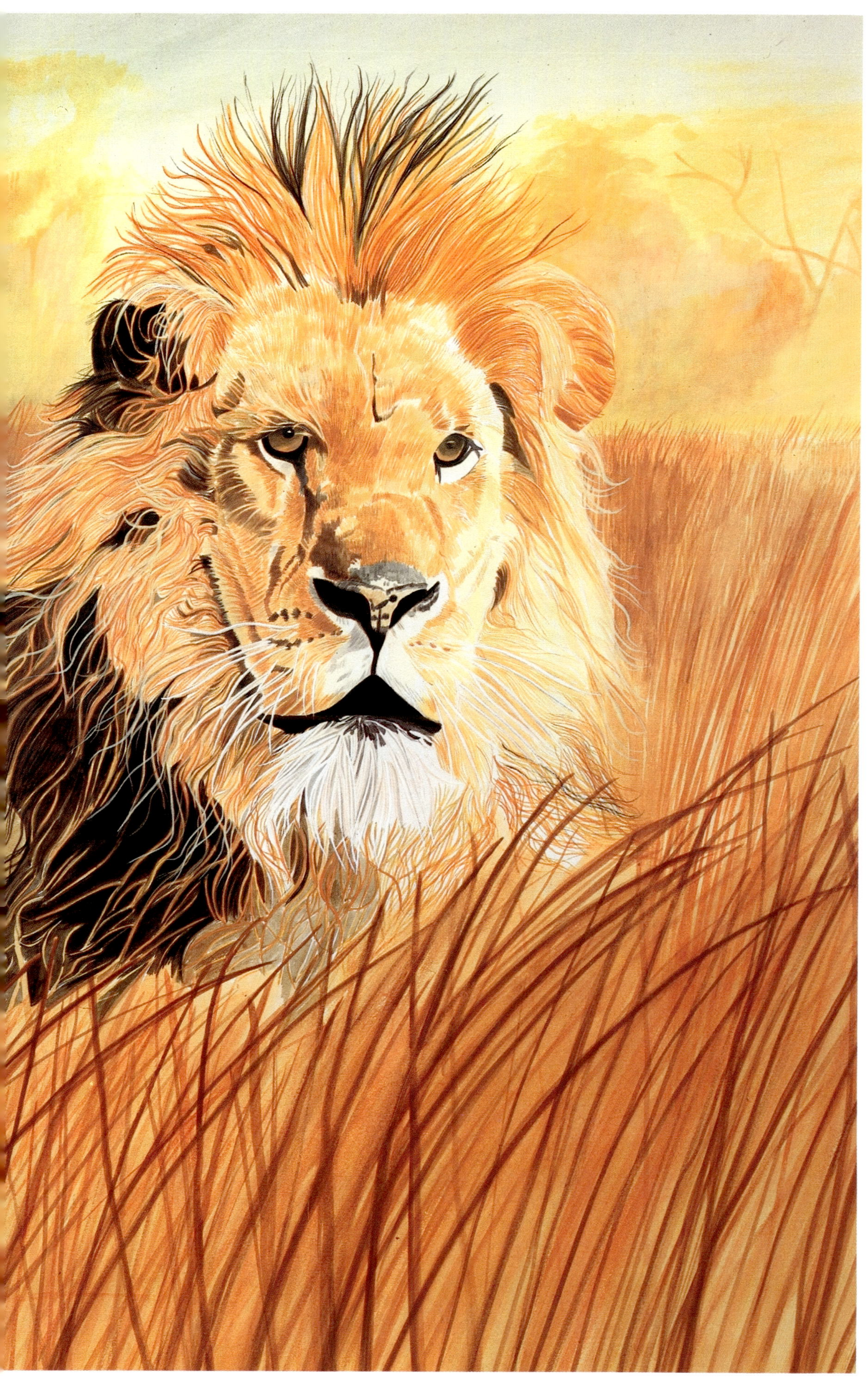

Siberian Tiger

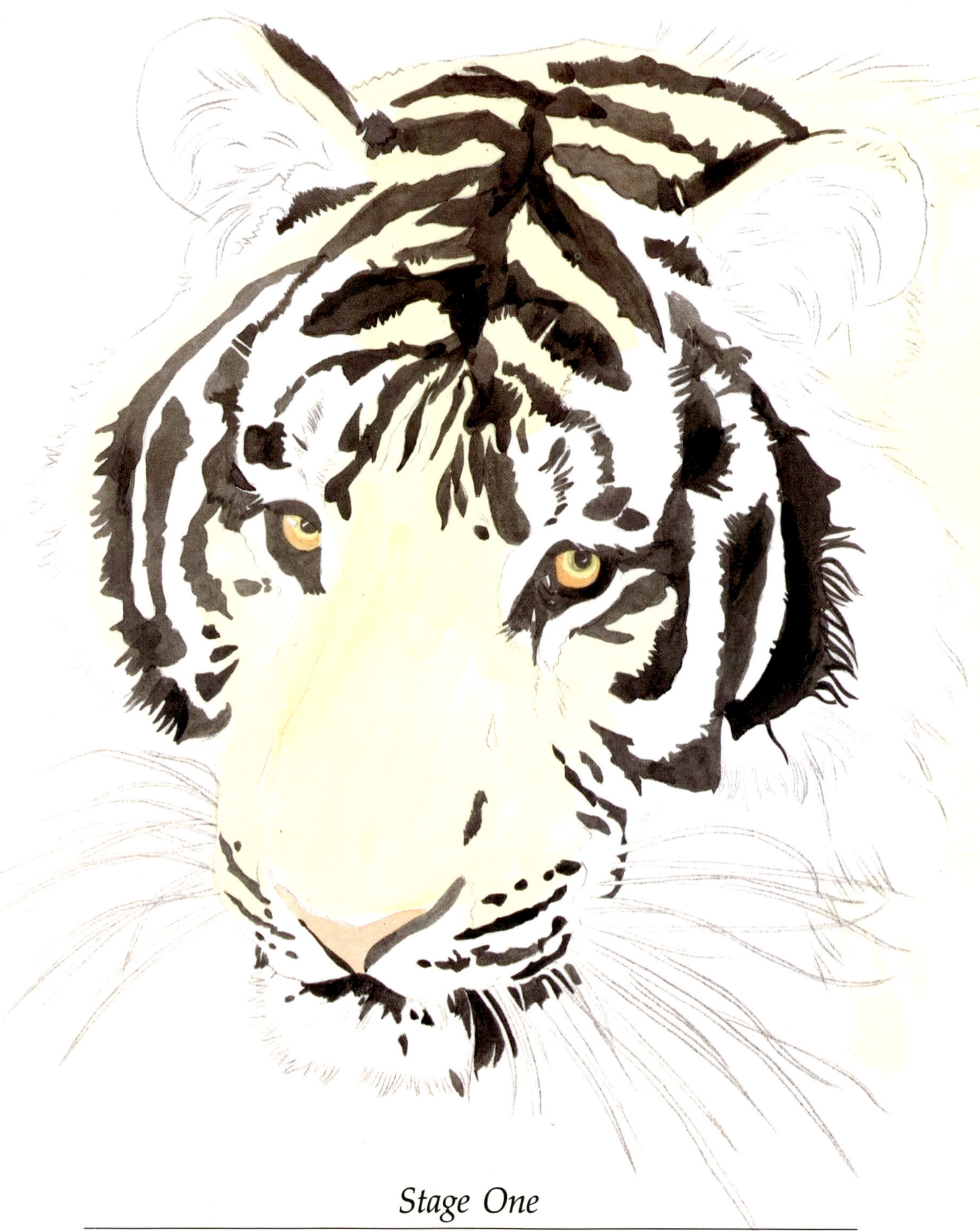

Stage One

After a careful drawing, use a ¼″ (6mm) flat sable brush to wash in a base of Naples yellow, leaving the whites uncovered. Then put a very thin wash of Chinese white over the white areas. With a no. 0 round sable brush, fill in the black stripes as accurately as possible, not as a solid color, but underpainted. A no. 2 round brush is best for the larger areas of black stripes.

With cerulean blue and cadmium yellow deep, paint the area surrounding the pupil, blotting the excess color on the brush before you get to the next color. Next paint the pupils lamp black and the surrounding eye area cadmium lemon with a speck of light red, using a no. 00 brush. (Notice that I have left the eye highlight unpainted and the whole of the eye area undetailed.) Finally, wash in the nose with a watery mixture of Chinese white, bright red, and lemon yellow and a no. 2 brush.

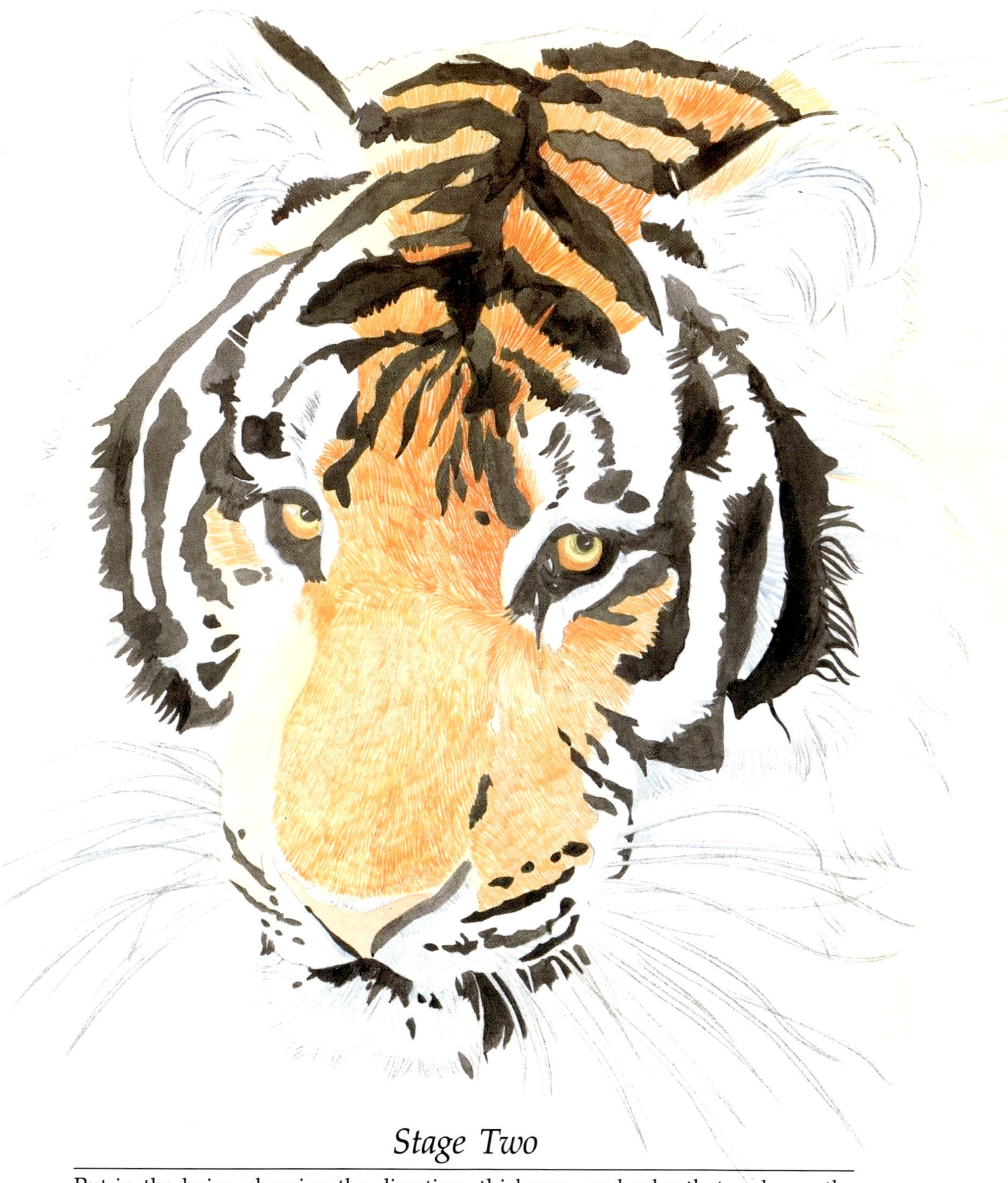

Stage Two

Put in the hairs, showing the direction, thickness, and color that make up the essence of the tiger. I use a fine-pointed no. 00 for the fine detail and a no. 2 round for the longer, thicker hairs. With a fairly generous amount of cadmium yellow, a little bright red, and a medium amount of light red on the palette, mix just enough orangy color to do only the part you're immediately concentrating on. (I start on the forehead, since the hair shapes and direction here help shape the whole face.) A fairly watery solution gives more brush control and creates long, crisp strokes. Take careful note of the length, weight, and direction of the hairs and remember that the space in between them is also important as it allows the lighter wash to show through. Putting the detail of white hairs onto white paper sounds difficult, but if you paint the gap between the hairs with a shadow effect, the white of the board creates the white hairs. (I always use a fine brush for this very careful work.) Mix a little cerulean blue with Chinese white for subtle touches on the ears, nose, chin, and elsewhere.

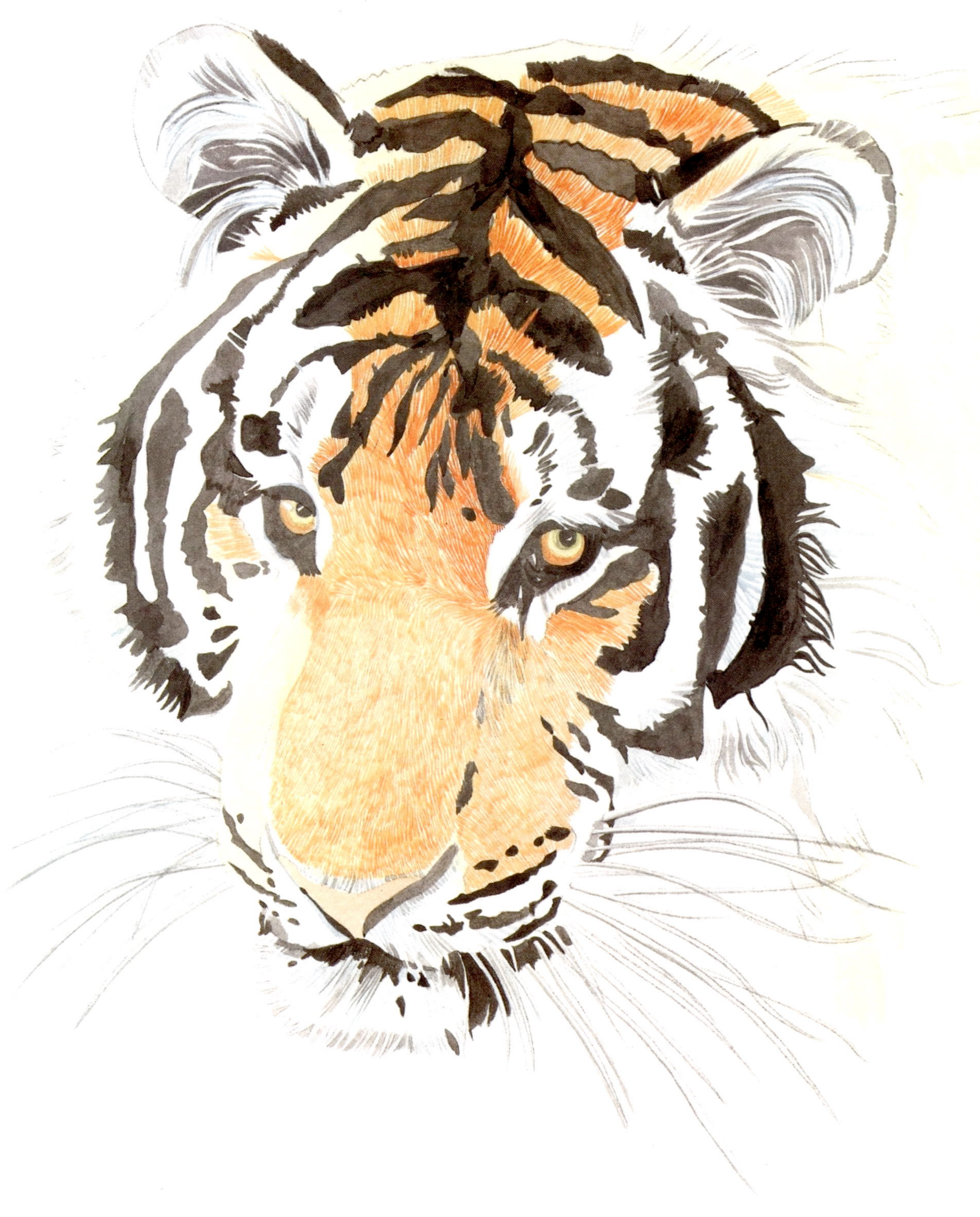

Stage Three

Concentrate on the darker shadows (such as those of the ears and outer face and below the eye) using a mix of lamp black and Chinese white, alternating the strength of the black according to the density of the shadow required. I use a no. 2 brush for the large strokes and a no. 0 brush for the finer detail. This stage is all-important, adding depth and delineating the white hairs that will come later.

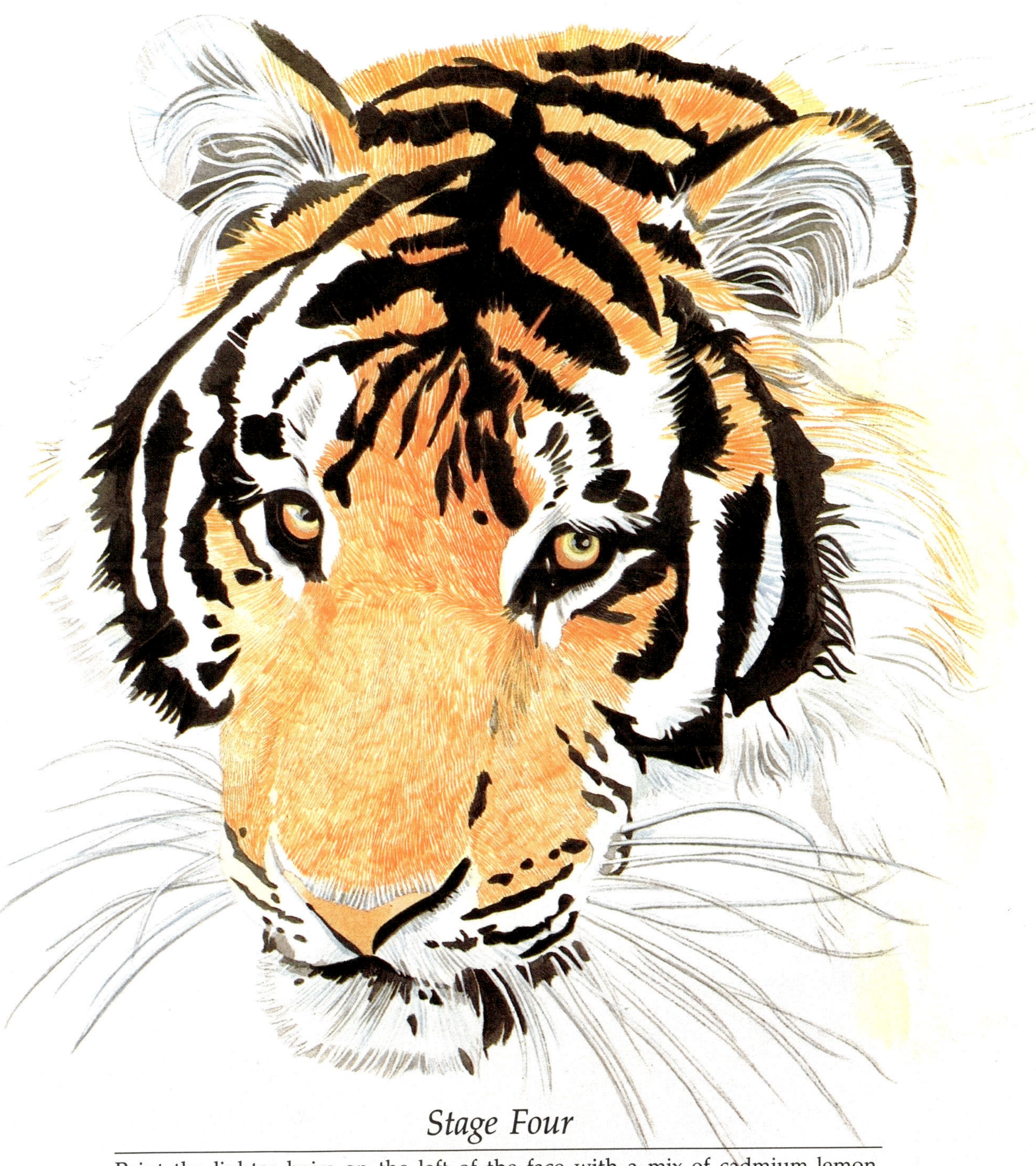

Stage Four

Paint the lighter hairs on the left of the face with a mix of cadmium lemon, chrome orange and light red, using a fine no. 0 brush. Then mix cobalt blue and lamp black and darken the black stripes. It is important to follow the hair direction and not just solidly fill in the black stripes. Use the same mix to define the eye pupils and, with white, to strengthen the shadows on the ears. Wash in a light shadow onto the nose, using a mix of yellow ochre, light red, and black.

Concentrate on the white hairs, using a fairly thick, but smooth, mix of process white and a well-pointed no. 0 brush. Notice the highlights in the eyes and the way the opaque process white allows white strokes to be applied over a darker color. I have used very weak Chinese white to soften the blend of the colors in the eye. When the white highlights dry, with a mixture of cerulean blue and Chinese white, soften all but the brightest shine with a faint blue wash. Finally, with a mixture of cerulean blue and a tiny amount of Chinese white, reinforce the shadows on the nose, whiskers, and ears.

Tropical Fish

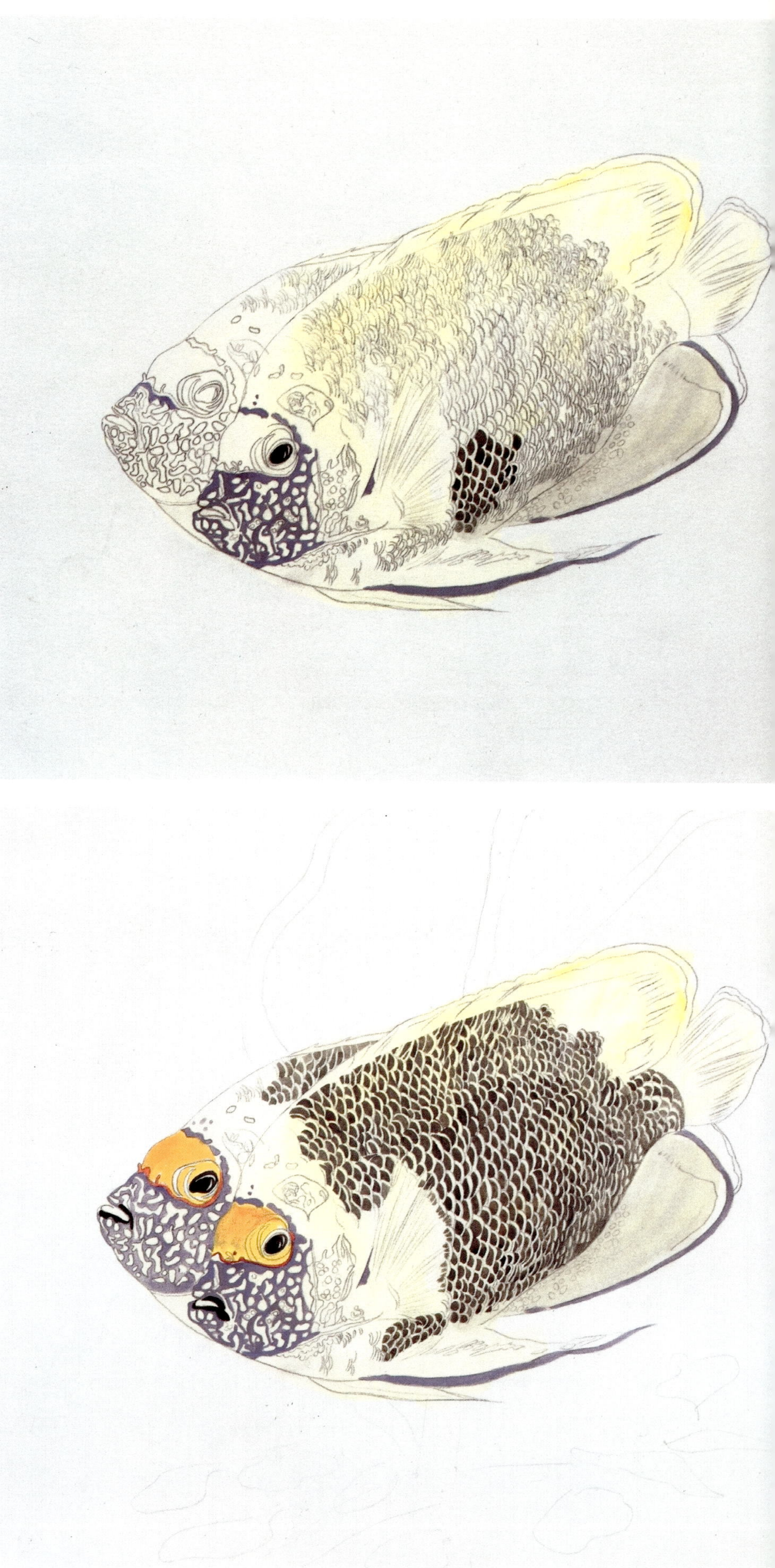

Stage One

To fix the very detailed drawing, wash the whole area with a very watery solution of process white and cadmium pale yellow, using a ½″ (13mm) flat sable brush. This not only protects the paint line of the drawing, but also provides a good foundation color for the fish. While the wash is still wet, tint the base fin with a weak cobalt blue. As a compass reference, paint the eye of the nearest fish in black, using a no. 0 brush. To capture the brilliant luminosity of the tropical fish, mix a cobalt blue gouache with a watercolor Chinese white for the nose pattern color, and apply it carefully with a well-pointed no. 0 sable brush. (I only painted the nearest fish so that you can still see the drawn detail of the pattern.) With a weak solution of raw umber and black, paint the flat areas of the body scales using a very finely pointed 00 brush—don't use too much water for this technique. (Again, I completed only part of the work so you could see the process.)

Stage Two

The scale pattern is now complete and the nose of the background fish has been painted with a no. 2 brush and pure cadmium lemon. Paint the area next to the front fish's eye, then add some cadmium yellow pale to make the mixture more orangy and add it to both background fishes. With a pure bright red, paint a line around the base of the yellow area on the nearer fish and then add white to the red and do the same on the second fish.

Stage Three

With a mixture of raw umber and black, paint the area above the eyes of the fish. As yet, little of the brilliant color has been added. So, in order to start hardening up the image, brush on an underwash of chrome orange and cadmium yellow pale around the fins using somewhat wet, weak color and a no. 2 brush.

Stage Four

With a well-mixed, thick wash of cerulean blue and white, paint the top line of both fish. Then, using a well-blunted no. 00 brush, paint the bed of the waterscape, making sure the lines follow the swirl of water above. Then add the background of the bed area. It will need finer treatment than the foreground floor in order to give an impression of distance. Notice that the lines in the distance are shorter and their direction has changed to give a contoured look to the ocean floor. I painted it with a blunt 0 brush (but just the point), and added a little lamp black to a mix of cerulean blue and Chinese white. With Chinese white and a touch of alizarin carmine and a little cerulean blue, using a no. 00 brush—but this time allowing each stroke to overlap—paint the pinkish underwater vegetation, aiming for slightly varying but similar shades of the color combined with strength of line and direction to create this imaginary underwater landscape.

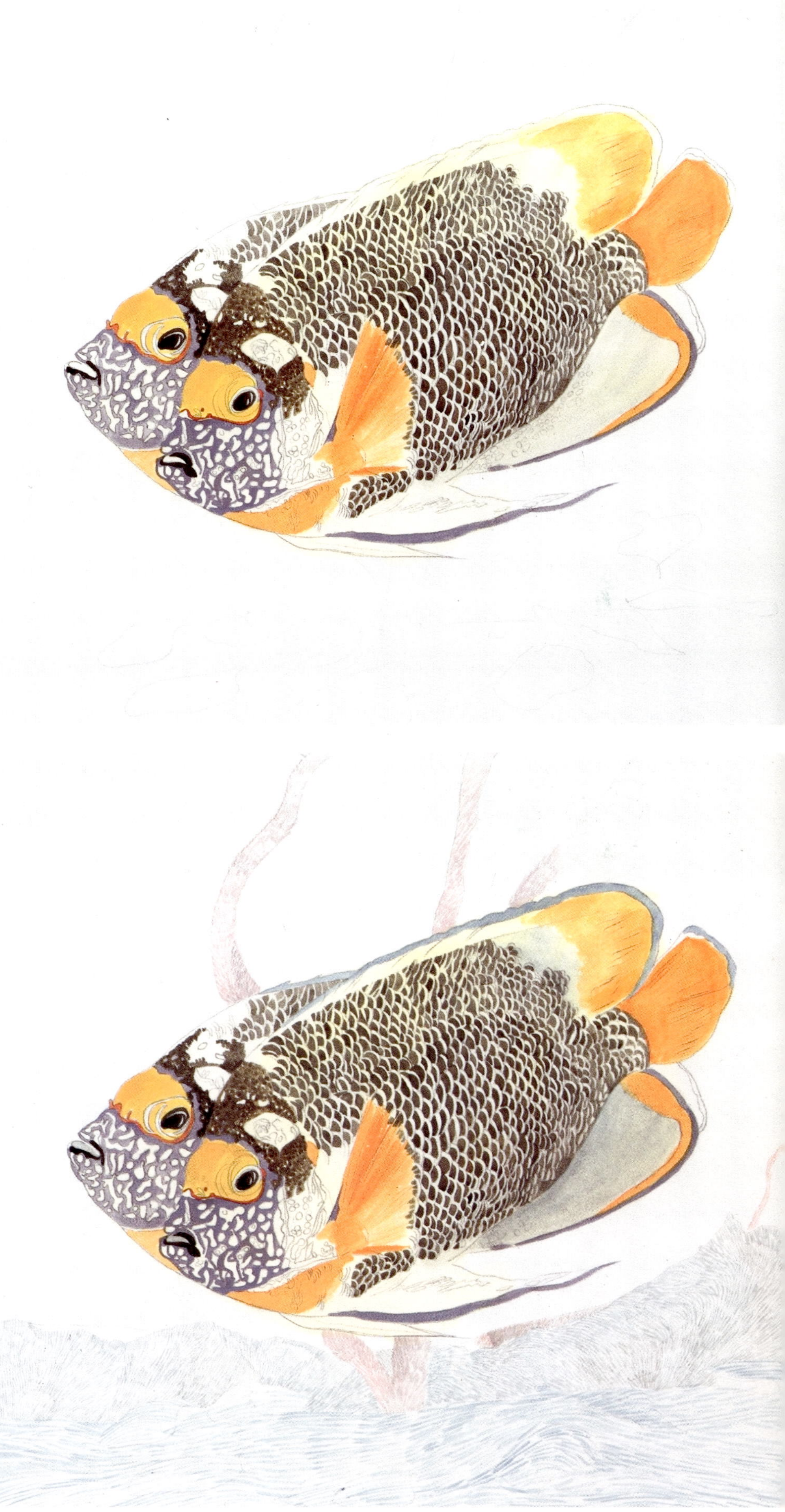

Stage Five

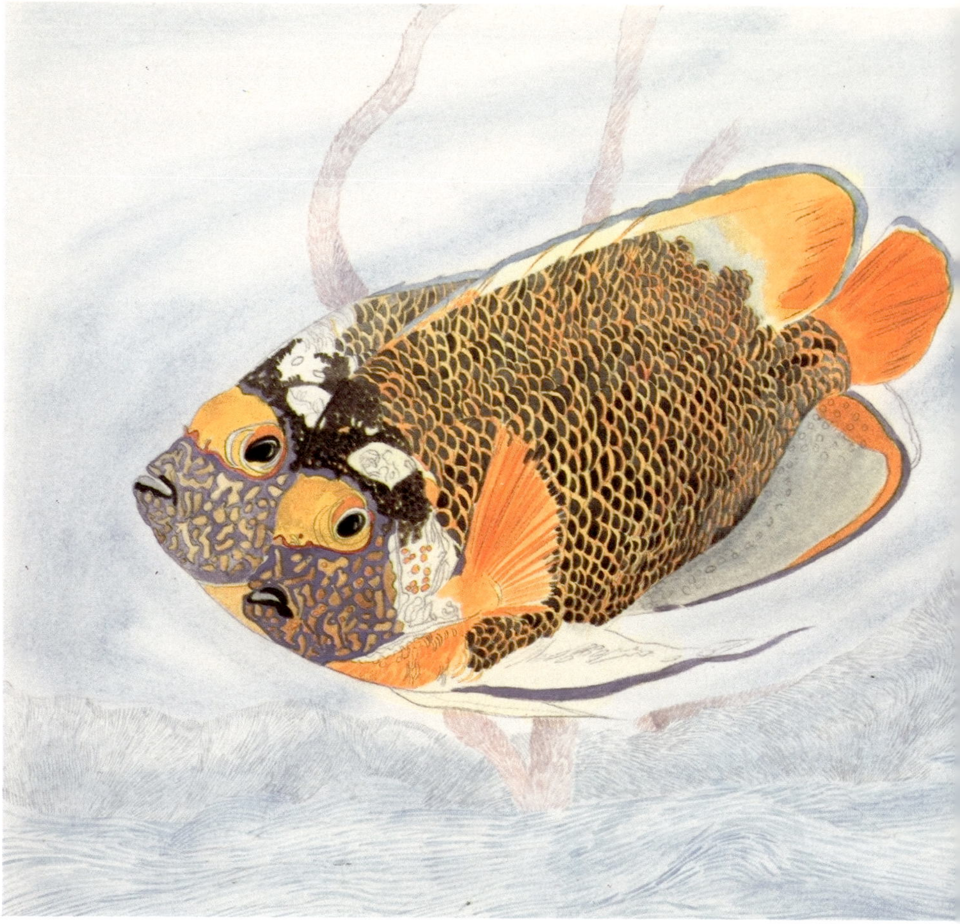

With a mixture of sepia and lamp black, complete the missing body scales, using a fine, no. 0 brush. Then darken the area above the first fish's head, using the same mix, but employing only the point of the brush. Now rework the rest of the scales to darken them down. With a watery mix of cadmium yellow pale, chrome orange, and Chinese white, fill in the scale edges, using a fine, no. 0 brush, never overloaded, to avoid the risk of smudging. (I use a weaker mix of the same colors for the second fish.) With a stronger mix, strengthen the fins and add color to both heads. Then, with a weakish black, increase the density of the eyes. Using a mix of sepia, cadmium yellow pale, and chrome orange, fill in the pattern area of the heads using just the tip of a no. 0 brush. Finally rub a piece of fine absorbent cotton on a stick of phthalo blue pastel (I use a soft Rembrandt-brand pastel) and gently smooth this onto the picture to create a waterlike effect, and then fix it with a water-resistant fixative spray. The technique is unorthodox, but it does give the desired effect.

Stage Six

With sepia and Chinese white, using a no. 0 brush, paint the fin, complete the heads of both fish, and put in round spots at the beginning of the upper and lower fins. Then, with a mix of Paynes gray, Chinese white, and cobalt blue, paint the area between the spots and then add more detail to the heads with Chinese white. The background of the heart shape on the head has been painted in with process white and gray. Finally, mix cadmium yellow dark and cadmium yellow pale, and highlight the eyes, then retouch some of the scales and detail with Paynes gray and white.

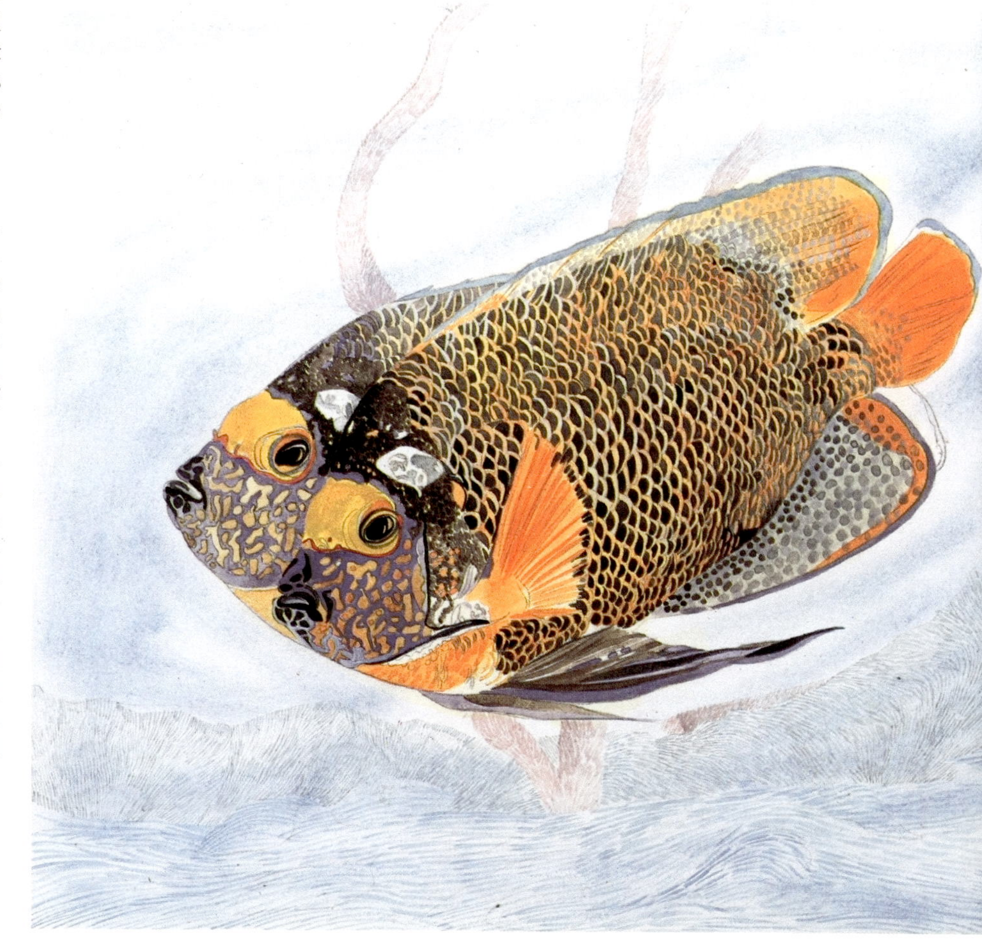

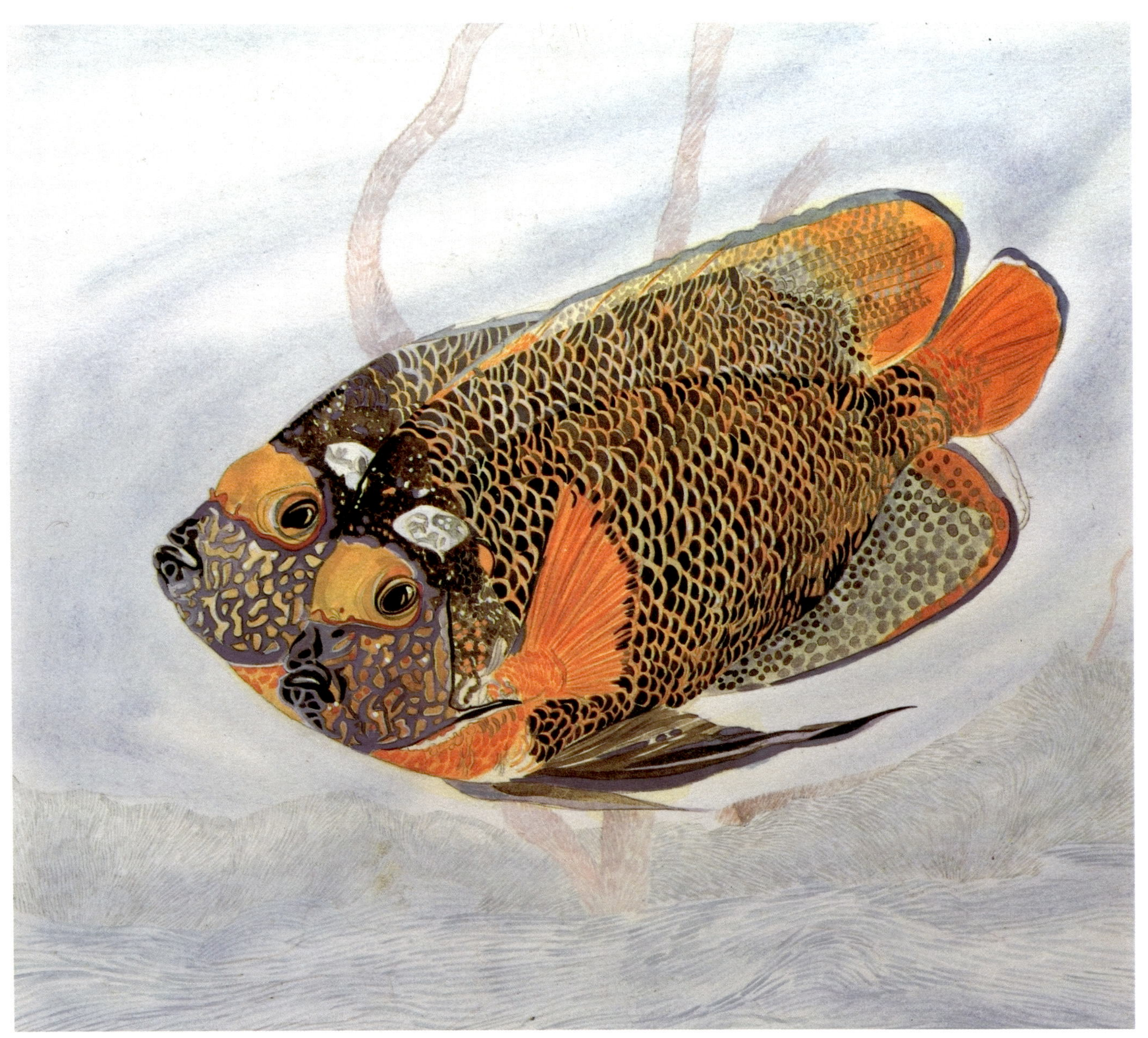

Stage Seven

Highlight the head pattern and fin outlines with two different blue pastels, then fix them with spray and overpaint the pattern with a pure cerulean blue. Even if you're very experienced, no painting you do is ever totally straightforward. But knowing what to do when you have a problem makes the difference.

Use pure Winsor red under the eyes, pure cadmium lemon around the eyes, and chrome orange to highlight the fins. Then draw a line on the first fish with a soft 3B pencil and trace the scales below the line with pure Paynes gray and add those above the line with Paynes gray mixed with process white. Paint the scale edges above the line with process white and add some touches of highlight. Finally, with a ¼″ (6mm) flat brush and a watery solution of process white, reduce the intensity of the blue background.

Mandrill

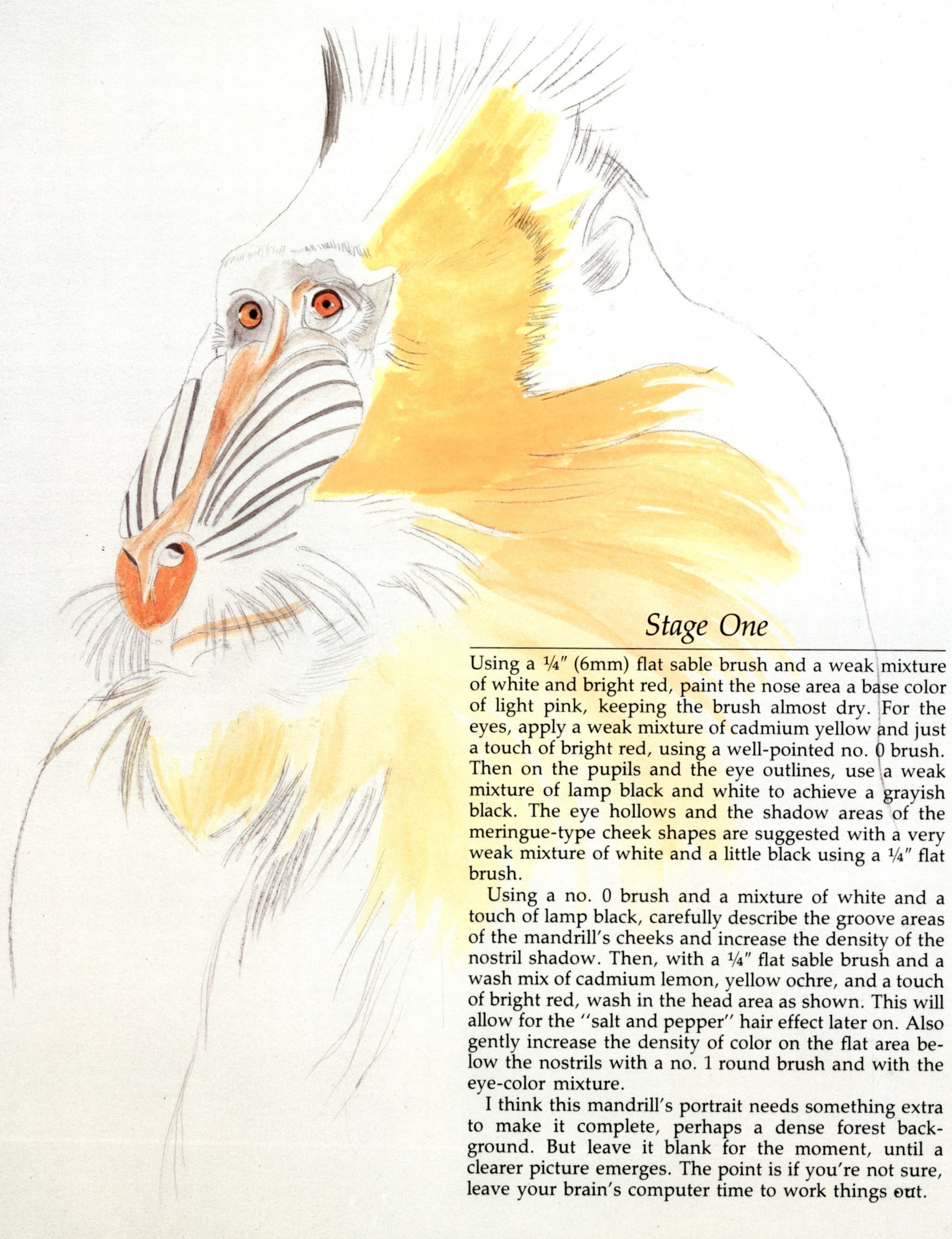

Stage One

Using a ¼″ (6mm) flat sable brush and a weak mixture of white and bright red, paint the nose area a base color of light pink, keeping the brush almost dry. For the eyes, apply a weak mixture of cadmium yellow and just a touch of bright red, using a well-pointed no. 0 brush. Then on the pupils and the eye outlines, use a weak mixture of lamp black and white to achieve a grayish black. The eye hollows and the shadow areas of the meringue-type cheek shapes are suggested with a very weak mixture of white and a little black using a ¼″ flat brush.

Using a no. 0 brush and a mixture of white and a touch of lamp black, carefully describe the groove areas of the mandrill's cheeks and increase the density of the nostril shadow. Then, with a ¼″ flat sable brush and a wash mix of cadmium lemon, yellow ochre, and a touch of bright red, wash in the head area as shown. This will allow for the "salt and pepper" hair effect later on. Also gently increase the density of color on the flat area below the nostrils with a no. 1 round brush and with the eye-color mixture.

I think this mandrill's portrait needs something extra to make it complete, perhaps a dense forest background. But leave it blank for the moment, until a clearer picture emerges. The point is if you're not sure, leave your brain's computer time to work things out.

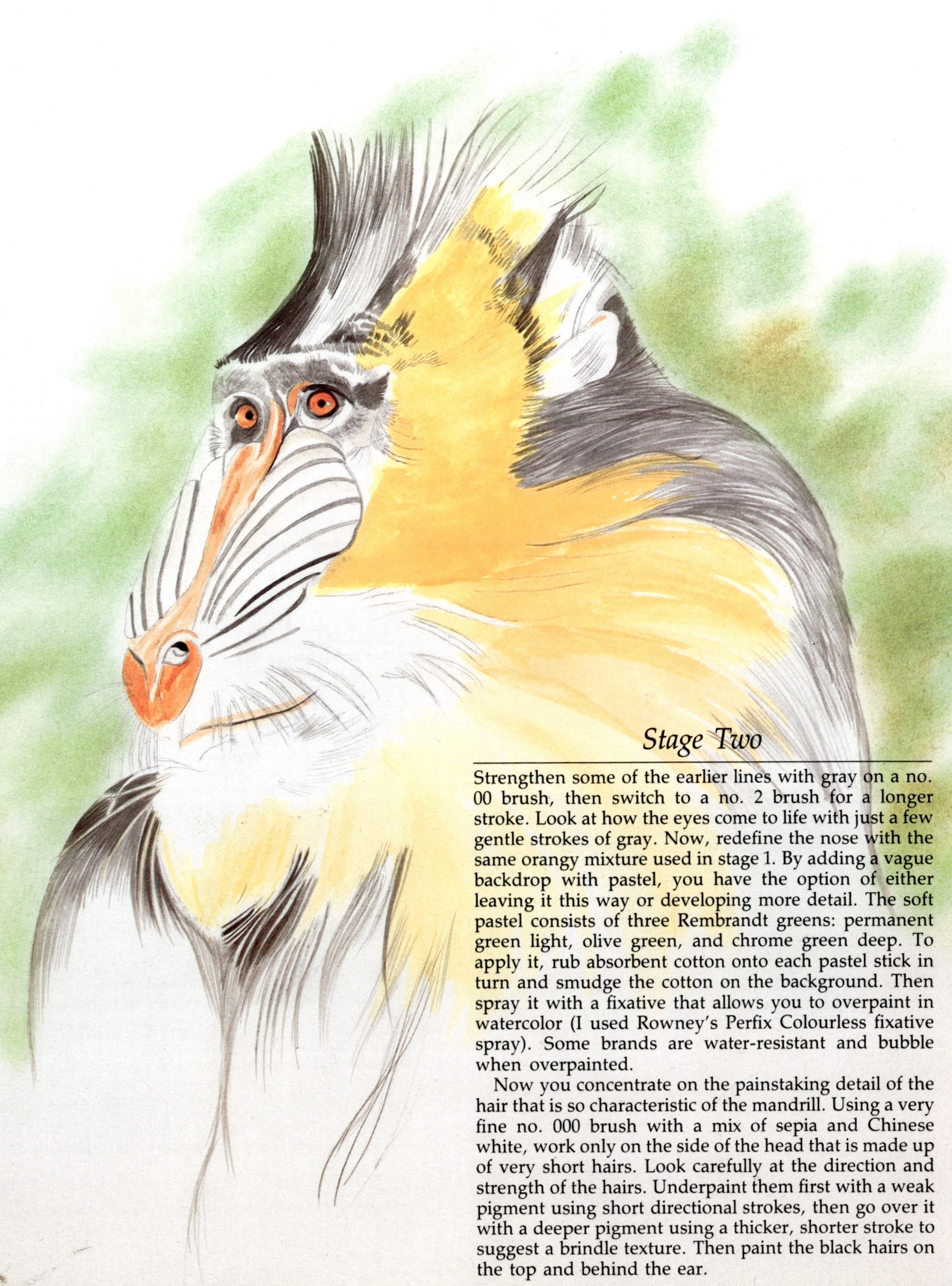

Stage Two

Strengthen some of the earlier lines with gray on a no. 00 brush, then switch to a no. 2 brush for a longer stroke. Look at how the eyes come to life with just a few gentle strokes of gray. Now, redefine the nose with the same orangy mixture used in stage 1. By adding a vague backdrop with pastel, you have the option of either leaving it this way or developing more detail. The soft pastel consists of three Rembrandt greens: permanent green light, olive green, and chrome green deep. To apply it, rub absorbent cotton onto each pastel stick in turn and smudge the cotton on the background. Then spray it with a fixative that allows you to overpaint in watercolor (I used Rowney's Perfix Colourless fixative spray). Some brands are water-resistant and bubble when overpainted.

Now you concentrate on the painstaking detail of the hair that is so characteristic of the mandrill. Using a very fine no. 000 brush with a mix of sepia and Chinese white, work only on the side of the head that is made up of very short hairs. Look carefully at the direction and strength of the hairs. Underpaint them first with a weak pigment using short directional strokes, then go over it with a deeper pigment using a thicker, shorter stroke to suggest a brindle texture. Then paint the black hairs on the top and behind the ear.

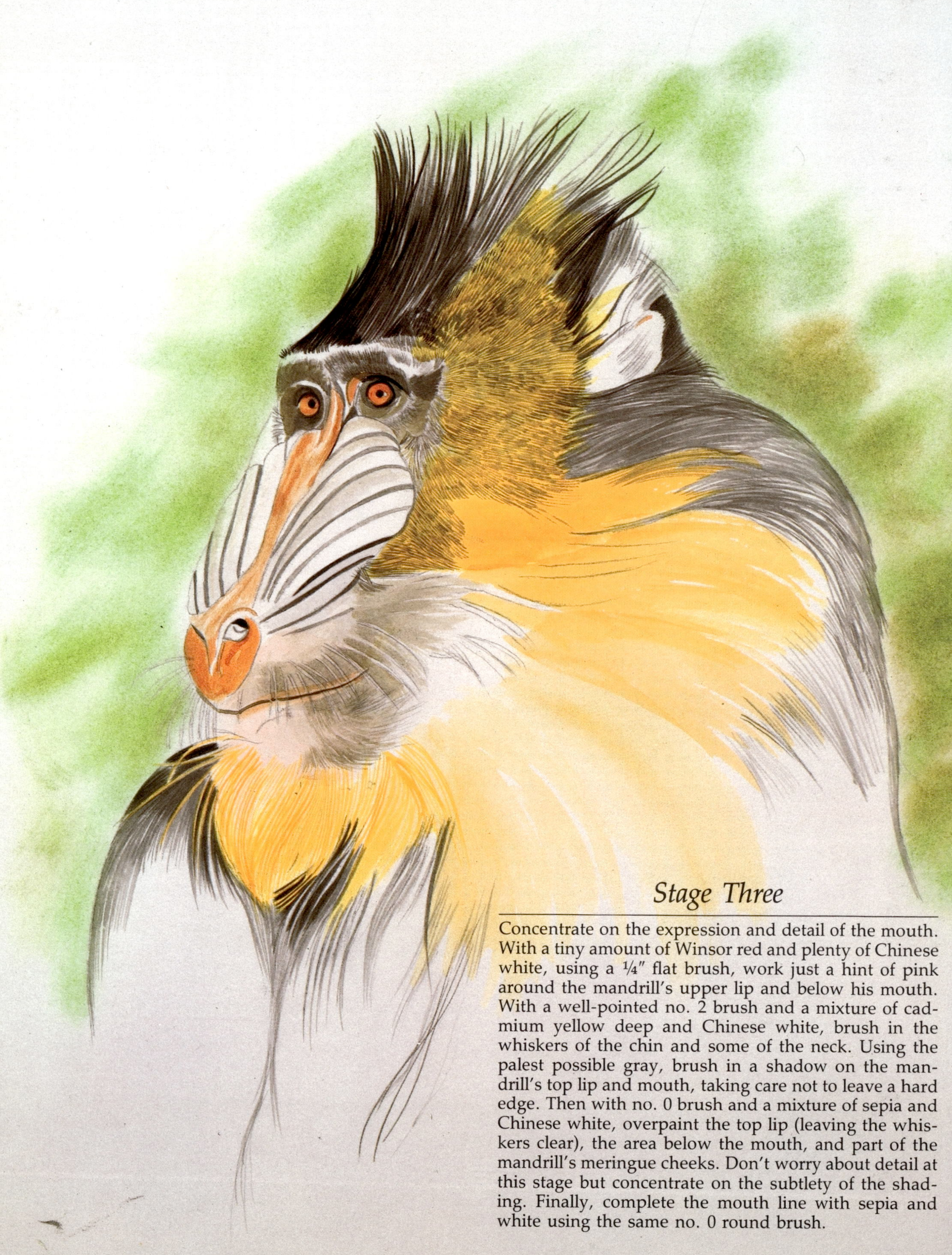

Stage Three

Concentrate on the expression and detail of the mouth. With a tiny amount of Winsor red and plenty of Chinese white, using a ¼″ flat brush, work just a hint of pink around the mandrill's upper lip and below his mouth. With a well-pointed no. 2 brush and a mixture of cadmium yellow deep and Chinese white, brush in the whiskers of the chin and some of the neck. Using the palest possible gray, brush in a shadow on the mandrill's top lip and mouth, taking care not to leave a hard edge. Then with no. 0 brush and a mixture of sepia and Chinese white, overpaint the top lip (leaving the whiskers clear), the area below the mouth, and part of the mandrill's meringue cheeks. Don't worry about detail at this stage but concentrate on the subtlety of the shading. Finally, complete the mouth line with sepia and white using the same no. 0 round brush.

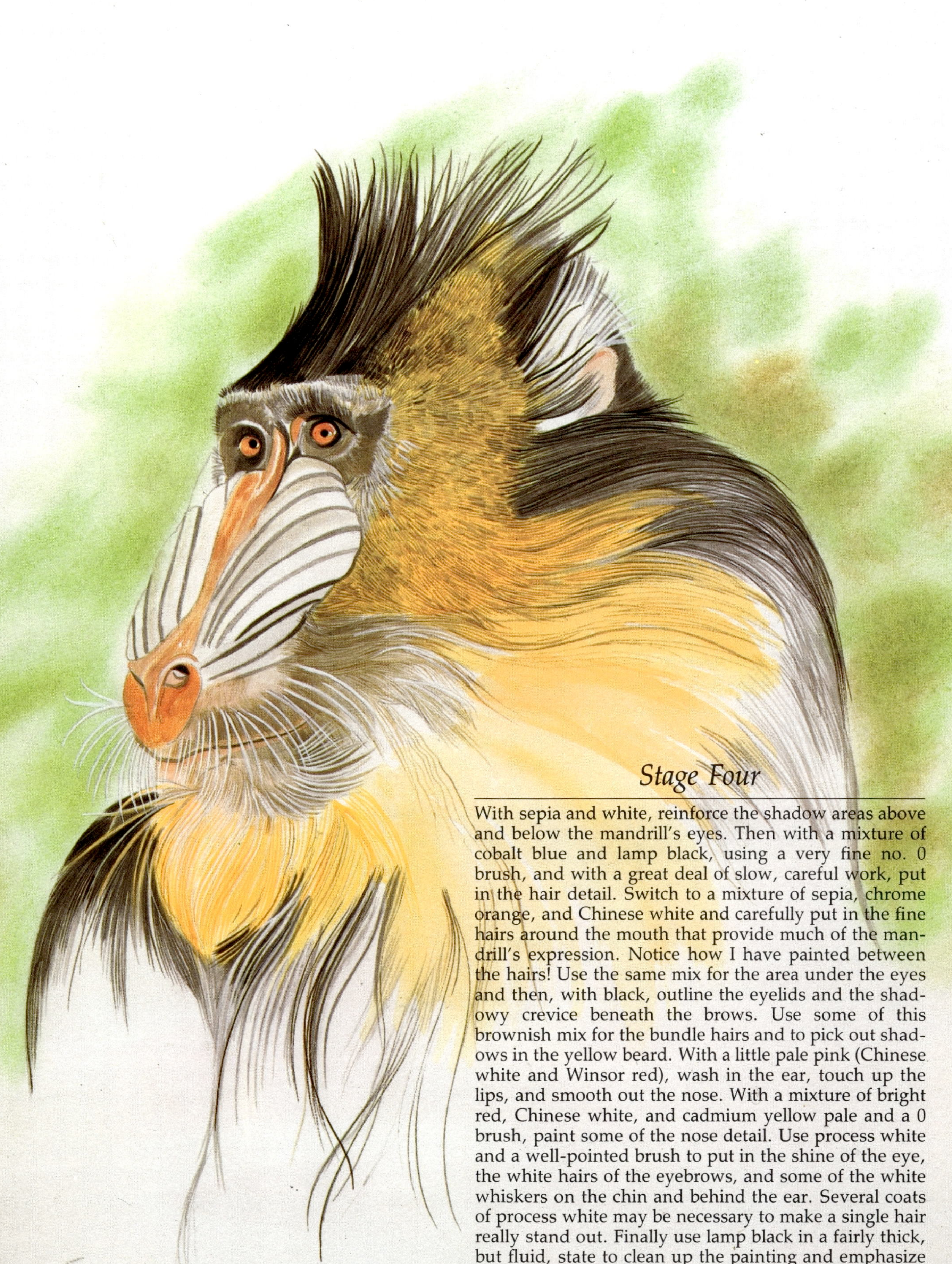

Stage Four

With sepia and white, reinforce the shadow areas above and below the mandrill's eyes. Then with a mixture of cobalt blue and lamp black, using a very fine no. 0 brush, and with a great deal of slow, careful work, put in the hair detail. Switch to a mixture of sepia, chrome orange, and Chinese white and carefully put in the fine hairs around the mouth that provide much of the mandrill's expression. Notice how I have painted between the hairs! Use the same mix for the area under the eyes and then, with black, outline the eyelids and the shadowy crevice beneath the brows. Use some of this brownish mix for the bundle hairs and to pick out shadows in the yellow beard. With a little pale pink (Chinese white and Winsor red), wash in the ear, touch up the lips, and smooth out the nose. With a mixture of bright red, Chinese white, and cadmium yellow pale and a 0 brush, paint some of the nose detail. Use process white and a well-pointed brush to put in the shine of the eye, the white hairs of the eyebrows, and some of the white whiskers on the chin and behind the ear. Several coats of process white may be necessary to make a single hair really stand out. Finally use lamp black in a fairly thick, but fluid, state to clean up the painting and emphasize some of the darker hairs.

Canada Goose

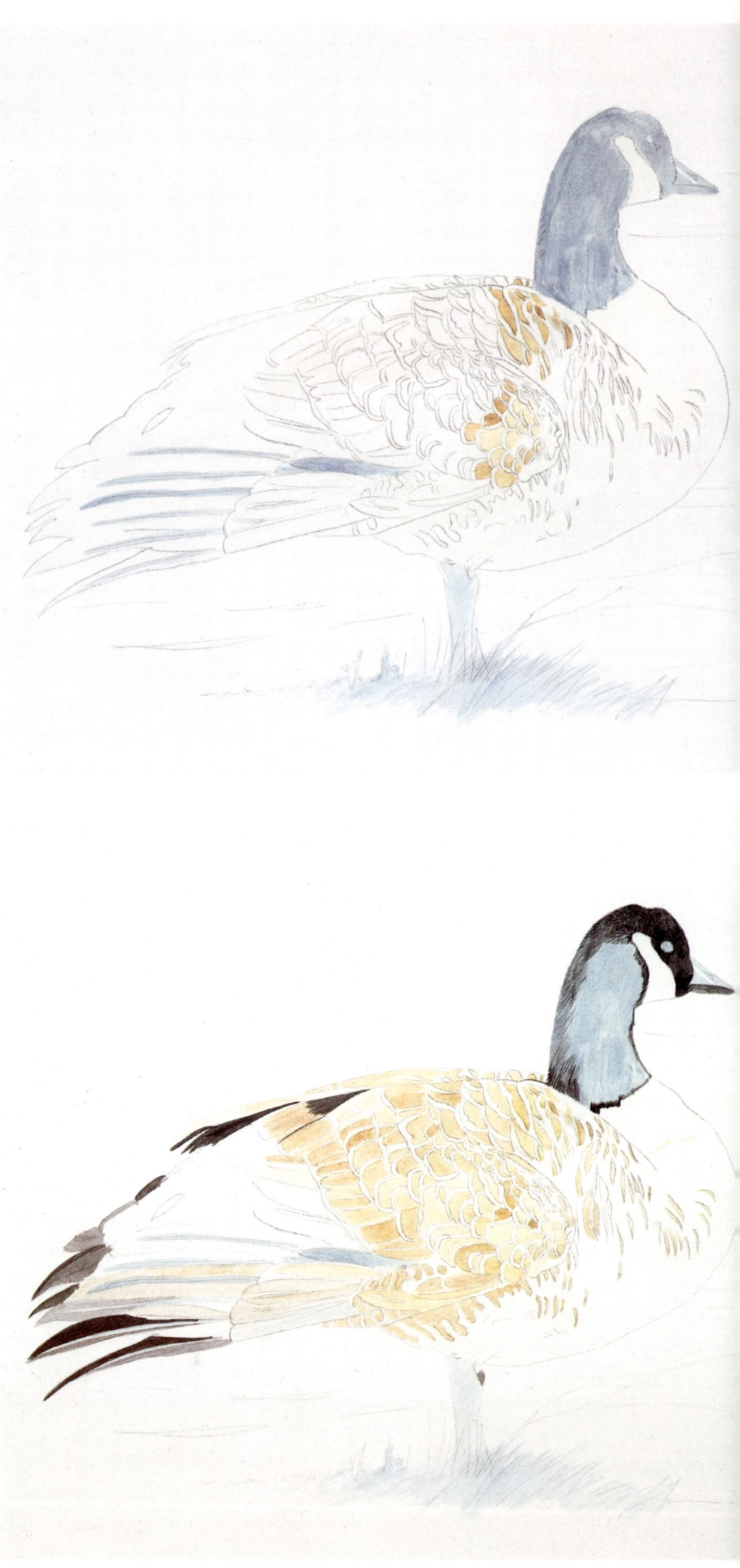

Stage One

Once the goose is clearly drawn, apply a wash of off-white (add the merest fleck of black) to fix the lines. Use a ¼″ (6mm) flat brush to wash in the whole of the body, head, and neck. While the wash is still damp, with a no. 2 round brush, apply a weak wash of cerulean blue and Chinese white to the neck, head, and beak, to provide bluish highlights later on. (The goose has a black neck and head, but solid black tends to look overly heavy and unnatural if it's painted just black.) Still using a no. 2 brush, this time with a weak solution of raw umber, sketch in the feather shapes. (Make sure your brush contains very little water, or precision will not be possible.) I have not completed all of the feathers at this stage so that you can clearly see the process.

Stage Two

With a well-pointed no. 0 brush, using a weak solution of lamp black, outline the eye, and then with short, careful strokes, start to fill in the black plumage of the neck and head. Use cerulean blue with Chinese white and lamp black on the back of the neck because the light catches here and the individual plumage lines can be seen. Whether or not plumage or hair detail can be seen, I find a more natural effect can be gained by imitating in action the detail that I know to be there. In other words, the plumage on the neck is fine and short, so use a short, chopping stroke rather than an overall solid. Notice the hairs extending beyond the outline of the bird's head and neck. With a no. 2 brush, using a mixture of cobalt blue, black, and white (with the cobalt dominant), start to sketch in the tail feathers.

Stage Three

With a well-pointed no. 0 brush, paint the solid of the eye and cover most of the head and neck with a weakish black. The chest of the bird is an off-white, so mix a little yellow ochre with Chinese white and 'tick in,' with short, fine strokes, the whitish plumage between the brown flecks of the chest. I could have saved both effort and time here with a wash, but individual strokes allow the white paper to show through and help not only the fine down effect, but aid form on what would otherwise be a fairly bland and uninteresting shape. Finally, with a mix of sepia, Chinese white, and yellow ochre, using a very fine no. 0 brush, paint in some of the feathers.

Stage Four

Using a no. 1 round brush and a mix of sepia and Chinese white, roughly paint the tail feathers. I have left white margins between some, in order to leave my basic plan clear. Then complete the body feathers with sepia, Chinese white, and yellow ochre. Achieving a realistic impression of feathers is always difficult, so whatever you do, avoid overpainting—there are many refining stages to come! Finally, with a weak black, intensify the darker shade of the eye.

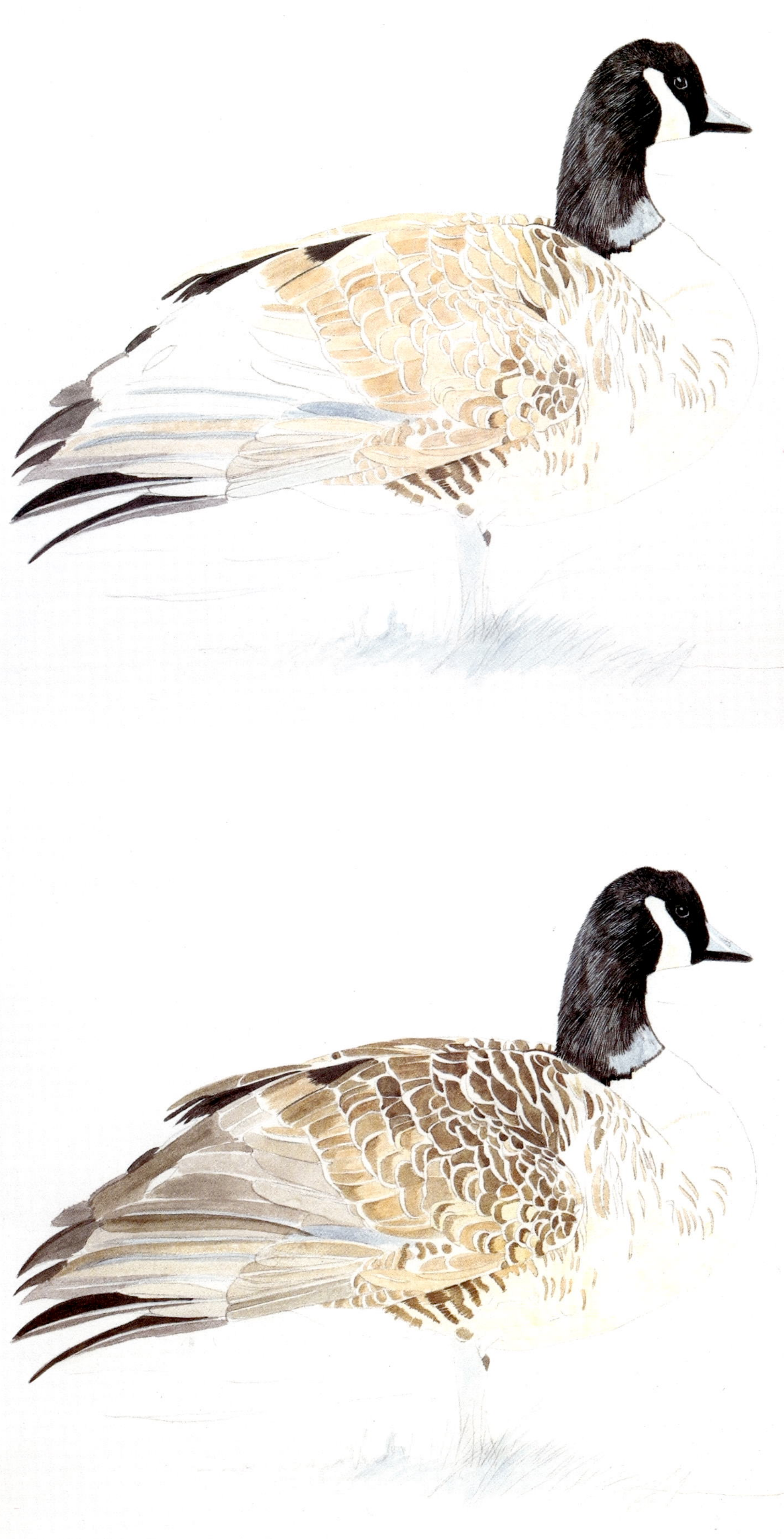

Stage Five

Add just a touch of grass with a mix of cadmium lemon and Hookers green dark, and a couple of twigs made from a mix of Hookers green and Paynes gray. To put a little more life into some of the feathers, mix light red and cadmium yellow pale, and 'warm up' several of the darker feathers. I painted the beginning of the leg with Chinese white, lamp black, and cobalt blue, and some of the nearer feathers in gray (Chinese white and lamp black) using a no. 0 brush and a hairlike stroke.

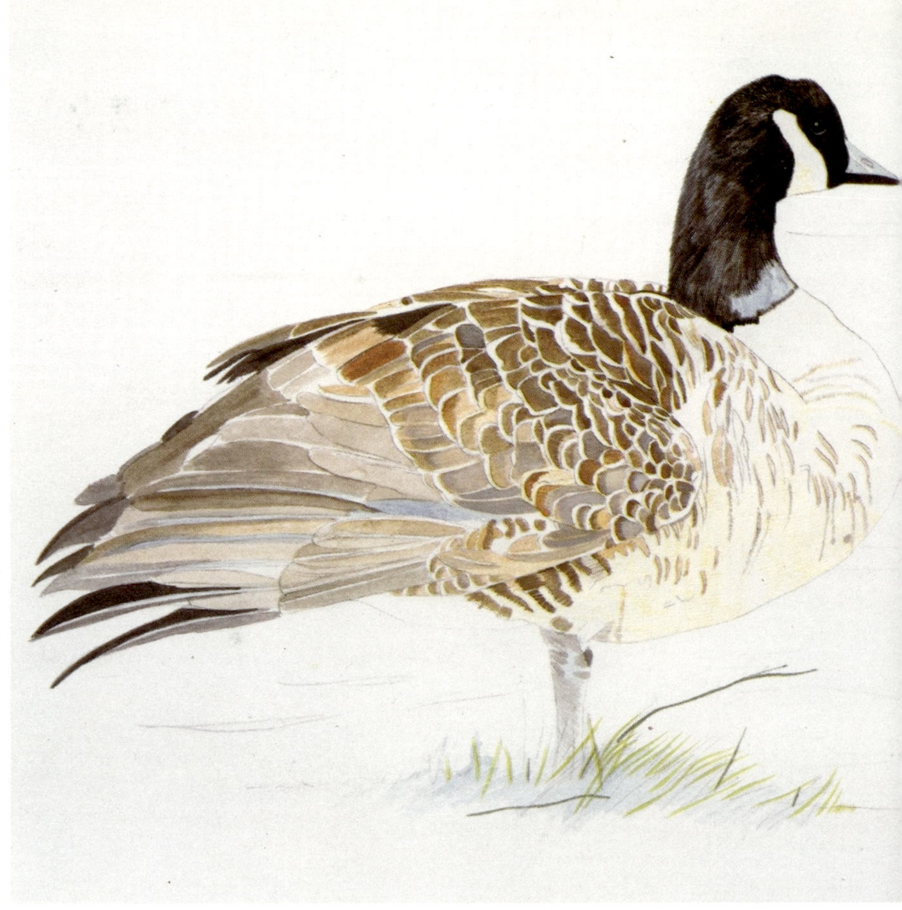

Stage Six

Use a no. 2 round brush for the whole of this stage. Darken the tail feathers with a mixture of cobalt blue and lamp black (not in one coat, but in several thin washes, to avoid pure and uninteresting solids). With the same mix, add shadow beneath the bird's wing and strengthen the tone of the leg and neck. Redefine the blue tone and black shadow of the beak and add the breathing hole. Add small lines to the chest area to give some interest to this area. Use a mix of sepia and Chinese white to darken the plumage beneath the wing, thereby increasing both shadow and dimensional effect. With Naples yellow and light red add a little detail to the unfinished feathers on the shoulder. Then, with just small touches of pure, but fairly watery Naples yellow, add detail to the chest plumage.

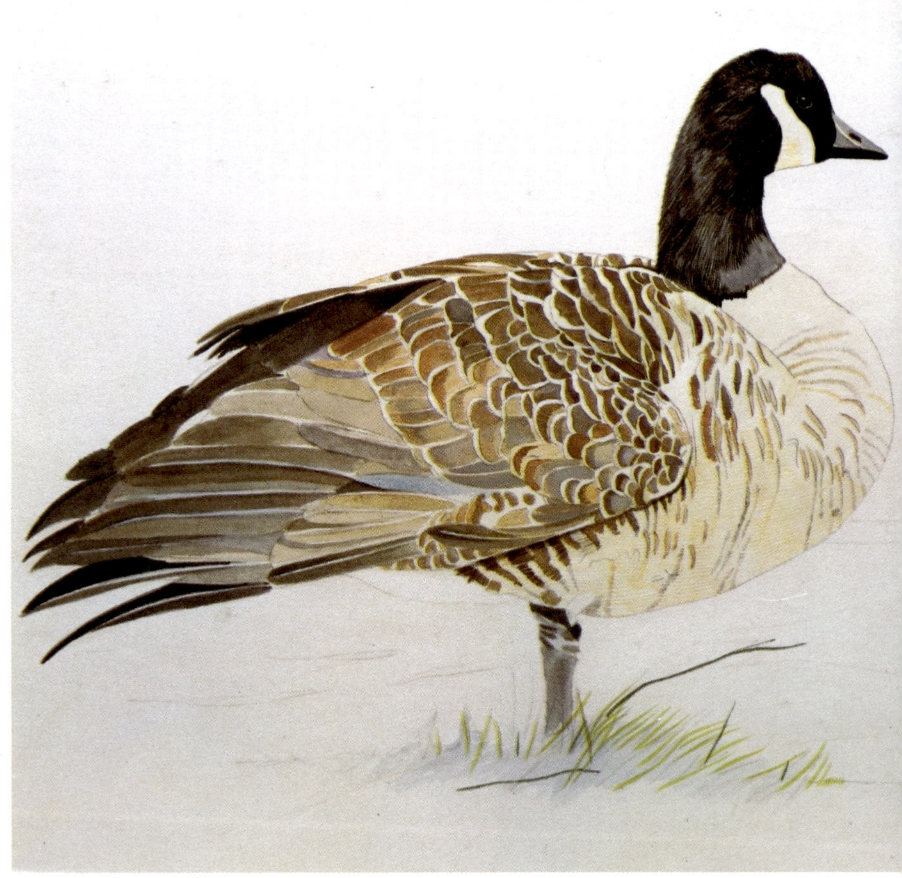

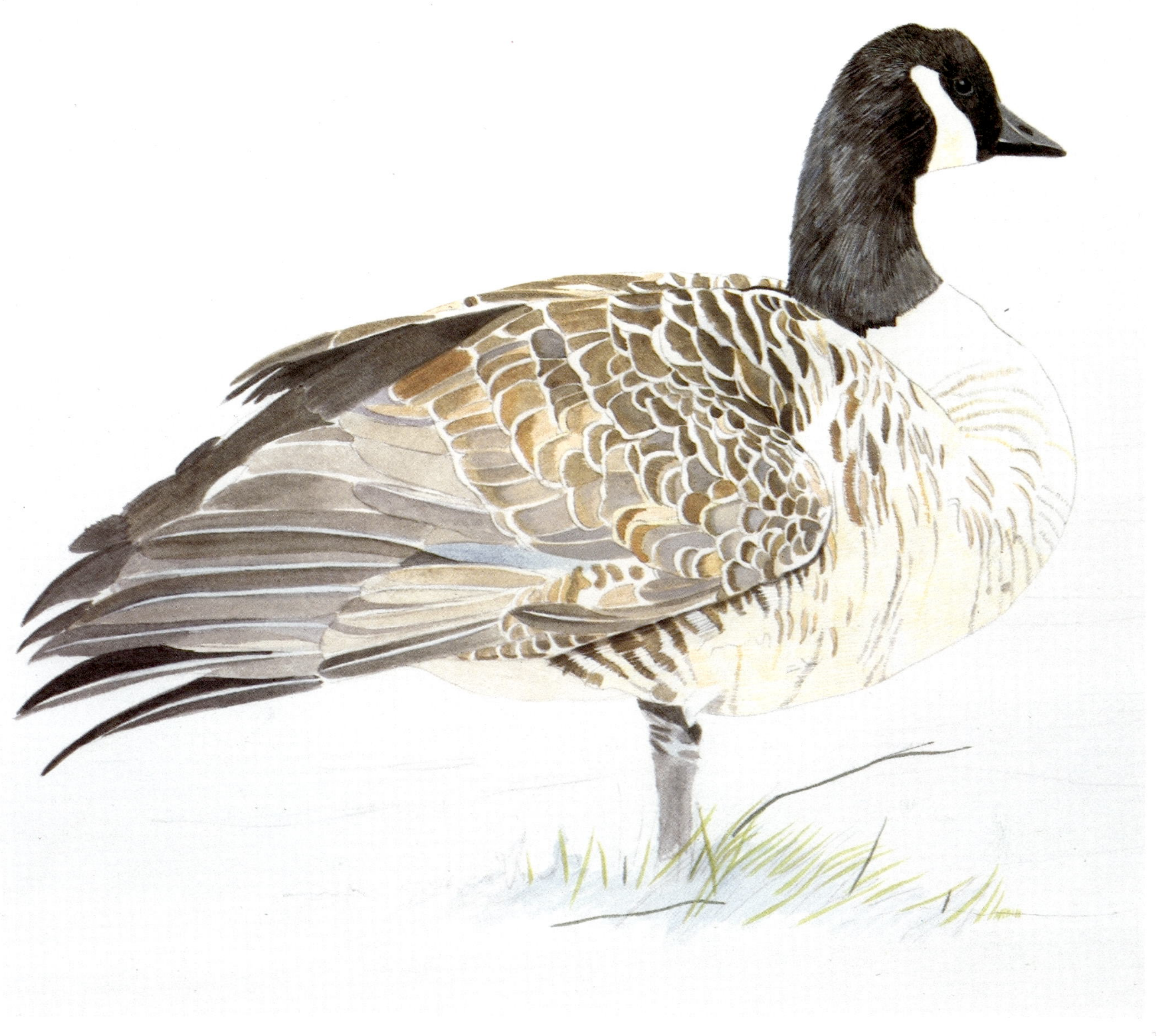

Stage Seven

Using a no. 0 brush and a mixture of lamp black and just a little Chinese white and sepia, darken some of the feathers on the back and around the junction of the wing. Also put touches of this mix immediately below the bottom edge of the wing to add dimension. With cerulean blue and a touch of lamp black, darken the highlights of the goose's eye and redefine the top of the beak. Then, with a slightly darker mix of the same two colors, complete the neck and darken the breathing outlet. Add a few touches of pure cerulean blue in a watery solution with a well-pointed brush to the gaps between the neck feathers and to the beak and eye. Use pure process white (in a very restrained fashion) to redefine and highlight feathertips and the spines of the tail feathers; and use process white, a touch of Naples yellow, and a speck of lamp black in a well-mixed solution to paint in the farthest wing hanging down below the body.

Penguin

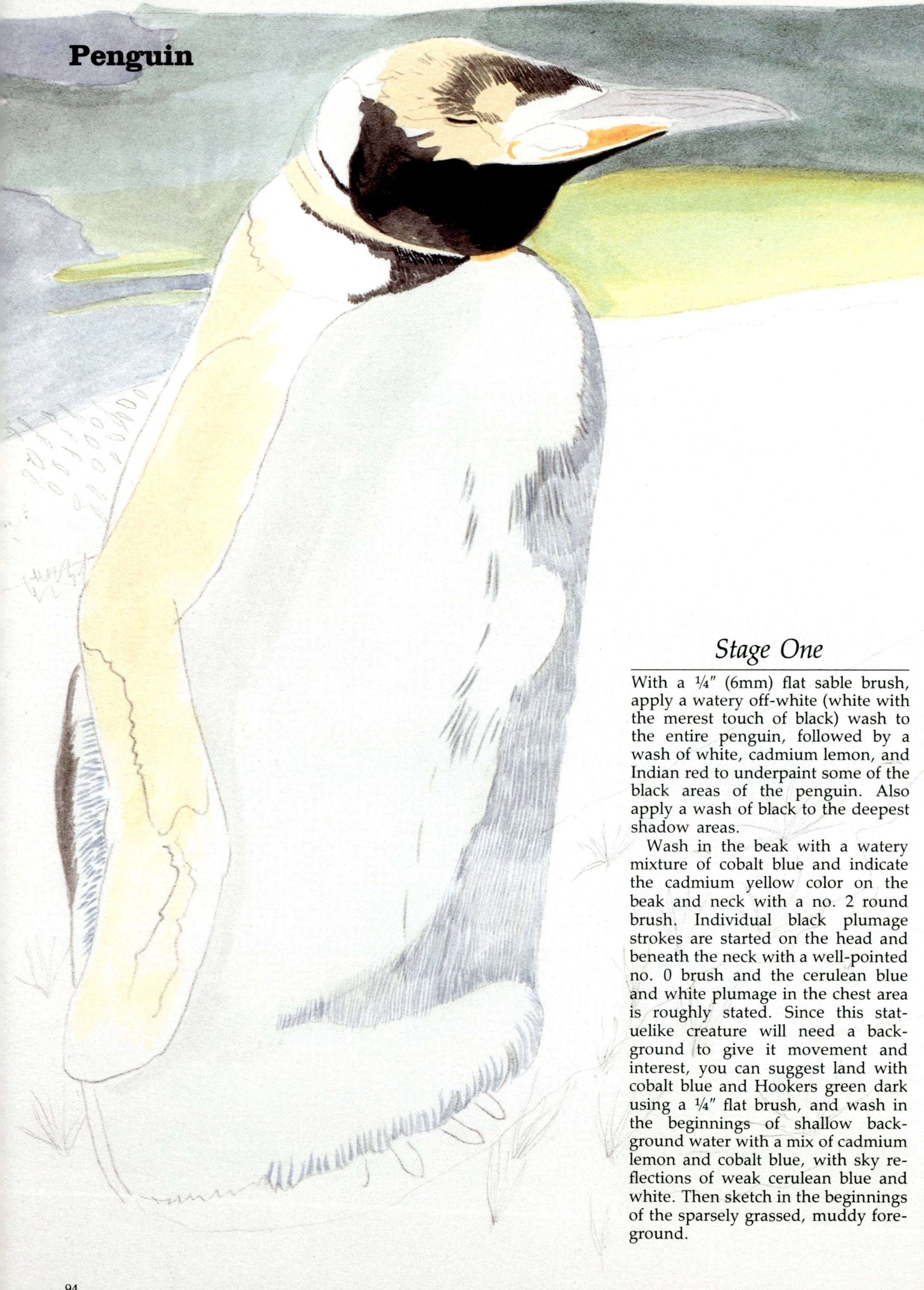

Stage One

With a 1/4″ (6mm) flat sable brush, apply a watery off-white (white with the merest touch of black) wash to the entire penguin, followed by a wash of white, cadmium lemon, and Indian red to underpaint some of the black areas of the penguin. Also apply a wash of black to the deepest shadow areas.

Wash in the beak with a watery mixture of cobalt blue and indicate the cadmium yellow color on the beak and neck with a no. 2 round brush. Individual black plumage strokes are started on the head and beneath the neck with a well-pointed no. 0 brush and the cerulean blue and white plumage in the chest area is roughly stated. Since this statuelike creature will need a background to give it movement and interest, you can suggest land with cobalt blue and Hookers green dark using a 1/4″ flat brush, and wash in the beginnings of shallow background water with a mix of cadmium lemon and cobalt blue, with sky reflections of weak cerulean blue and white. Then sketch in the beginnings of the sparsely grassed, muddy foreground.

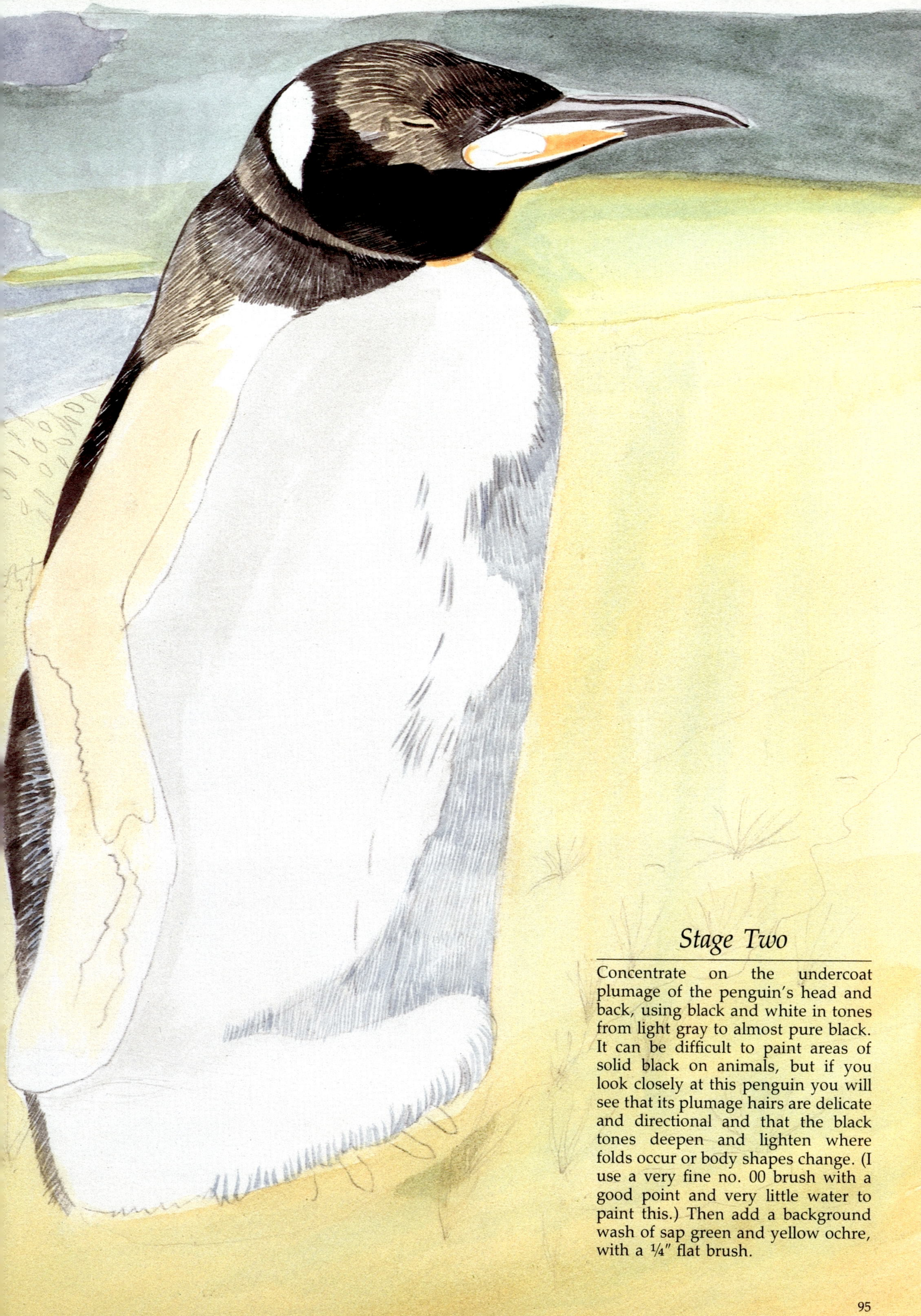

Stage Two

Concentrate on the undercoat plumage of the penguin's head and back, using black and white in tones from light gray to almost pure black. It can be difficult to paint areas of solid black on animals, but if you look closely at this penguin you will see that its plumage hairs are delicate and directional and that the black tones deepen and lighten where folds occur or body shapes change. (I use a very fine no. 00 brush with a good point and very little water to paint this.) Then add a background wash of sap green and yellow ochre, with a ¼″ flat brush.

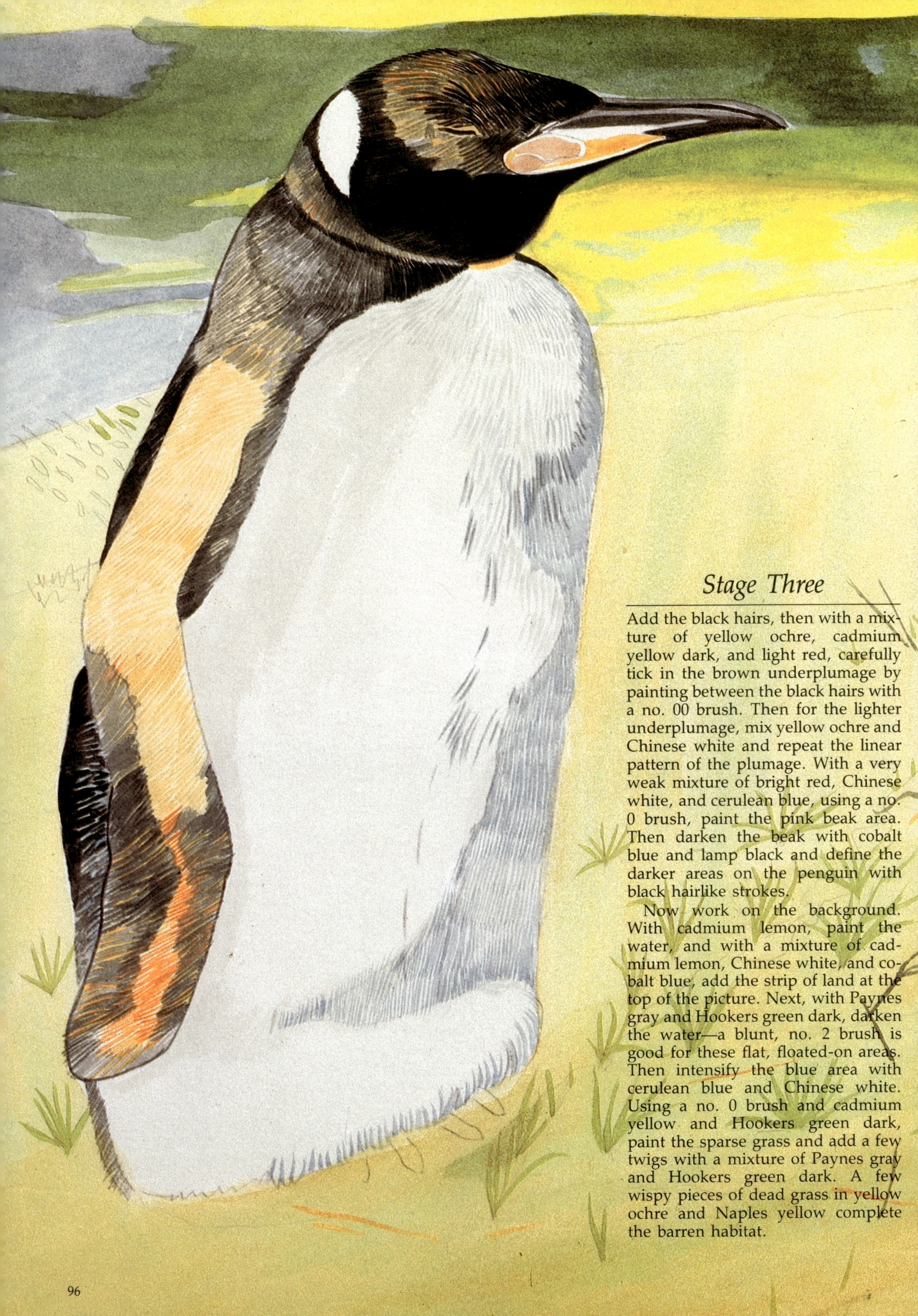

Stage Three

Add the black hairs, then with a mixture of yellow ochre, cadmium yellow dark, and light red, carefully tick in the brown underplumage by painting between the black hairs with a no. 00 brush. Then for the lighter underplumage, mix yellow ochre and Chinese white and repeat the linear pattern of the plumage. With a very weak mixture of bright red, Chinese white, and cerulean blue, using a no. 0 brush, paint the pink beak area. Then darken the beak with cobalt blue and lamp black and define the darker areas on the penguin with black hairlike strokes.

Now work on the background. With cadmium lemon, paint the water, and with a mixture of cadmium lemon, Chinese white, and cobalt blue, add the strip of land at the top of the picture. Next, with Paynes gray and Hookers green dark, darken the water—a blunt, no. 2 brush is good for these flat, floated-on areas. Then intensify the blue area with cerulean blue and Chinese white. Using a no. 0 brush and cadmium yellow and Hookers green dark, paint the sparse grass and add a few twigs with a mixture of Paynes gray and Hookers green dark. A few wispy pieces of dead grass in yellow ochre and Naples yellow complete the barren habitat.

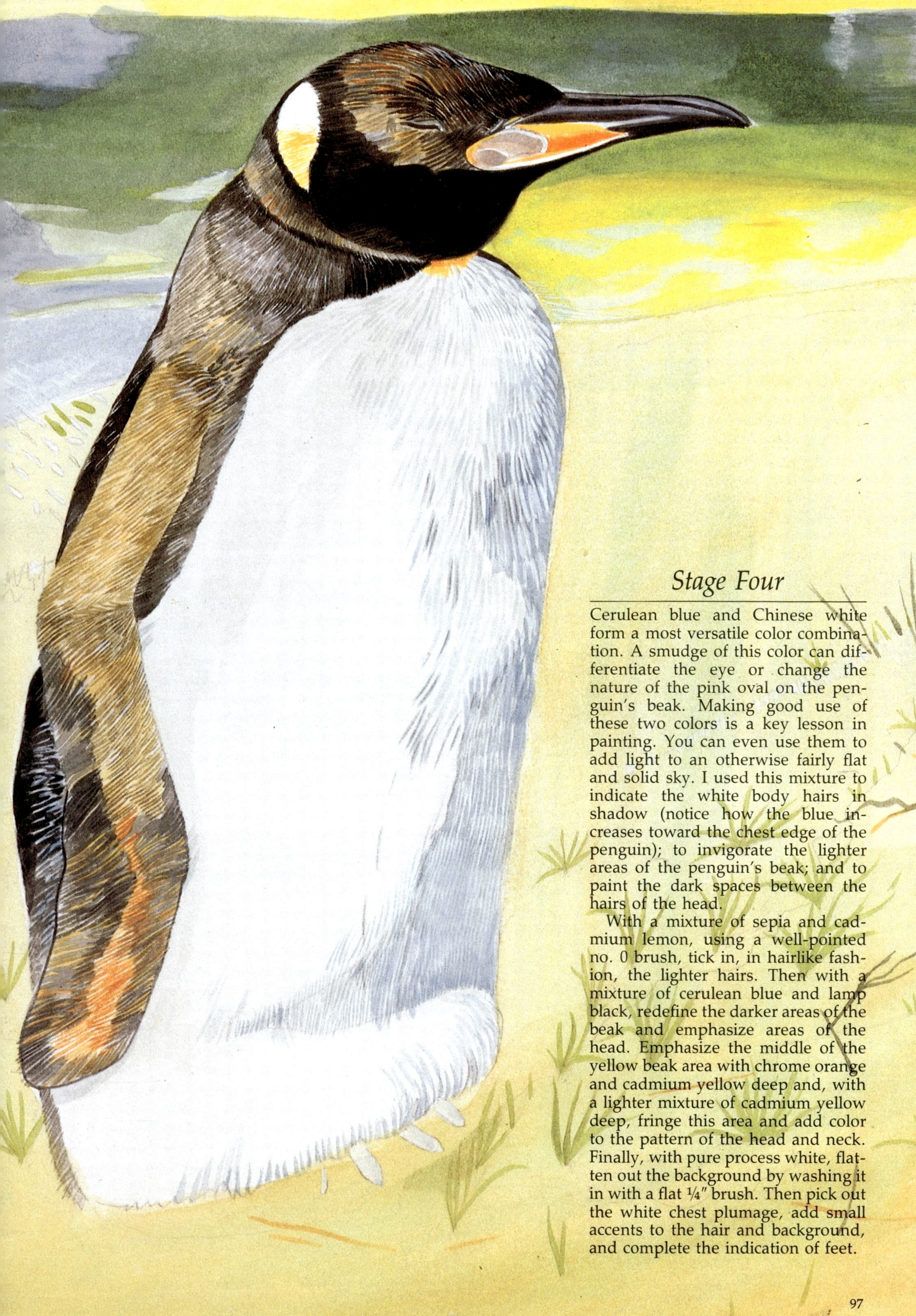

Stage Four

Cerulean blue and Chinese white form a most versatile color combination. A smudge of this color can differentiate the eye or change the nature of the pink oval on the penguin's beak. Making good use of these two colors is a key lesson in painting. You can even use them to add light to an otherwise fairly flat and solid sky. I used this mixture to indicate the white body hairs in shadow (notice how the blue increases toward the chest edge of the penguin); to invigorate the lighter areas of the penguin's beak; and to paint the dark spaces between the hairs of the head.

With a mixture of sepia and cadmium lemon, using a well-pointed no. 0 brush, tick in, in hairlike fashion, the lighter hairs. Then with a mixture of cerulean blue and lamp black, redefine the darker areas of the beak and emphasize areas of the head. Emphasize the middle of the yellow beak area with chrome orange and cadmium yellow deep and, with a lighter mixture of cadmium yellow deep, fringe this area and add color to the pattern of the head and neck. Finally, with pure process white, flatten out the background by washing it in with a flat ¼″ brush. Then pick out the white chest plumage, add small accents to the hair and background, and complete the indication of feet.

Ducks

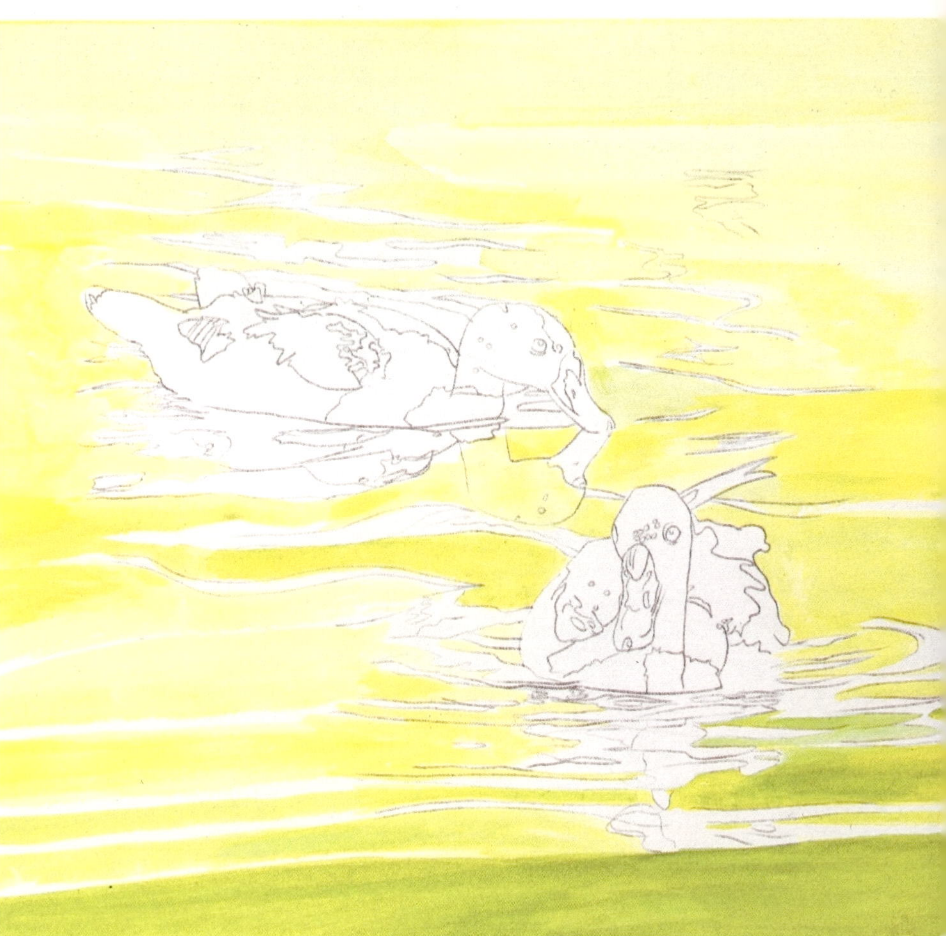

Stage One

The compositional balance of this picture is carefully in the preliminary pencil drawing, as water is extremely difficult to paint and even harder to change at a later stage, though plants or reeds can always be added. Soften the pencil lines with a kneaded eraser so they don't show through the watercolor.

Because water is so difficult to paint, you should build it up gradually with a series of light washes because it's easier to add color than take it away. Here the wash is a mixture of olive green and cadmium yellow. Use a no. 2 round brush for the intricate (between reflections) section in front of the foreground duck and a 1/4″ (6mm) flat brush for the larger open areas. Absolute consistency of color at this stage is less important than smoothness of application. It's also easier to apply washes around an animal or bird if not too much water is used. Make the swell water in the foreground slightly darker because it is closer.

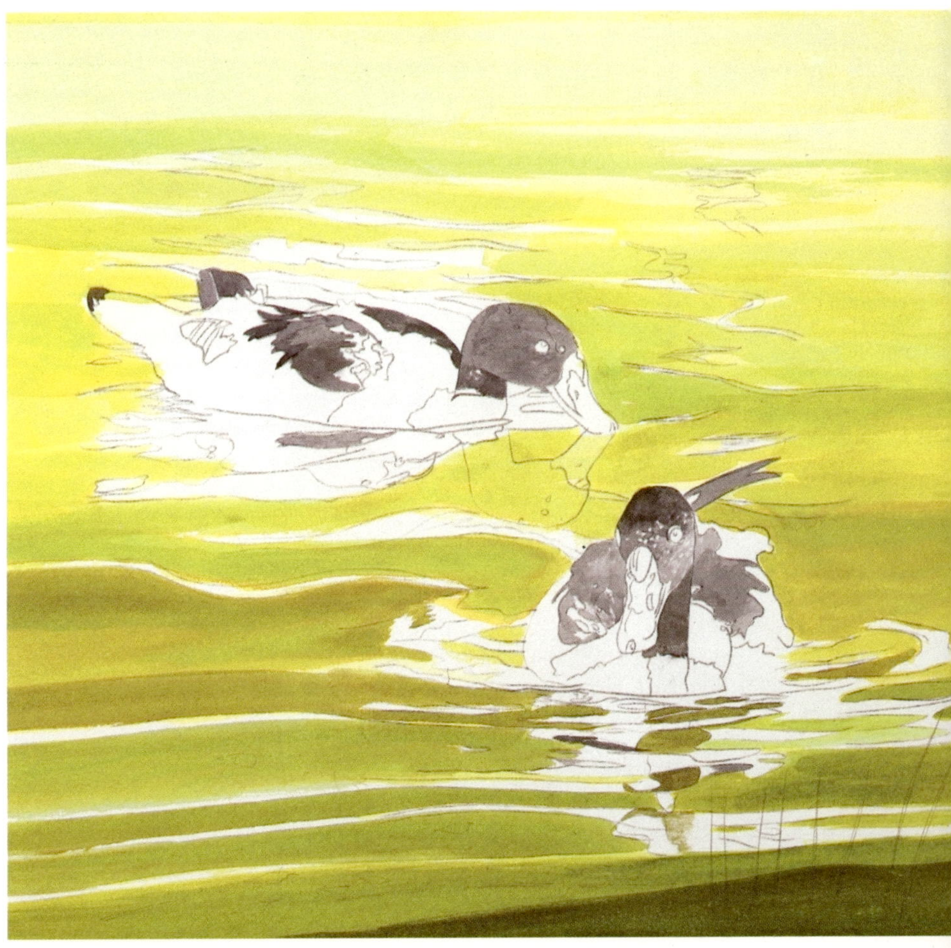

Stage Two

The foreground reflections are a mixture of sap green, yellow ochre, and a touch of lamp black, put on with a fine, no. 00 brush. Paint the ducks with a mixture of lamp black and cerulean blue, varying the color to show tonal differences between the neck and head. The foreground water is overwashed with a mixture of cobalt blue, sap green, and burnt sienna, with sap green and cadmium yellow used in the background.

Stage Three

With a weak mixture of bright red and Chinese white, use a fine no. 0 brush to fill in the first wash of the ducks' bills and their reflections. Paint the lighter strips of water with cerulean blue and Chinese white. A thin wash of yellow ochre provides the undercolor of the ducks' plumage, eyes, and some reflections, while white with a touch of cerulean blue and the merest speck of lamp black form the shadow on the nearest duck's neck.

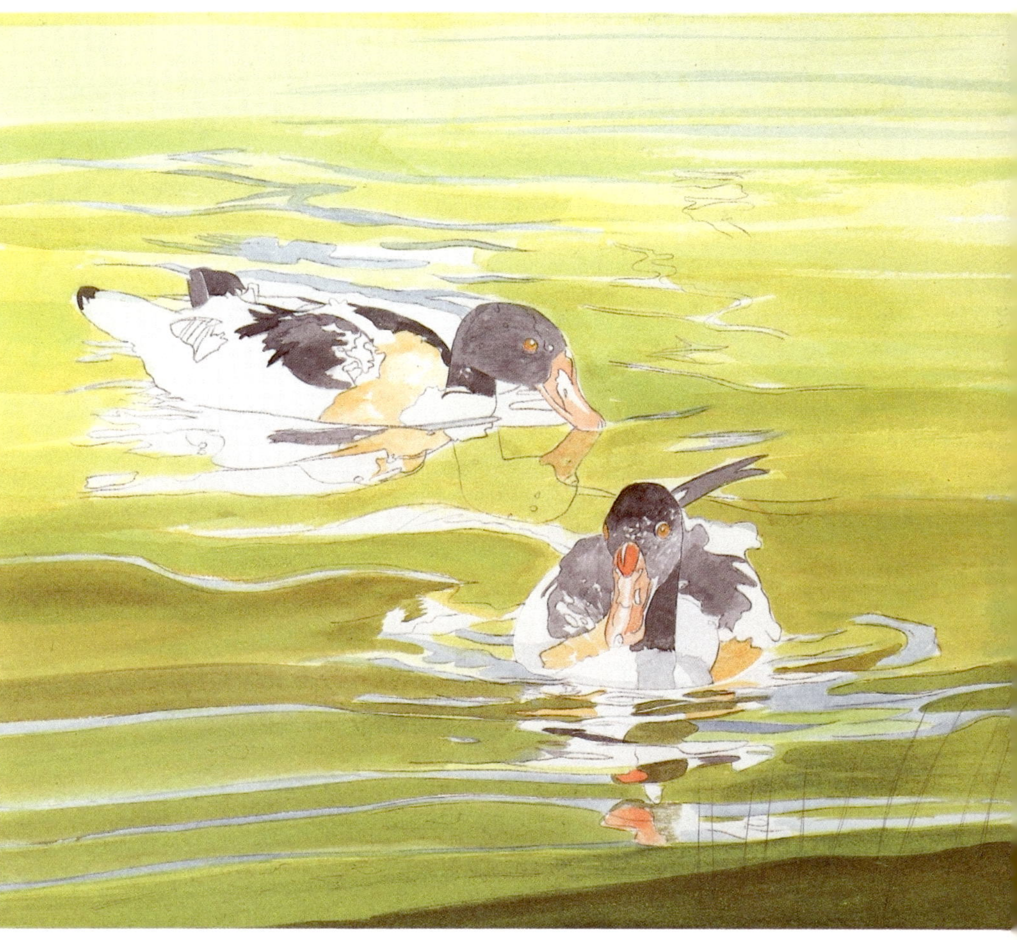

Stage Four

Using a very well-pointed no. 0 brush and a mixture of cobalt blue and lamp black, paint the head of the nearest duck using fine, hairlike strokes, favoring the blue of the mixture for lighter sections and the black for darker areas. Model the folded back wings of the nearest duck with Paynes gray and Chinese white to prevent head, neck, and wings from merging. With a weak solution of yellow ochre and sepia, darken the eye. Then paint the main hump of the duck's beak with Winsor red and Chinese white and add the surrounding area with a weak solution of Chinese white and a mere fleck of bright red. With a watery mixture of yellow ochre and cadmium yellow dark, paint the shoulder on the left and use the same color for reflections and fallen leaves. Then mix cerulean blue, Chinese white, and lamp black for the bluish-gray shadow of the chest, upper eyelid, water droplets on the head, and some of the swells in the water. Deepen the water reflections and add some debris with olive green and yellow ochre. Paint the darks of the second duck with Paynes gray, and underpaint the head reflection water a watery mixture of cobalt blue, lamp black, and white, using a blunt no. 2 brush. Add reflections with cerulean blue and white and put reeds in the background with weak sepia and Chinese white.

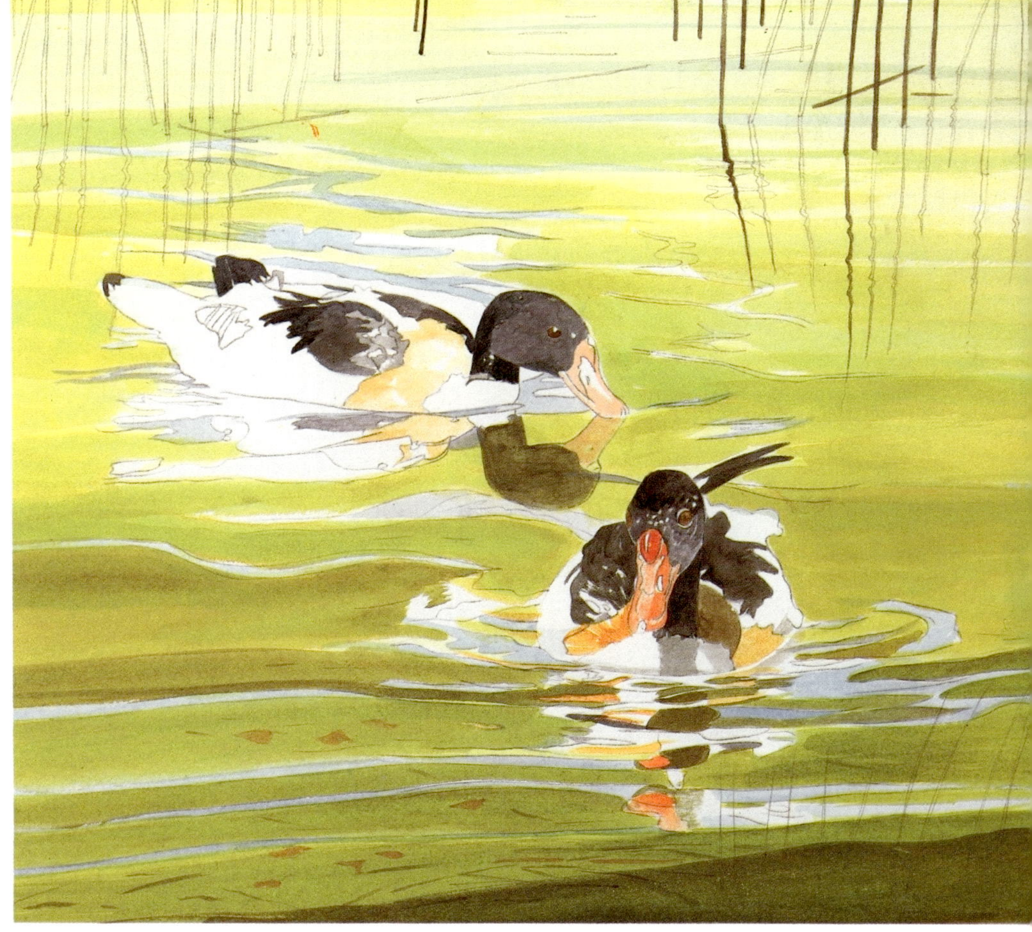

Stage Five

Finish putting in the reeds, warm up the back feathers of the leading duck, and strengthen some of the reflections with a light red and a cadmium yellow dark. Also use lamp black and Chinese white on the reflections, followed by process white to lighten the white plumage reflections. With a mixture of cobalt blue and black, paint the dark on both bills, and use various shades of this mixture to darken the front duck's head and back plumage. The plumage, head, back, and tail of the background duck are darkened with cobalt blue, lamp black, and Chinese white. A mixture of light red and sepia is used for the rear features and lighter mixes of both of these combinations are repeated in the water reflections. With light red and cadmium yellow, add a few distant reeds and more floating debris. A couple of extra leaves are also added with a mixture of Hookers green dark and cobalt blue.

Add more ripples with Chinese white, with cerulean blue and a little process white for body. Then add some squiggles with a watery mixture of Hookers green dark and cadmium lemon. Intensify the beaks and their reflections with bright red and Chinese white. With cerulean blue and lamp black, redefine and strengthen areas on both ducks and in the water. Use a pure solution of process white to redefine both plumage and water reflection. Finally, draw additional reeds and paint them with a strong mixture of sepia and Chinese white, and add a few touches of pastel yellow pencil to the water.

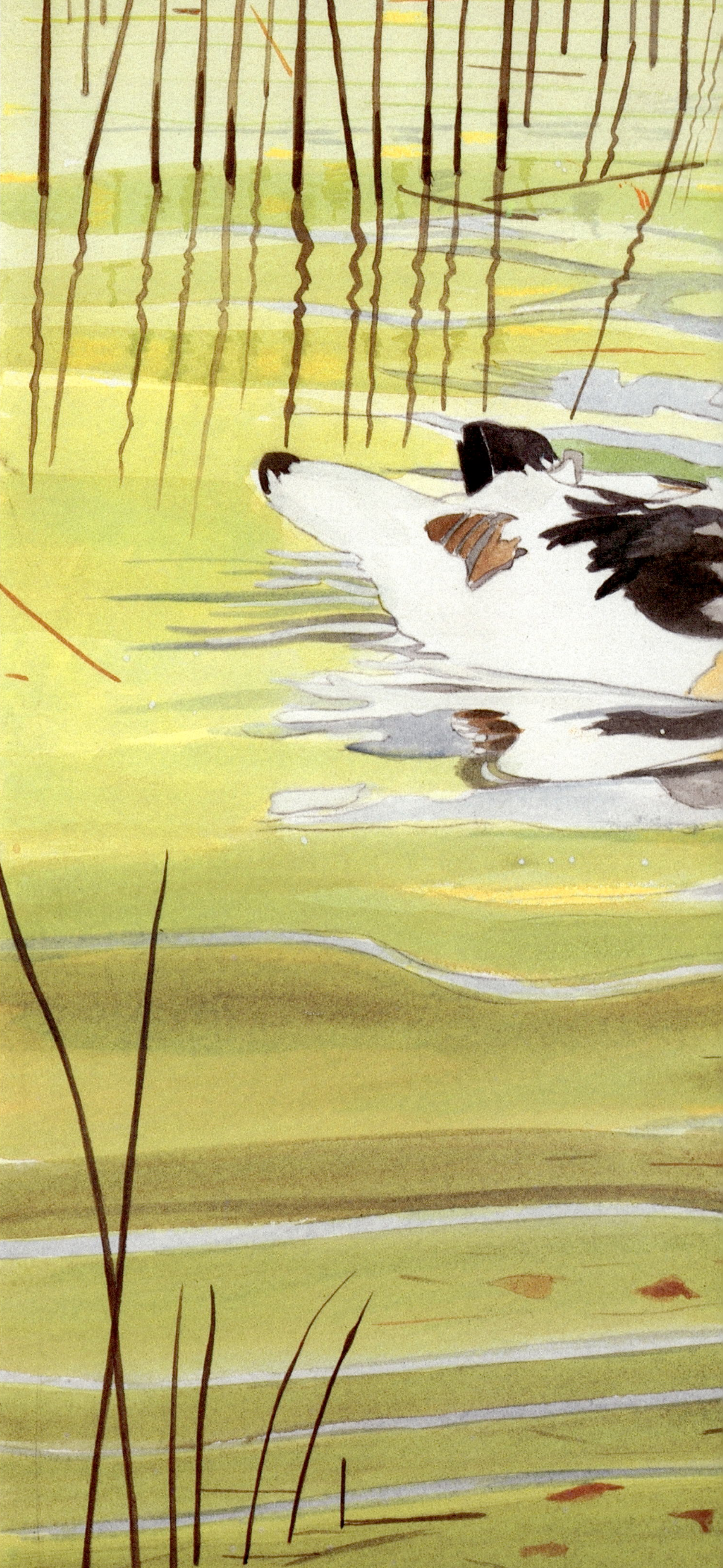

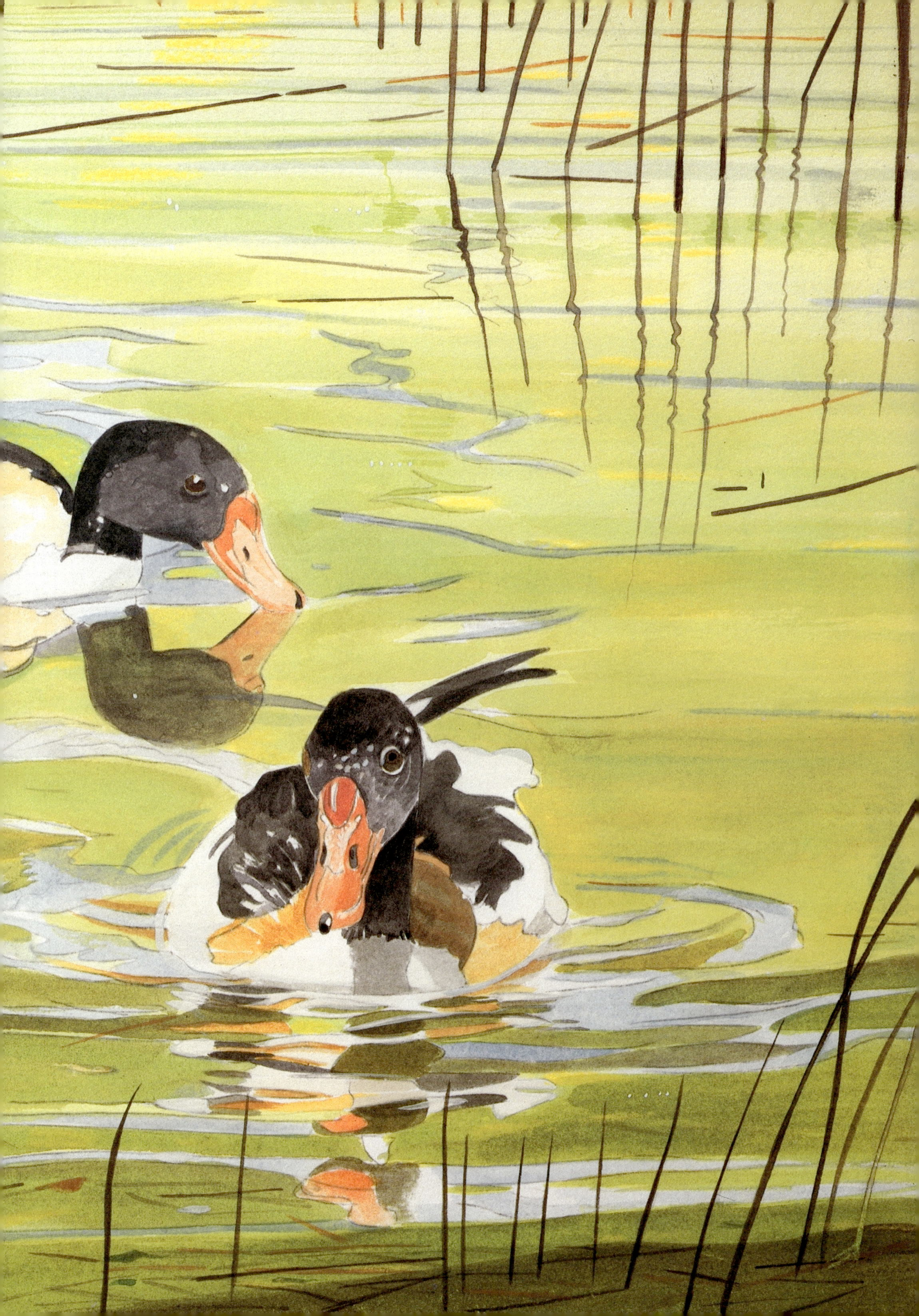

Peacock

Stage One

I wanted to include an exercise of a different kind, one with a carefully designed composition, and compare its decorative quality with the "natural," or photographic, results of the earlier demonstrations. This demonstration is based on a painting I did for a large European manufacturer to advertise the colors of its housepaints. The composition was carefully constructed, after many trial sketches, to achieve a perfect balance. I began with an extensive, detailed drawing. In copying it, don't be put off by its apparent complexity. Treat one component at a time, and make it fairly large or detailed brushwork will be difficult. Try the head first, then the neck, and then the surrounding detail. The identikit drawing method explained earlier is an excellent one to use.

Stage Two

To avoid smudging the drawing, wash the bottom half of the picture and the head and neck with a wash of Chinese white and a no. 2 round brush. Then wash the areas between the spines of the display feathers with a mixture of sap green and yellow ochre. As you can see, I don't try to make each section identical in color value, preferring the subtle changes achieved by mixing the colors as I go along to the bland uniformity of a premixed wash. With a dense solution of lamp black, paint the "eyes" of the display roundels, using the tip of a well-pointed no. 00 round brush.

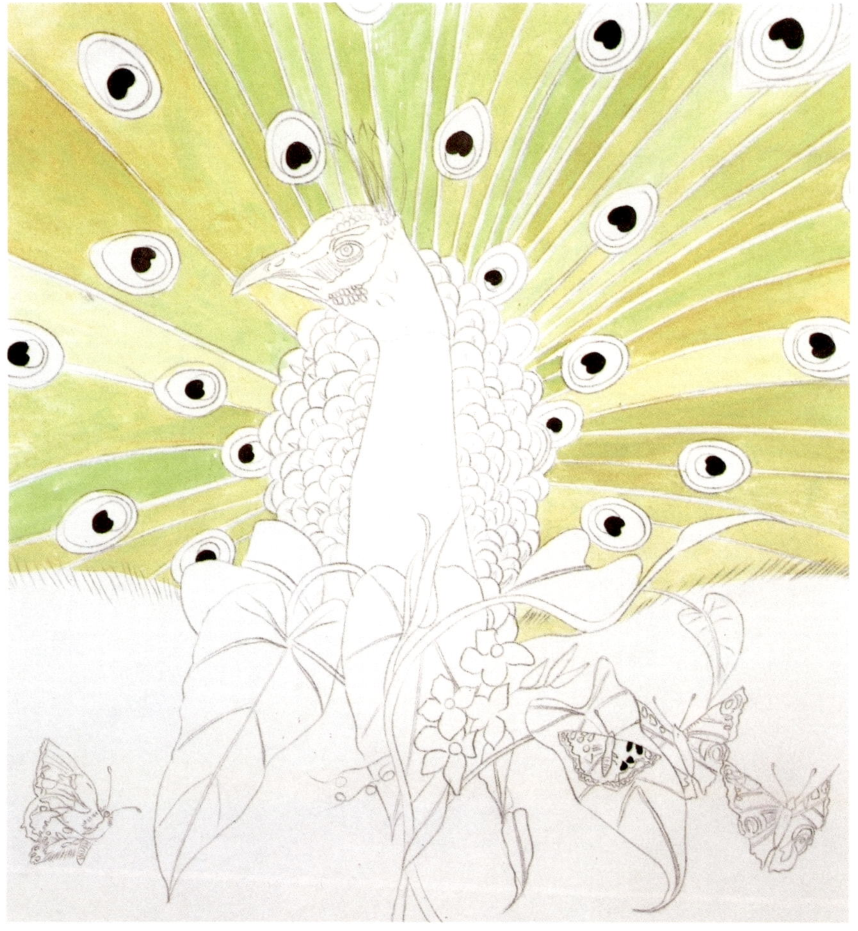

Stage Three

Mix cerulean blue, cobalt blue, and Chinese white to paint the outside of the peacock's display eye, and carefully apply it with a well-pointed no. 0 round brush. Then wash in the head and neck with a watery mixture of cerulean blue and Chinese white. With a well-pointed no. 2 brush and the strongest possible mixture of cobalt blue and purple lake, paint the two heart-shaped leaves that frame the peacock's emerging neck. Finally, with light red and cadmium yellow dark, wash the surrounding area of the peacock's eye.

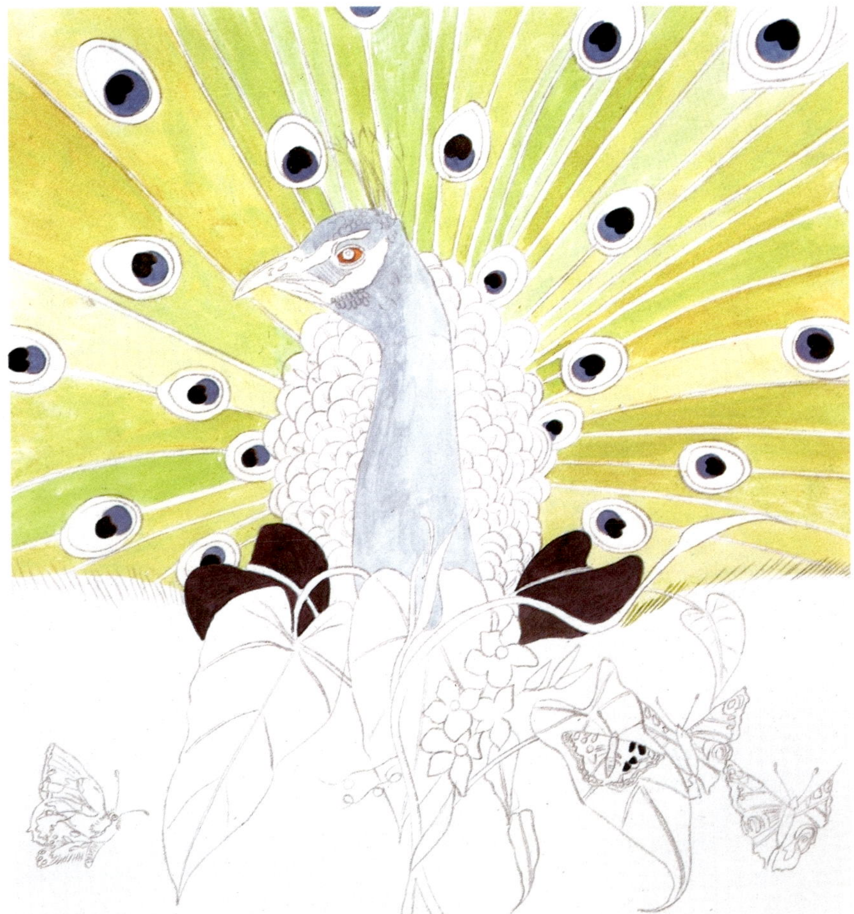

Stage Four

Mix a greenish wash of sap green and yellow ochre and, with a no. 0 brush, indicate tail feathers and greenish outer rings of the display "eyes." Next, mix cadmium yellow with just a dot of cadmium yellow dark and paint the inner yellow of the display "eyes." The tight, overlapping yellow feathers directly behind the neck and head are washed in with a watery mixture of cadmium pale and sap green (favoring yellow), using a no. 2 brush, and the outer rings of the display "eyes" are painted with a slightly yellower mix of these colors. With Hookers green, carefully wash in the two foreground leaves, then underpaint the small foreground seed pods in cadmium yellow pale.

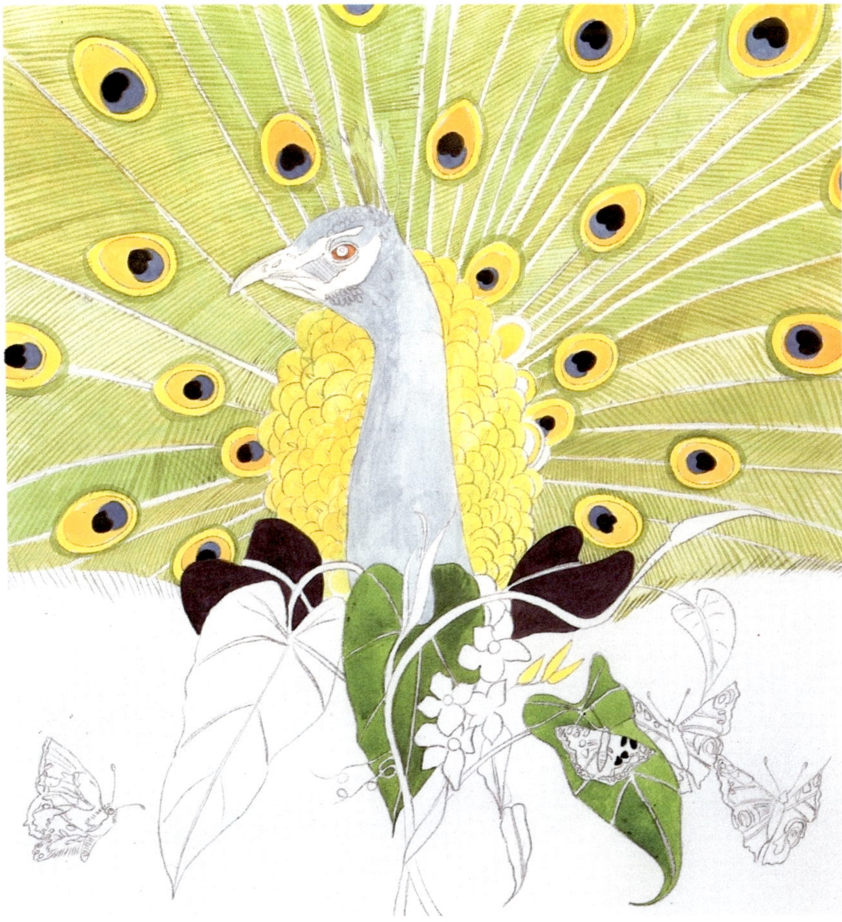

Stage Five

With a mixture of cobalt blue and Chinese white, tick in the undercoat of plumage on the neck and head, using a darker shade for accents. Because the tail-feather construction is complicated, I have rendered only part of it so you can see my method. With a watery mixture of Hookers green dark and a no. 0 round brush, put in a few of the background feather strokes. (Use a sweeping stroke and take care not to overdo either the pigment strength or the thickness of your stroke.) Next, with a mixture of Chinese white, Winsor red, and purple lake and a well-pointed no. 0 brush, paint the unfurled new leaves and the ribs of the large leaf. With a mixture of cerulean blue and Chinese white, wash in the flowers using a blunt no. 2 brush. Hookers green dark and a touch of sepia provide the color for the two small leaves at the bottom of the picture. The grass is of varying strengths of Hookers green and cadmium yellow deep. Notice how it radiates outward to draw attention to the center of the design. (Again I have not completed this process so that the technique remains easy to follow.) Finally, with a mixture of lamp black and Chinese white, paint the center of the bird's eye.

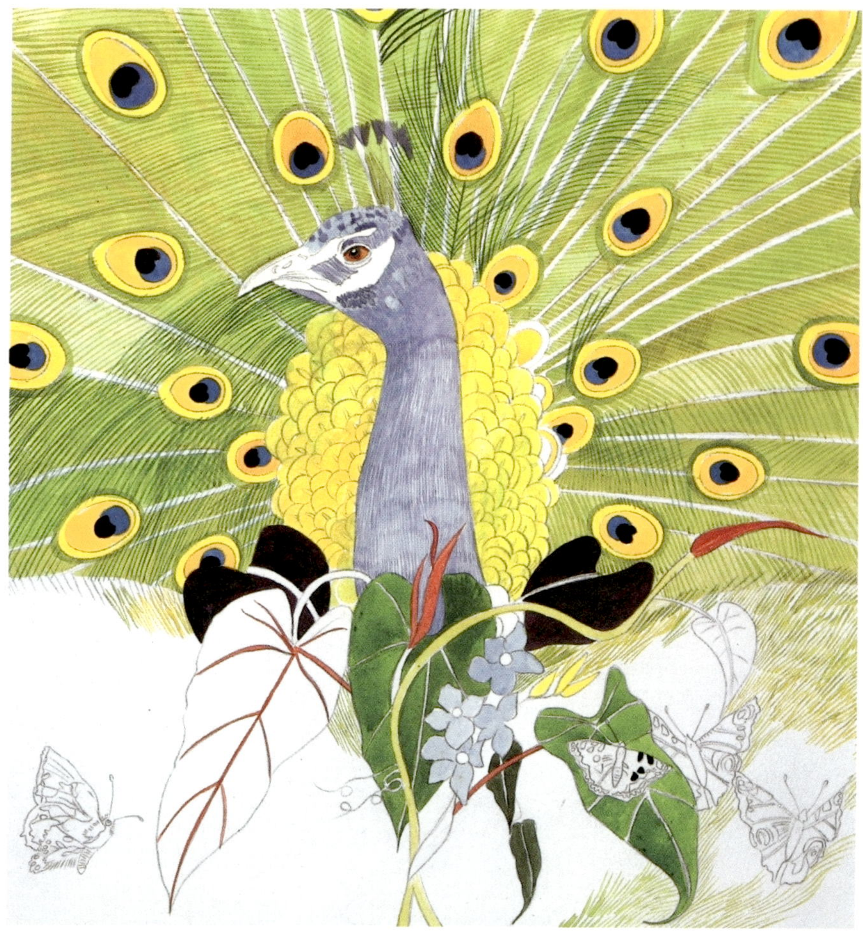

Stage Six

Complete the spray effect of the feathers, and, with a stronger mixture of the same color and a well-pointed no. 1 brush, indicate the direction of each display feather. With cerulean blue and cobalt blue, paint the fine 'hairs' on the peacock's head and neck. Paint the shadow areas on the head with a very light gray (lamp black and Chinese white), and increase the density of the black pupil. With pure lamp black, paint the pattern area on the wings of the butterflies. With cadmium lemon and Chinese white, paint the round feathers behind the head, treating each as a separate entity, and put in the leaf ribs and the long, twisted plant stem with the same mixture. The large leaf is washed in with pure Hookers green dark.

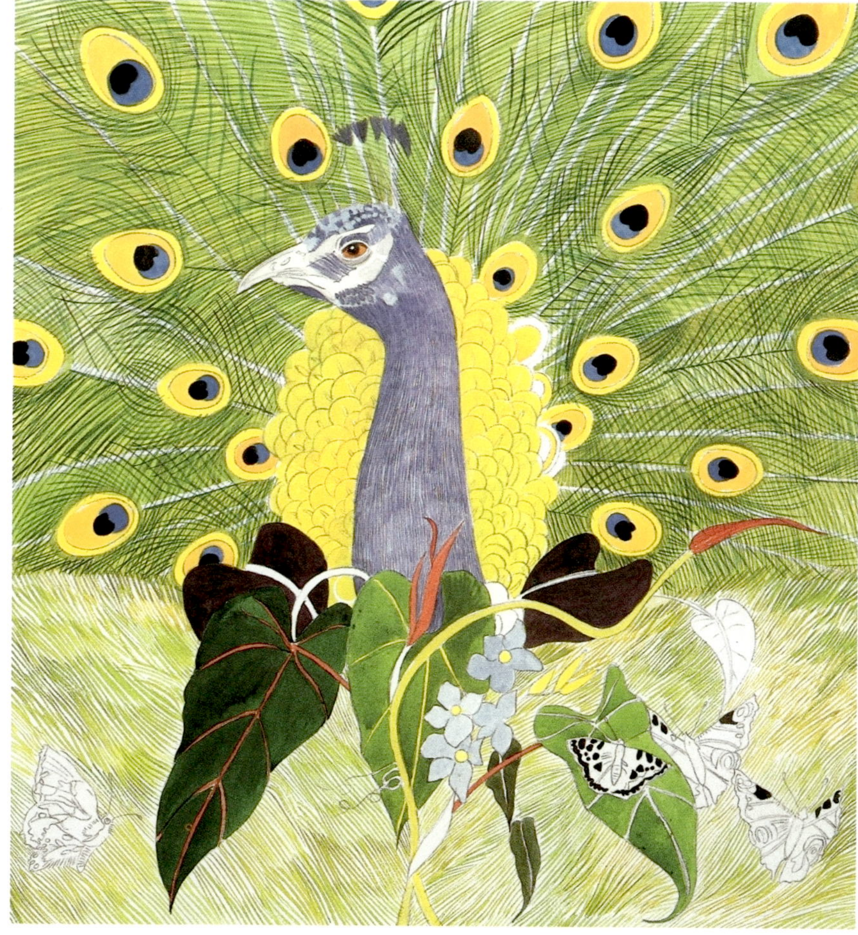

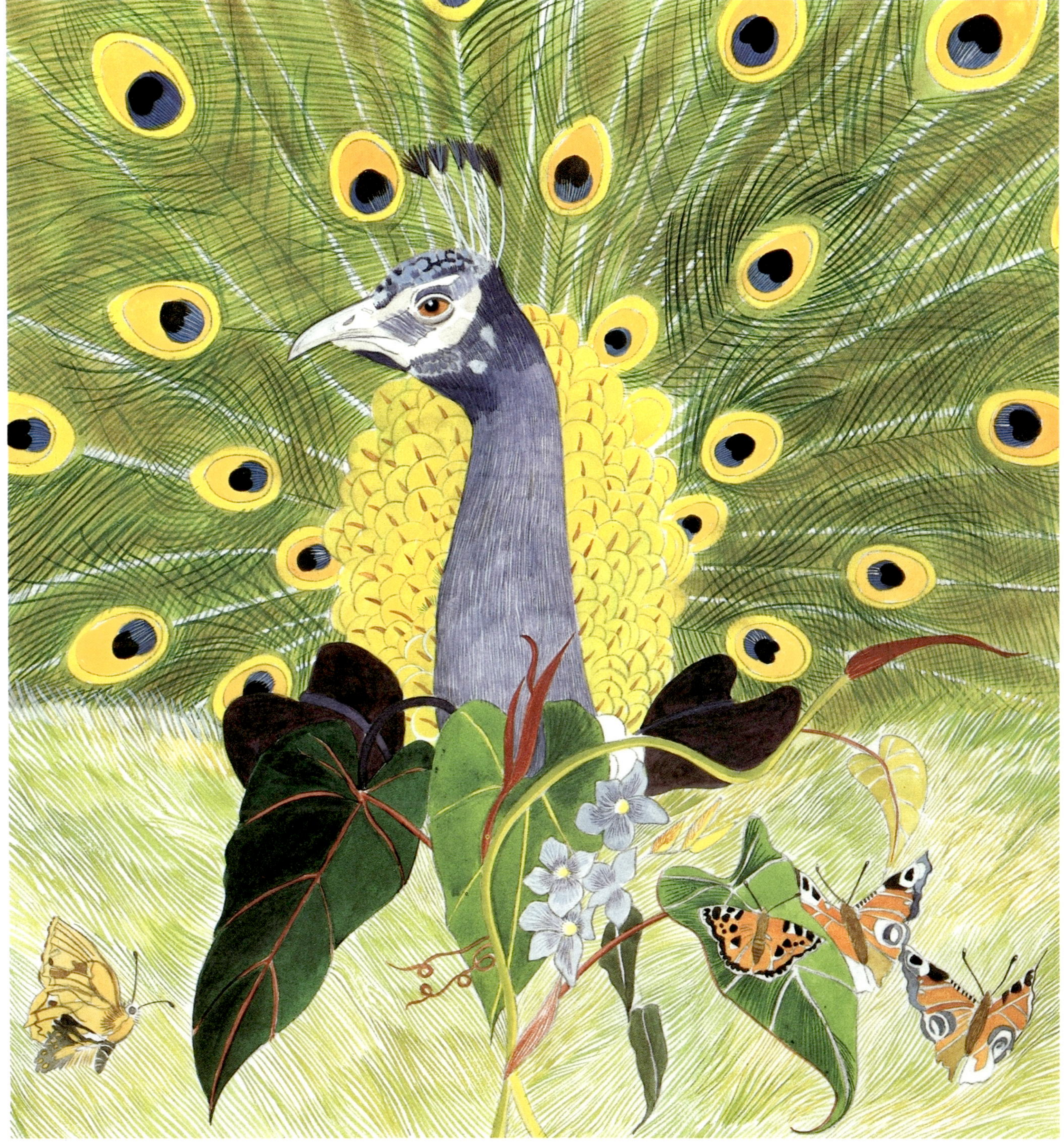

Stage Seven

Use a well-pointed no. 1 brush for the whole of this final stage. With a mixture of cadmium yellow deep and light red, tick in the feather spines on the canopy structure behind the neck and head. Then paint in the base color of the three butterflies on the right using a mix of chrome orange and light red, and then add the pattern with cobalt blue, with light red and sepia for the bodies, and black details. Rub a small piece of absorbent cotton on an olive green pastel stick and then onto the painting to give the feathers a sense of bulk between the radiating main spines, and then fix it with a fixative spray. With a mix of French ultramarine and purple lake, redefine the detail on the flowers, head, neck, and crest, and add stems to the purple leaves. Then use Hookers green dark to retouch some of the display feathers and leaves. The butterfly on the left was painted with a Naples yellow wash and then detailed with a mix of sepia and light red (lighter pattern), and lamp black and Chinese white for the dark pattern. Use a mixture of cadmium yellow dark and Hookers green dark to reinforce the leaf stems and add a few more display feathers. Finally, add highlights with process white and mix it with previous mixtures to get lighter tints of refining details. For example, look at the main feather spines to see the light effects gained by adding small touches of process white.

Part Five

Working Out a Composition

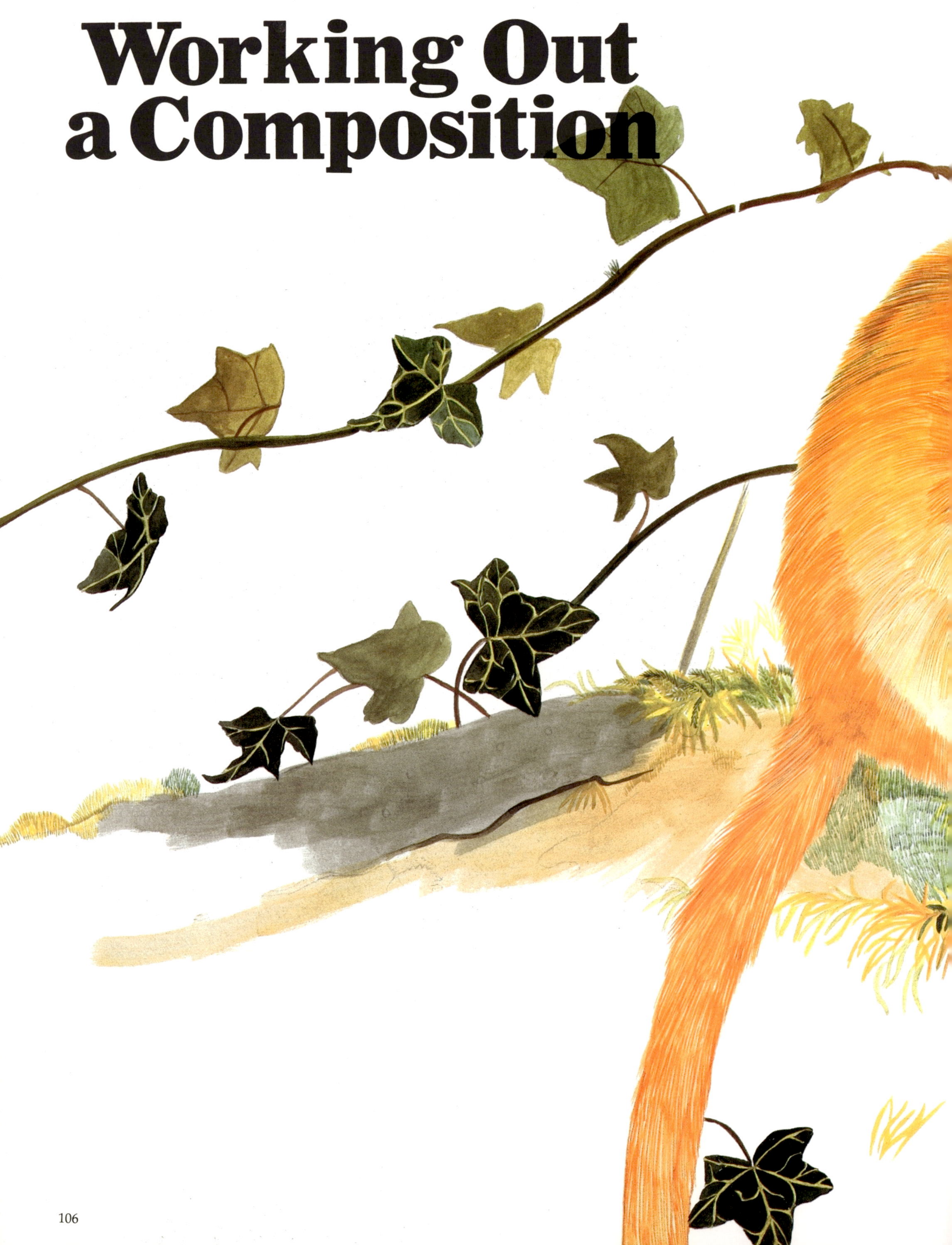

WHENEVER FOREGROUNDS and backgrounds are talked about, especially in relationship to wildlife painting, it is almost impossible not to wander into areas that have much to do with composition. In wildlife painting where the animal is the hero, the surrounding environment is used to emphasize that fact. In general, scanty foreground and background aids tension, drama, or alertness or unifies the main story and makes it more appealing. But sometimes in some cases the reverse is true. For example, *The Storm Tiger* (page 110) has a heavily painted habitat that aids the quiet loneliness of the painting. And the peacock (page 105), which carries around its own habitat, needs a more detailed background to knit it into a well-rounded and integrated design. In the end, choosing the right foreground or background is a question of personal taste, but I suggest that you begin by understating them at first as you experiment to find out what suits your needs. In this section we will examine two related compositional problems: where to place the subject in the composition and how to choose a foreground and background.

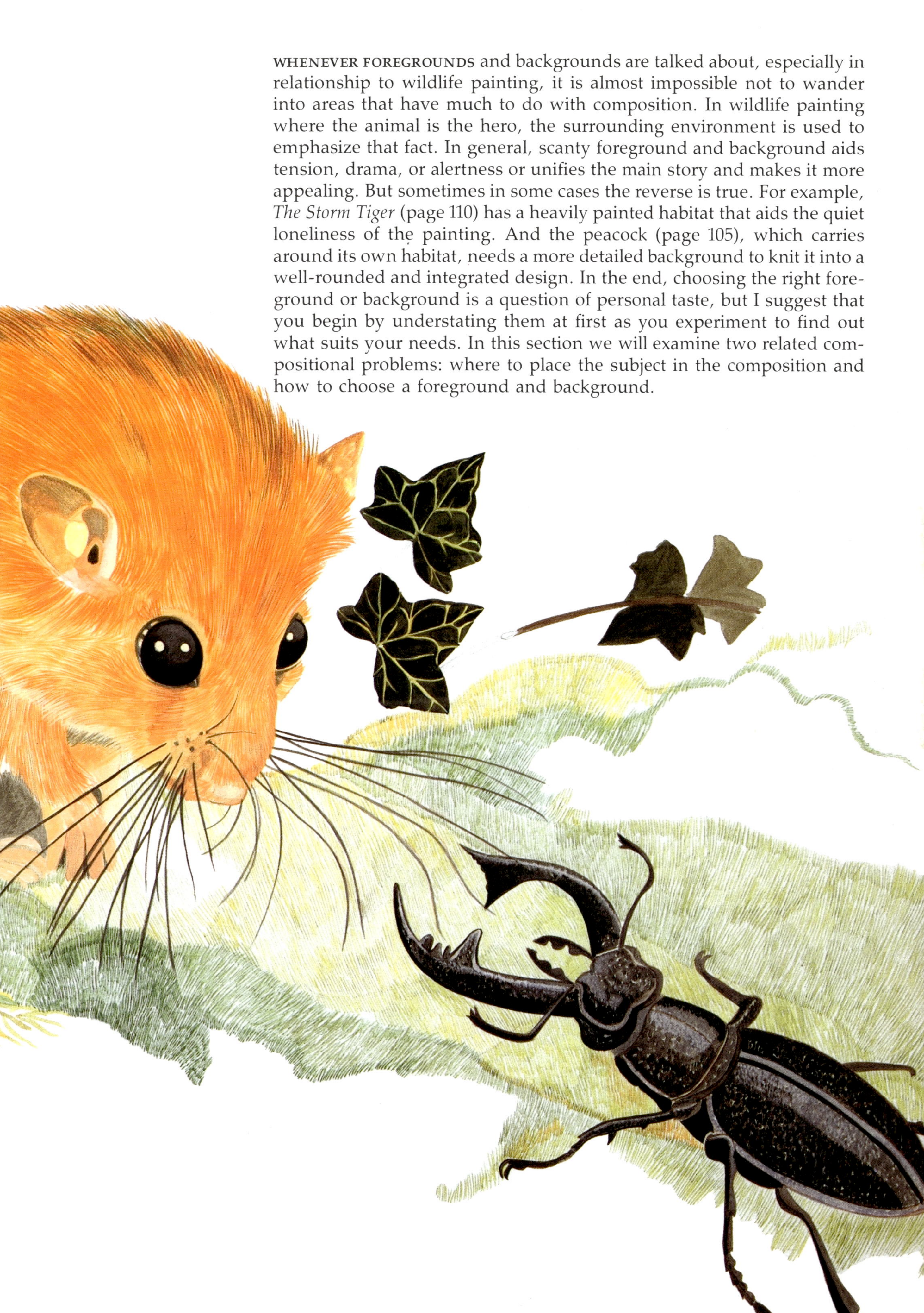

Placing Subjects in a Composition

Animals should be placed within the borders of your painting to create a certain effect: to suggest an emotion, create a strong compositional line, or convey a point of view, the way the artist perceives the subject.

Central placements tend to focus all-over attention on the animal. It has the same undivided attention as, for example, a tiger coming toward us in the wild (if we are lucky enough to spot him). This central placement is also effective in an animal portrait, where the animal is obviously the focal point. It not only makes life easier to place the head in the center in that case, but it is also a good placement for beginners, who may have difficulty making a decision. (I would suggest that beginners place the animal in or near the center, with the focal point two-thirds of the way up the picture.)

But the center is not the only major focal point. If you want to create a certain tension, you can move the animal to the left or right. This way, our eye and head must move slightly to focus on the animal and this very process of our eye movement adds to our sense of the animal's movement. It also avoids the static, formal quality of the central placement. Placing the animal above or below the center can also make a point. When the animal is placed low on the paper, it suggests the equivalent of something barely glimpsed—and the quick glance of your eye is always more alerting than the a head-on view, which encourages a more studied look.

Position can also emphasize the moving quality of the animal. For instance, a stalking tiger in long grass would be best placed low in the center of the picture so attention is focused on the drama of its approach, whereas a tiger about to spring or actually in the act of springing should be placed high within the borders of the picture. Placing the subject two-thirds of the way up on the paper also creates a certain feeling, like looking into the face of a person who is just the right height for you . . . comfortable!

In the long run, if you feel strongly that a certain position is right, then put your subject there. Don't worry too much about rules. There is too much emphasis on calculated logic these days, obscuring our ability to feel naturally, through hunch or inspiration, how things should be. You can always sketch your compositional options very rapidly before you start painting and pick the one that appeals most.

The following are examples of some of my older work, selected because I can still clearly remember the thoughts that ran through my mind at the time.

THE OWL AND THE MOUSE

This picture is a good example of a situation where the composition contributes greatly to the finished picture and the clarity of the communication. I wanted to create drama, not just in a theatrical sense, but in a knowledgeable, realistic fashion. The concept of this picture is that the owl, after hunting all night, is returning to its rest and at the same moment a mouse is beginning to start its own hunt for food. The picture therefore has to say all of this clearly. But because I wanted the mouse to live, I made the owl miss the mouse.

The picture is divided into three more-or-less equal parts symbolizing the areas of life occupied by the three subjects:

1. *The owl as seen from below (by the mouse?), and suspended in its own environment.*
2. *A clearly designed fern forest, another world.*
3. *The forest floor, where the mouse is foraging.*

The third of the page devoted to each subject and its area enhances the feeling of menace in the picture.

The dark silhouetted foliage around the edges of the picture draw the eye to the owl, the ferns give the impression that the owl is several feet above the ground, and the distant tree trunk (the owl has just come from there), together with the ferns, demonstrate that the owl is moving quickly, silently, and purposefully. This picture was constructed with space to dramatize a situation, and to portray it accurately. It would not have been as clear if I had used a landscape shape, or had I not divided the three environments so equally.

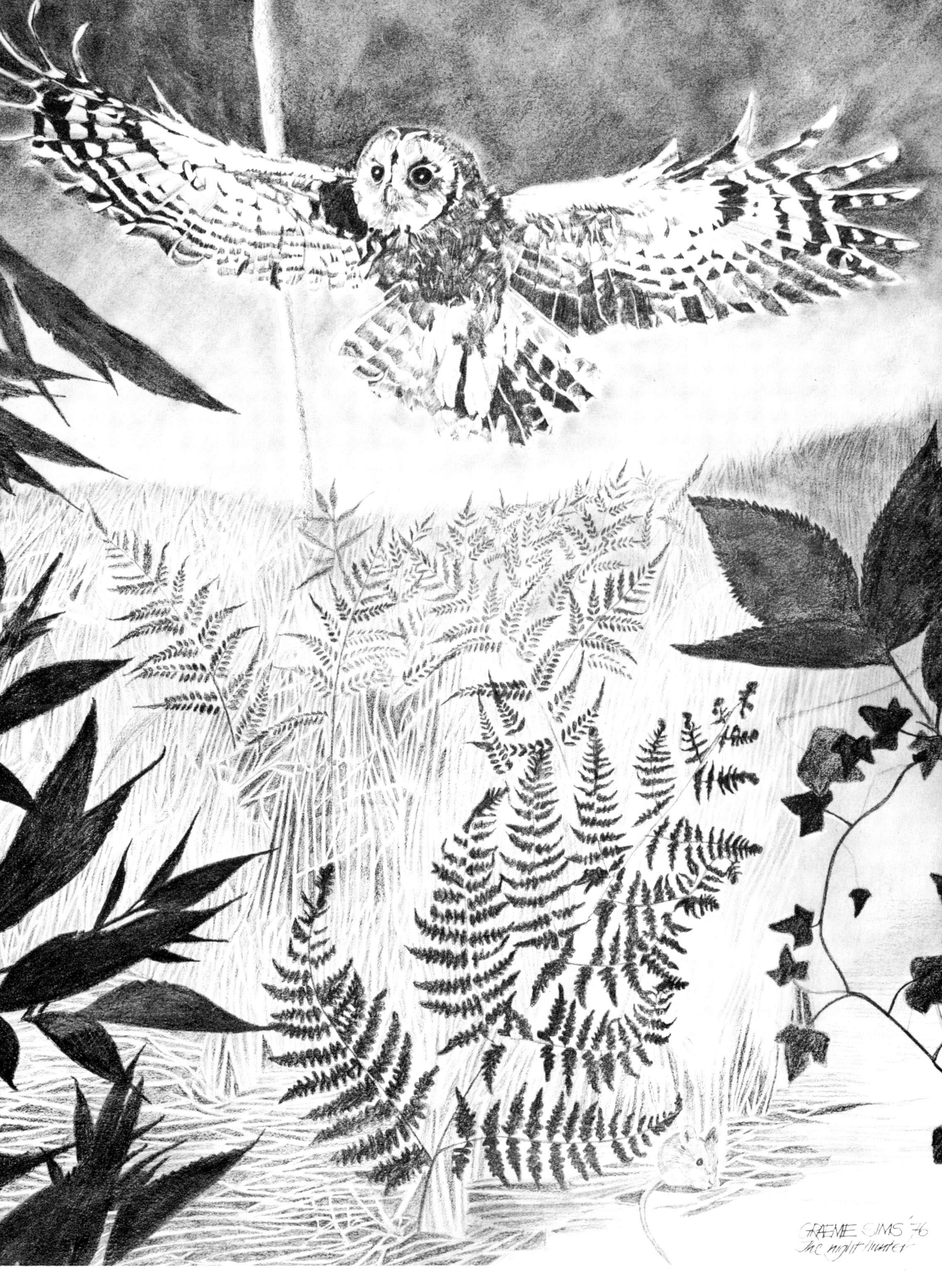
GRAEME SIMS '76
The night hunter

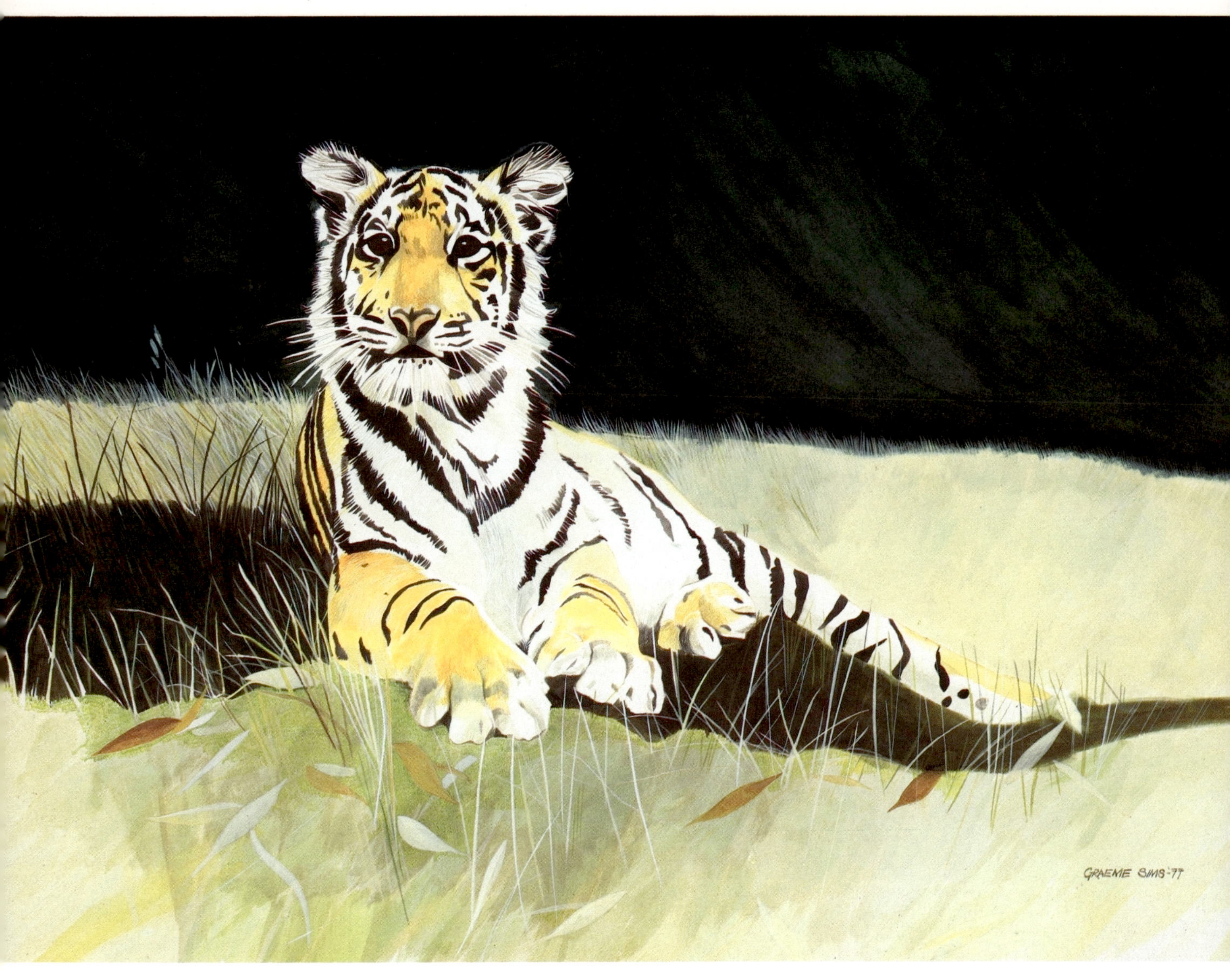

STORM TIGER
Collection of the artist

Storm Tiger *depicts the opposite emotion of the* Owl and the Mouse. *The subject is a very young tiger that was born in captivity, and then released into the jungle in India. It has not yet become wild and still knows how to totally relax in the presence of humans. It was obviously friendly with the person who took the picture, because it is looking playfully and with curiosity at the photographer. I moved the tiger over to the left of the picture, which had the effect of making it look as though it would or could move out of the picture more easily than if it were placed in the middle. While there is no menace in the painting, there is pent-up energy, and the placement of the tiger enhances this wound-up springlike element.*

The sky in the photograph was a beautiful blue, but I wanted to emphasize the alertness of the tiger, so I divided my picture just below the tiger's head (this is where the energy manifests itself) and made the sky a stormy color in order to emphasize the tiger's head, neck, and shoulders. Notice how the tiger's paws are flat on the ground, with the paw divisions separated, suggesting that fast movement would shortly follow. Also, all of the grass is blown to the left, suggesting more tension and tending to give the effect of pushing the tiger to move to the left.

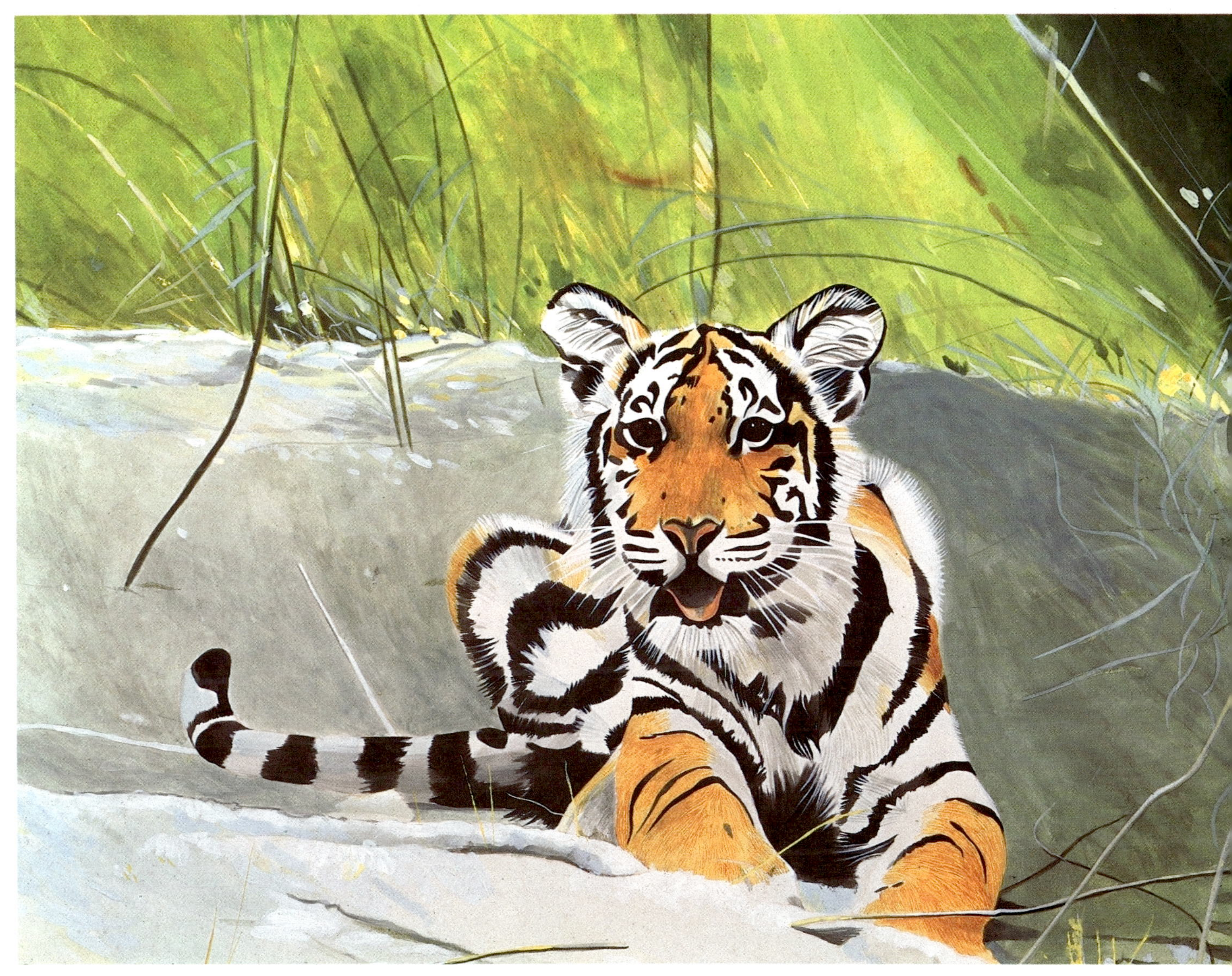

TIGER IN A CLEARING

There is an interesting comparison to be made here between this painting and Storm Tiger, *opposite. Both are of the same tiger cub, yet their painting styles and moods differ enormously. I wanted the mood of* Storm Tiger *to be serious, with that strange, clear light that precedes a storm matching the tiger's attentive mood in order to give the painting an earnest and disturbing quality. I had just heard that the young tiger, Tara, had died after an attempt to resettle her in the jungle. Fortunately, the story turned out to be untrue. But my mood upon hearing it was reflected in* Storm Tiger.

Tiger in a Clearing, *on the other hand, is simply a picture of a carefree and mischievous cub playing tiger hide-and-seek in a safe, sun-dappled clearing. It is also a study of the tiger's natural camouflage that makes it so successful as a predator. The painting style is looser than in* Storm Tiger, *with less definition of the animal. This not only helps to emphasize its unformed and undefined youth (see the section on eyes), but also effectively keeps the mood of the painting carefree.*

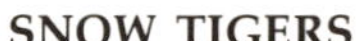

SNOW TIGERS

Original in the collection of Mr. Ian Wilkinson

Another example of where a composition is used to create a story or a feeling is in the painting, Snow Tigers. *I wanted this picture to express the natural unity between a male and a female tiger, and I wanted to make the picture depict calm security. So I placed the subjects very close to each other, with the central point of the picture being more or less between the two creatures. The male tiger is turning to look at the female and to emphasize this, the very simple and understated background springs from the direction of the turning male tiger to lead over the head of the female, so the main subject is, if you like, pleasantly gift-wrapped in a very secure fashion into a friendly environment.*

In some ways I have cheated, or shall we say used more license, as neither of the tigers is a Siberian and would not in fact be living in a snow-clad coniferous forest. But I had a strong image in my mind and just had to paint it, with habitat accuracy taking second place. The essence here is the simple, counter-balanced composition of two unadorned tiger heads with a very underpainted habitat indication. All of my attention therefore went into the very careful rendering of the heads. It was important to the composition that only one tiger look directly at the viewer. The reasons for placing the subject in a particular spot are thus straightforward—straightforward, that is, when related to wildlife art.

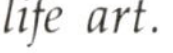

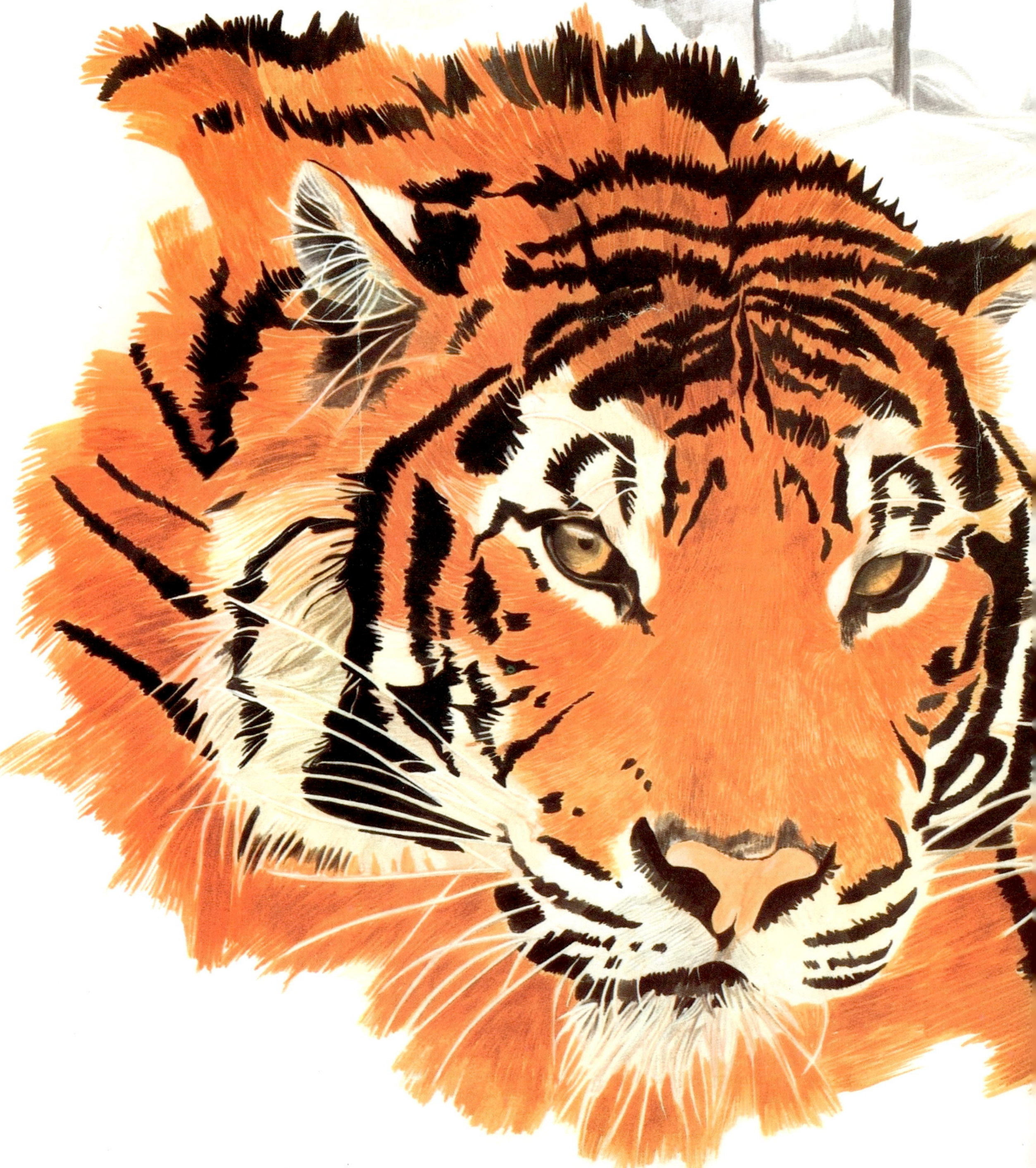

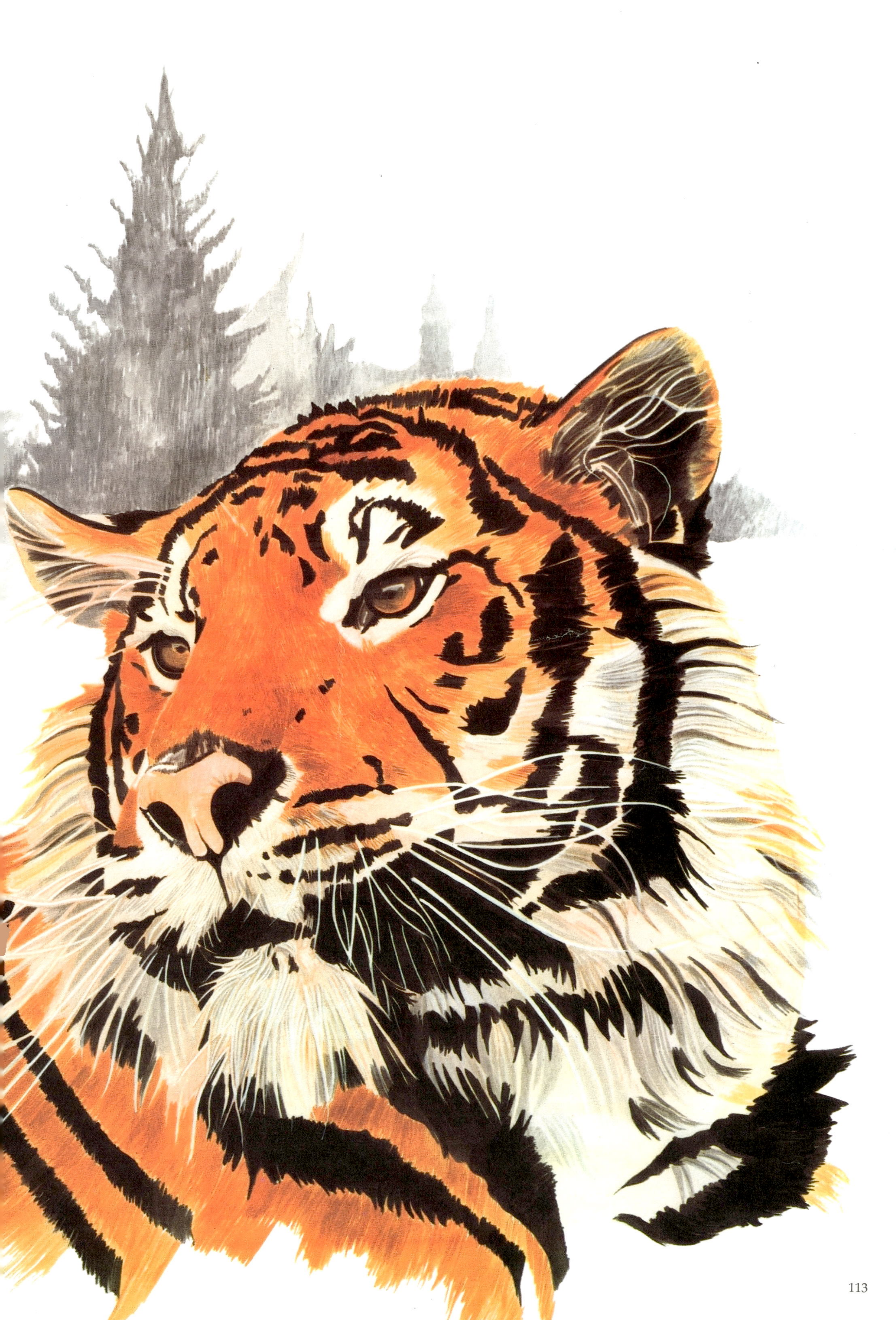

Choosing Foregrounds and Backgrounds

Selection of the animal's environment—where to place it, how much of it to include, what colors or mood to express—is also essential to the compositional process. My views on this subject are colored by my own approach to painting. I believe that the animal I'm portraying is of prime interest and attraction. Therefore backgrounds and foregrounds should be placed and executed in order to best project the central subject of the picture. For that reason, many elements should be considered before a foreground or background is selected. For example, if the animal itself is dramatic in both pose and character, background or foreground can best be kept to a minimum in order to gain emphasis. But if the subject is to be portrayed as a component part of its habitat, greater detail and coverage of the surroundings will be needed. By looking at examples, each with its own rationale, you will best understand how this works.

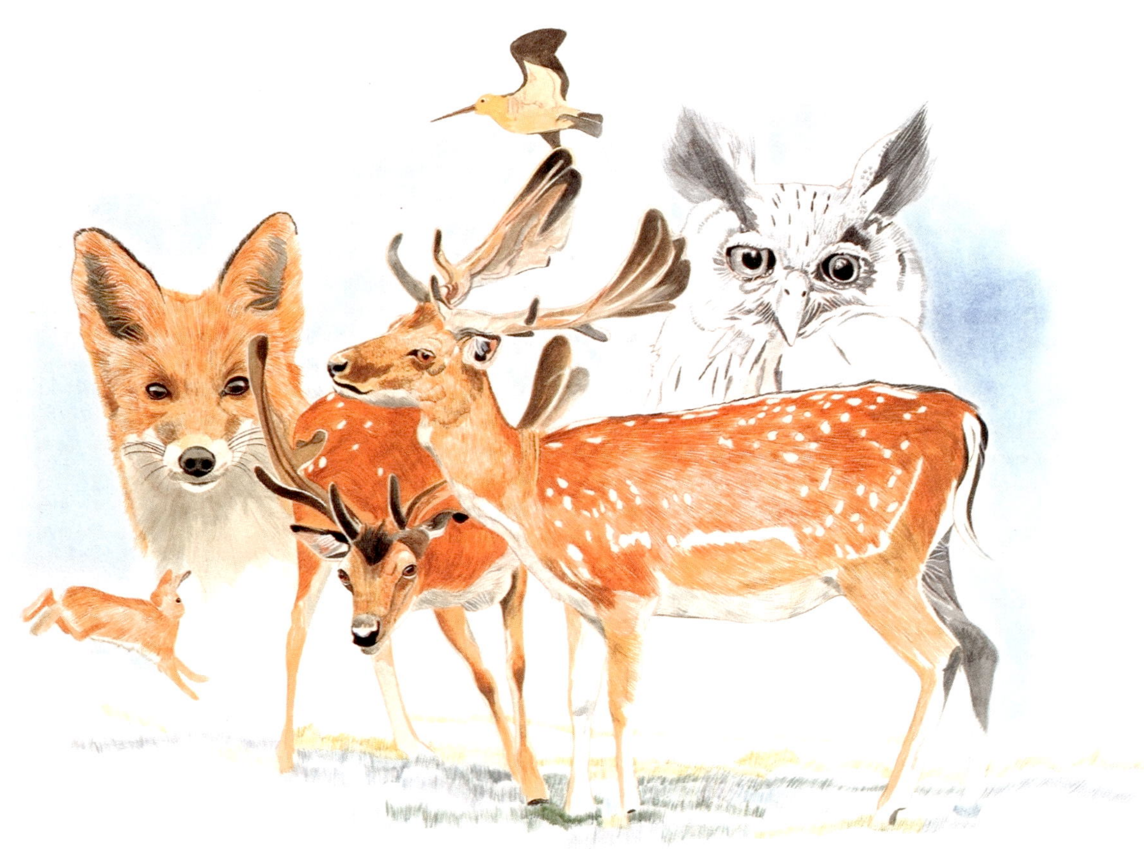

SIX ANIMALS

Brooke Bond Oxo wanted a picture full of animals to make into a Limited Edition Print. I included six separate creatures covering the central interest area of the picture. Even without environmental detail, the painting had a lot of interest, but it needed something to anchor the animals to the ground and to unify them into not only a tight composition, but also a pleasing picture. Otherwise they would appear to float, disembodied, in the air. I added a very understated grass line under the feet of the two central characters to give them a base and to provide a perspective to all of the other studies. Then I finished the painting by rubbing pastel very gently into the background with absorbent cotton to provide a hint of blue sky. The addition of foreground and background grass together with the blue sky emphasized the setting and improved the picture dramatically.

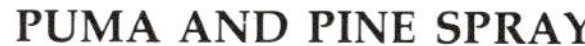

PUMA AND PINE SPRAY

My next picture illustrates a quite different use of foreground and background. I wanted to paint the head of a puma with the portrait of the creature being the essence of my picture, but I did not want it to look like a zoo study. Neither did I want to merge it into a habitat, which would have taken interest away from the attraction of the compelling eyes. In the end, I settled for a fairly detailed rendering of a pine tree spray for the foreground. This made the puma appear to look over the branch, giving an appearance of depth, as well as breaking the otherwise too vertical line of the animal. It also firmly established the fact that it was in the wild.

Selecting a good foreground and background is particularly important when a zoo animal is the model for the photograph because the area in front and behind the animal is usually unnatural and unphotogenic. It is also exceedingly difficult to combine a photograph of a zoo animal with that of a wild animal and make it look convincing. Also, straightforward copying of a picture in every aspect is most unsatisfying and neither stretches the imagination nor improves the skill.

CHEETAH AND CUB

I wanted the animals to be watching and alert for danger in the middle of an open plain. They have seen something, and the baby cheetah moves in closer to the mother, either in excitement or for protection. They have chosen to rest on a small hillock that has been burned leaving just a few stalks of scorched, dry grass, and twigs. The background was painted in very small, almost vertical, strokes, using colors that grow fainter as they move toward the horizon.

Much of the landscape has been left out because once a certain lie of land has been suggested, the eye tends to fill it in. But because of the incompleteness of this background, the eye can fill it in with different details every time.

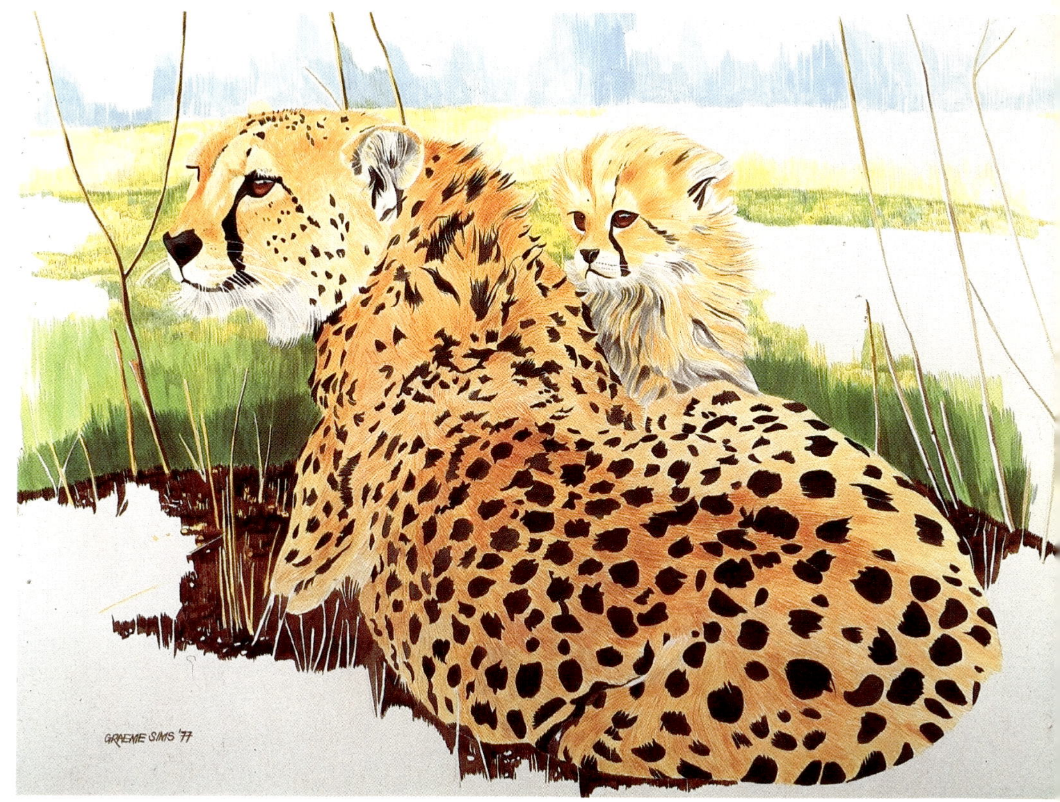

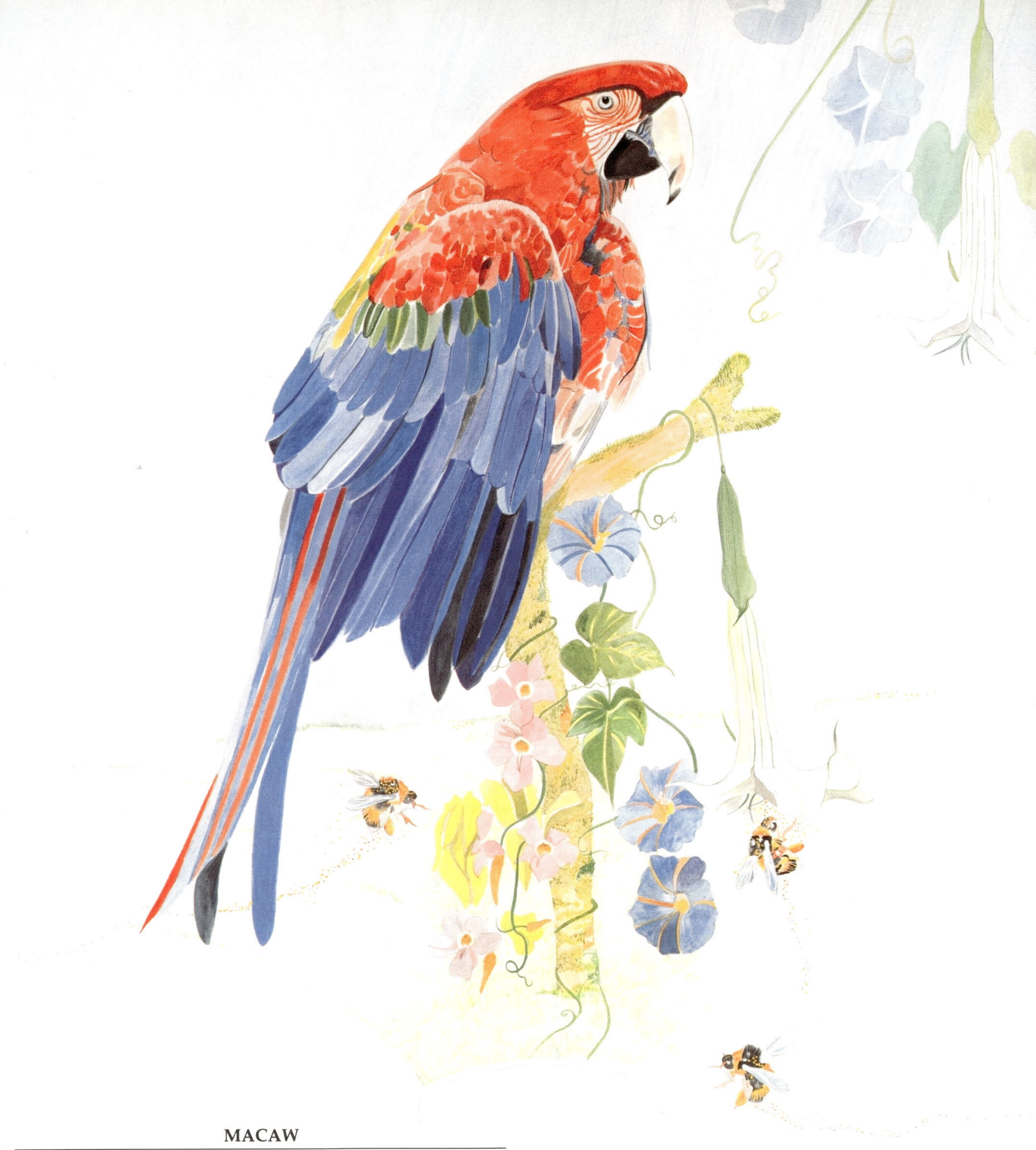

MACAW

This picture was commissioned by I.C.I. Paints Division and needed to tell a story. I wanted both habitat and creature to emerge from an exact area in order to do a particular job, so a composition involving the central subject and its habitat, both foreground and background, became a design.

I selected a macaw that was in an interesting position but it had to sit on something, and because I needed to lead the eye to a certain point, I wanted a vertical composition. But vertical compositions are notoriously difficult to make interesting because they lead the eye up and down in far too mechanical a fashion and do not provide sufficient activity.

To paint the macaw, I washed a very faint sky onto the background, moving across the picture diagonally from right to left. This provided a background that not only flattered the macaw, but also minimized the straight up-and-down effect of the central composition by providing lines of color that traveled in a different direction. The branch that the macaw is sitting on is covered in moss and the flowers extend wider than the actual branch, giving interest over more of the picture area as well as adding charm to a static object.

The moss or grass landscape again extends the area of interest. The bumblebees, with their pollen trails, also have been included to add a clearly focused additional area of interest and movement to what would have otherwise been not only a vertical picture but a static one as well. This kind of carefully thought out and designed picture has to be treated subtly in terms of its foreground and background. If too many creatures or too much habitat is added, or if the pigment or brushstrokes are too heavy, or if too many details are included, the picture would be ruined because background and foreground would distract from and minimize the eye-drawing appeal of the central subject.

LEOPARD ON A LOG

Collection of Mr. and Mrs. Michael Rabin

Here is another example of an understated use of foreground. Although a well-considered picture, actual detail is confined only to what is absolutely necessary. I wanted to emphasize the crouch of the leopard to give a sense of movement to the painting, so I decided to put him on a tree branch, with all of the bark lines leading down almost in the same direction as the leopard's stare. The area below the leopard has been painted only enough to let you know he is on a tree, but the tree is not completed to the extent that it locks the leopard in by making it appear static. The few blades of grass here add to the feeling of an impending rush of movement as they curl toward the leopard (and will obviously spring back as he dashes forward). I purposely left out sky and ground because I wanted to stress the oncoming movement of the leopard.

LEOPARD IN THE MOONLIGHT

In terms of selecting an appropriate background, Leopard in the Moonlight *presents an interesting example. It was one of my first attempts to paint a black animal against a night background. The essence of the painting was always intended to be dramatic. Leopards tend to be very fierce and aggressive, and this was the very mood that I wanted to communicate.*

The leopard itself was detailed only on the head and the muscular hump of back and the legs because I wanted to draw attention to these tension areas. The moon emphasizes the crouched position and picks up its mnemonic eye, thereby increasing the drama, almost as if the moon, too, is glaring at the viewer. I rubbed ground-up pastel onto both sky and ground, increasing the density of color on the ground areas. The moon, the rising ground, and the leopard's arched back converge to add weight to the picture, and this effect is intensified by the unfinished sky. This picture probably would have worked well even if the foreground and background had been painted in a detailed fashion, but then far less focus would have been directed to the central character and its all-important malevolence. The few blades of grass silhouetted against the moon work in shorthand fashion to reveal the setting as a wild and natural habitat.

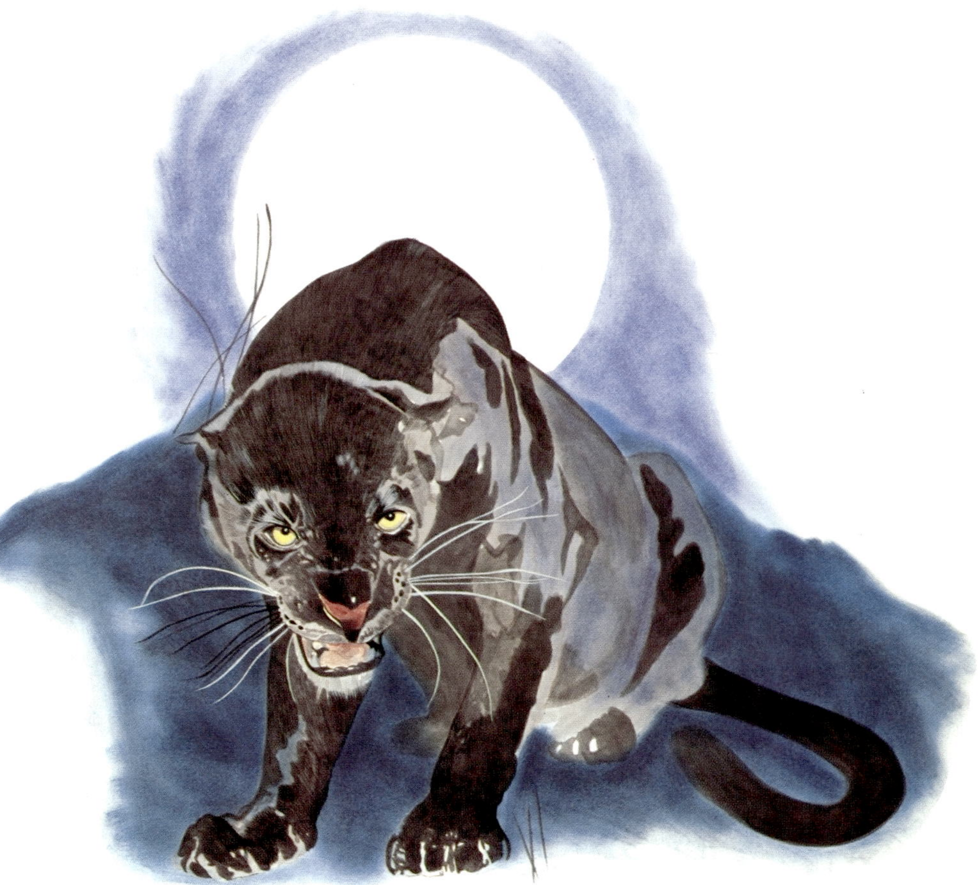

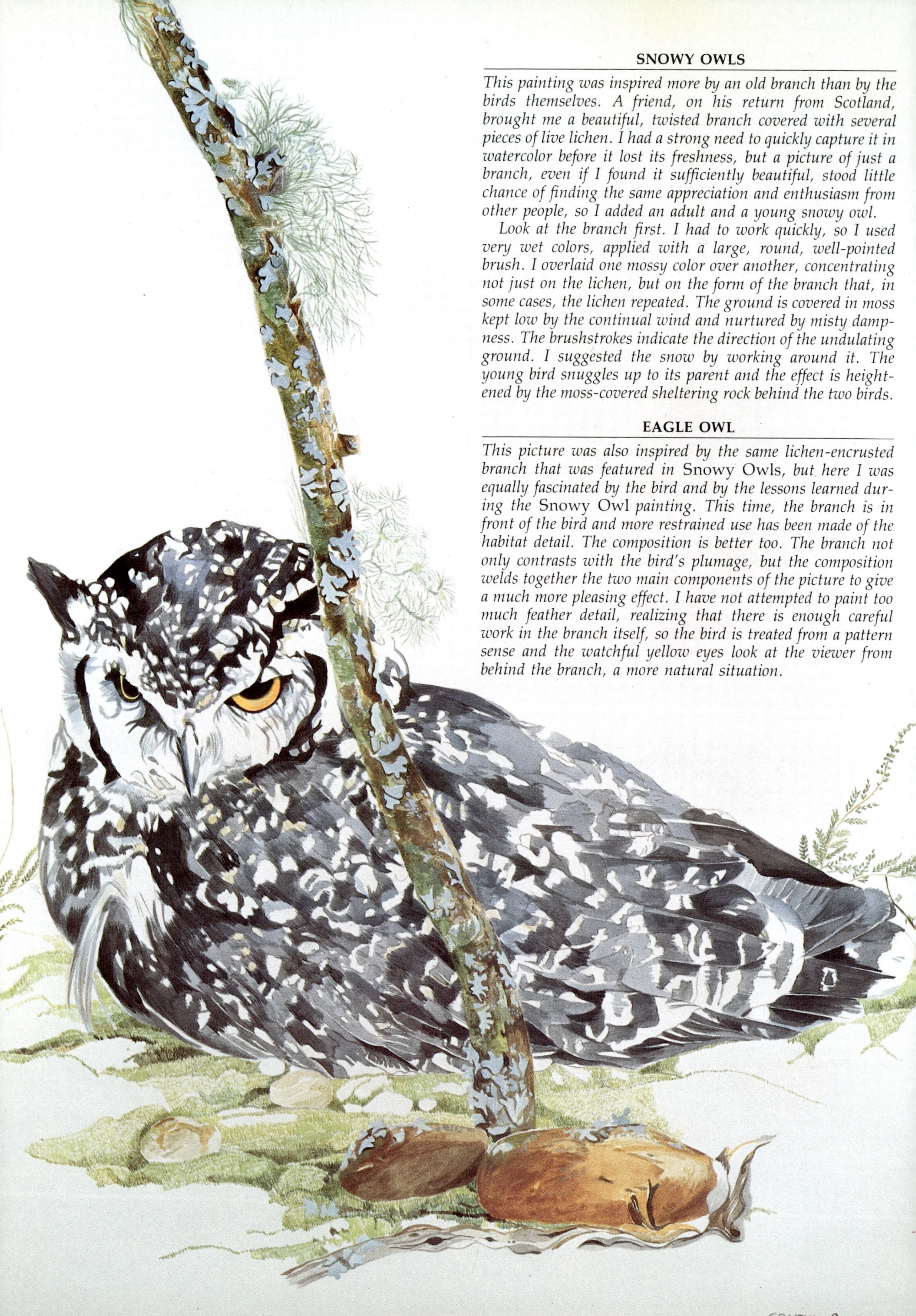

SNOWY OWLS

This painting was inspired more by an old branch than by the birds themselves. A friend, on his return from Scotland, brought me a beautiful, twisted branch covered with several pieces of live lichen. I had a strong need to quickly capture it in watercolor before it lost its freshness, but a picture of just a branch, even if I found it sufficiently beautiful, stood little chance of finding the same appreciation and enthusiasm from other people, so I added an adult and a young snowy owl.

Look at the branch first. I had to work quickly, so I used very wet colors, applied with a large, round, well-pointed brush. I overlaid one mossy color over another, concentrating not just on the lichen, but on the form of the branch that, in some cases, the lichen repeated. The ground is covered in moss kept low by the continual wind and nurtured by misty dampness. The brushstrokes indicate the direction of the undulating ground. I suggested the snow by working around it. The young bird snuggles up to its parent and the effect is heightened by the moss-covered sheltering rock behind the two birds.

EAGLE OWL

This picture was also inspired by the same lichen-encrusted branch that was featured in Snowy Owls, *but here I was equally fascinated by the bird and by the lessons learned during the* Snowy Owl *painting. This time, the branch is in front of the bird and more restrained use has been made of the habitat detail. The composition is better too. The branch not only contrasts with the bird's plumage, but the composition welds together the two main components of the picture to give a much more pleasing effect. I have not attempted to paint too much feather detail, realizing that there is enough careful work in the branch itself, so the bird is treated from a pattern sense and the watchful yellow eyes look at the viewer from behind the branch, a more natural situation.*

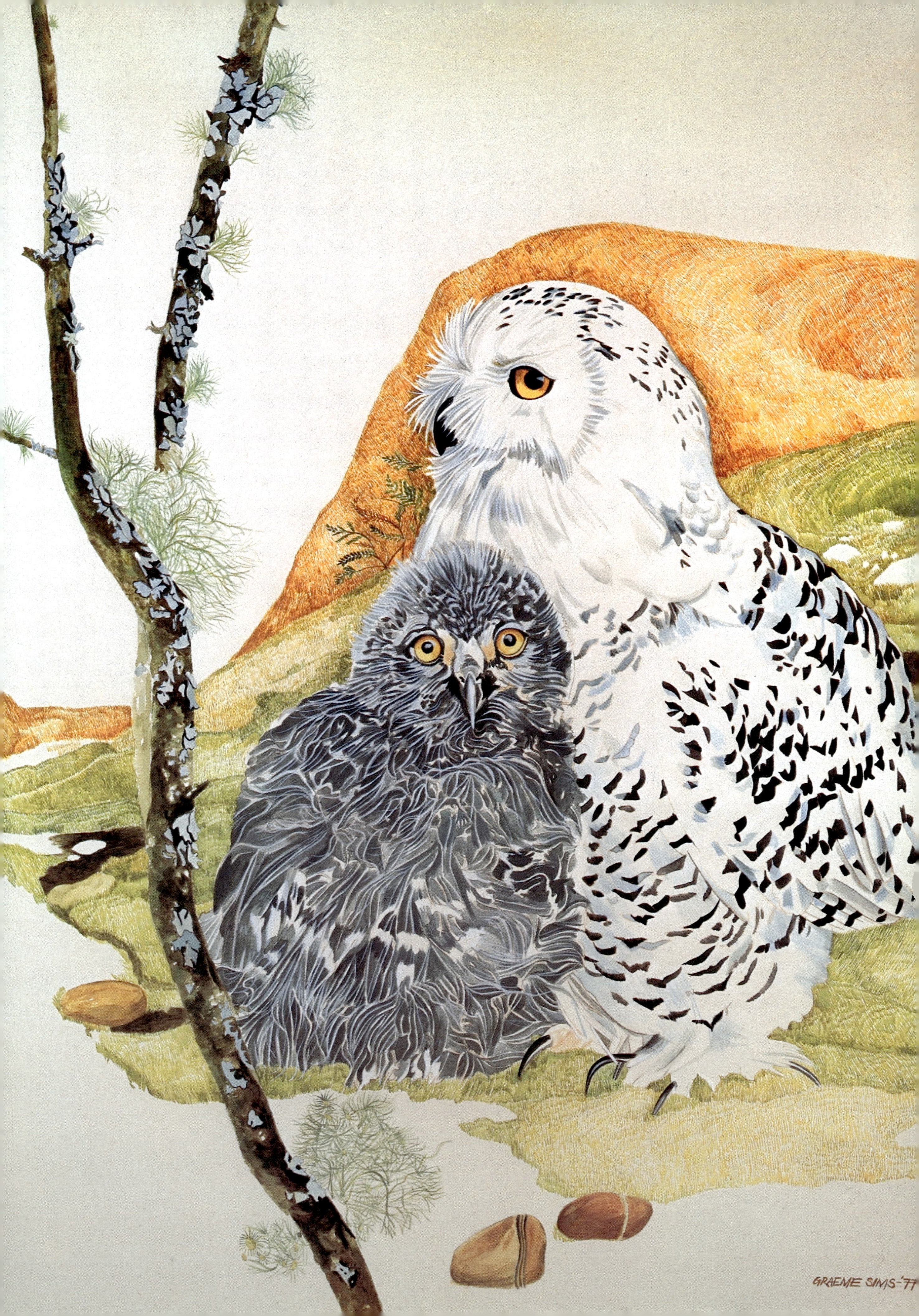
GRAEME SIMS-'77

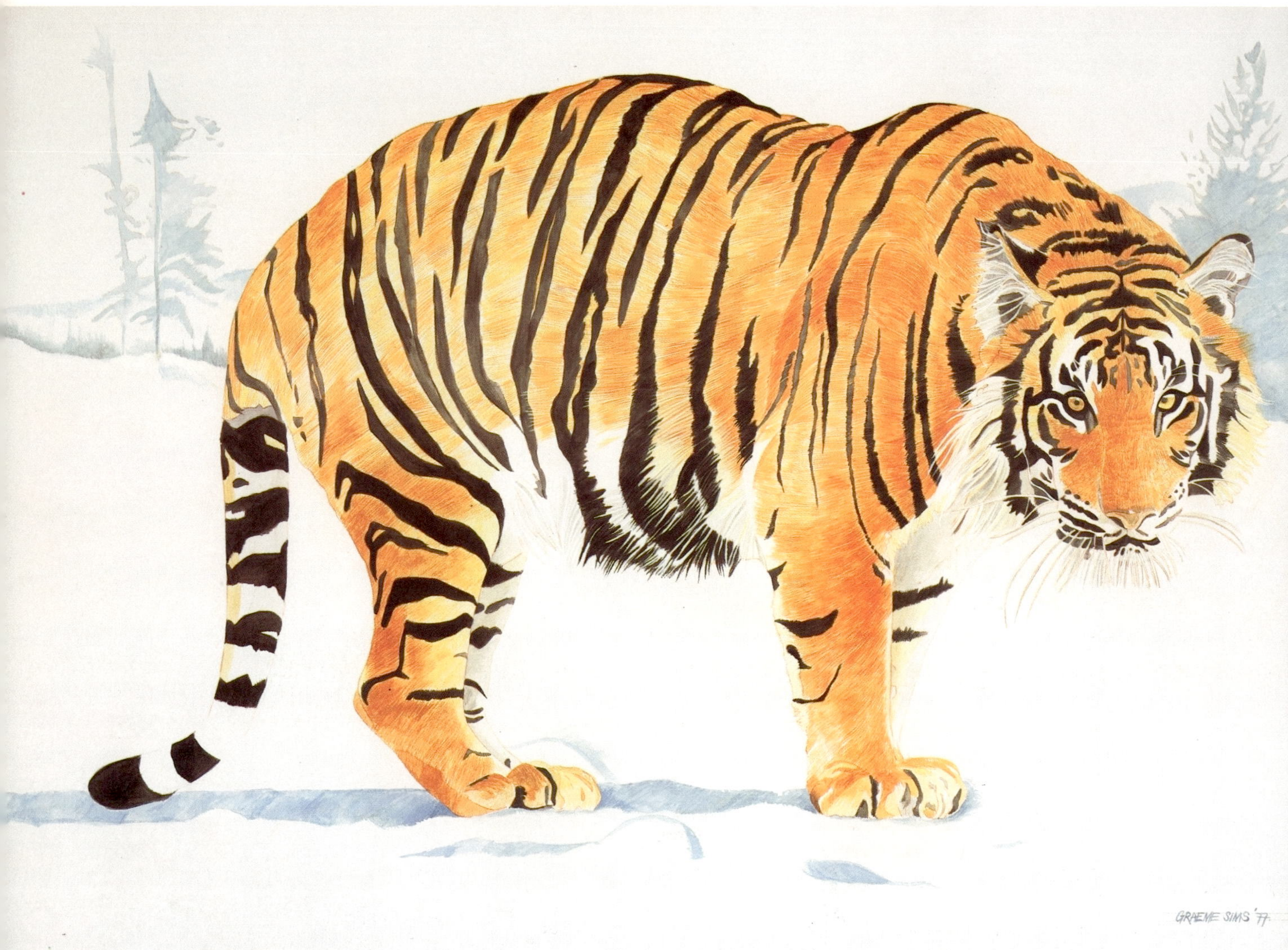

THE OLD TIGER

Collection of the artist

The old tiger is another painting that I like and have kept for myself. I try to paint pictures that are different and that tell a story, and the concept of an elderly tiger showing the same signs of old age that a person does pleases me.

His back is bent, his belly is sagging, and the expression in the eyes, though still very alert, is worldly wise. "I could charge if I wanted to, but I really can't be bothered," he seems to be saying.

As with several other paintings, the central character contained the message and so there was no need for an overly intricate background.

CHIMP

This painting, one of a series, was produced for an English company in order to sell matches and raise money for the World Wildlife Fund. I obviously had to take great care to produce a very accurate and well-defined chimpanzee, as the painting became an advertisement not only for the client, but for me, too.

Care has been lavished on the face of the chimp to capture the expressive and lustrous eyes that reflect the animal's curiosity and intelligence, the wrinkles that make him look so much like an old man, and the mouth. The rest of the head has been treated in a freer manner. I find it difficult to remember the stages of this painting, as it was one of the first of the big commercial series I later became involved with. All I remember now is the fear of having to produce, in a limited time, a good piece of work of an enormously difficult subject.

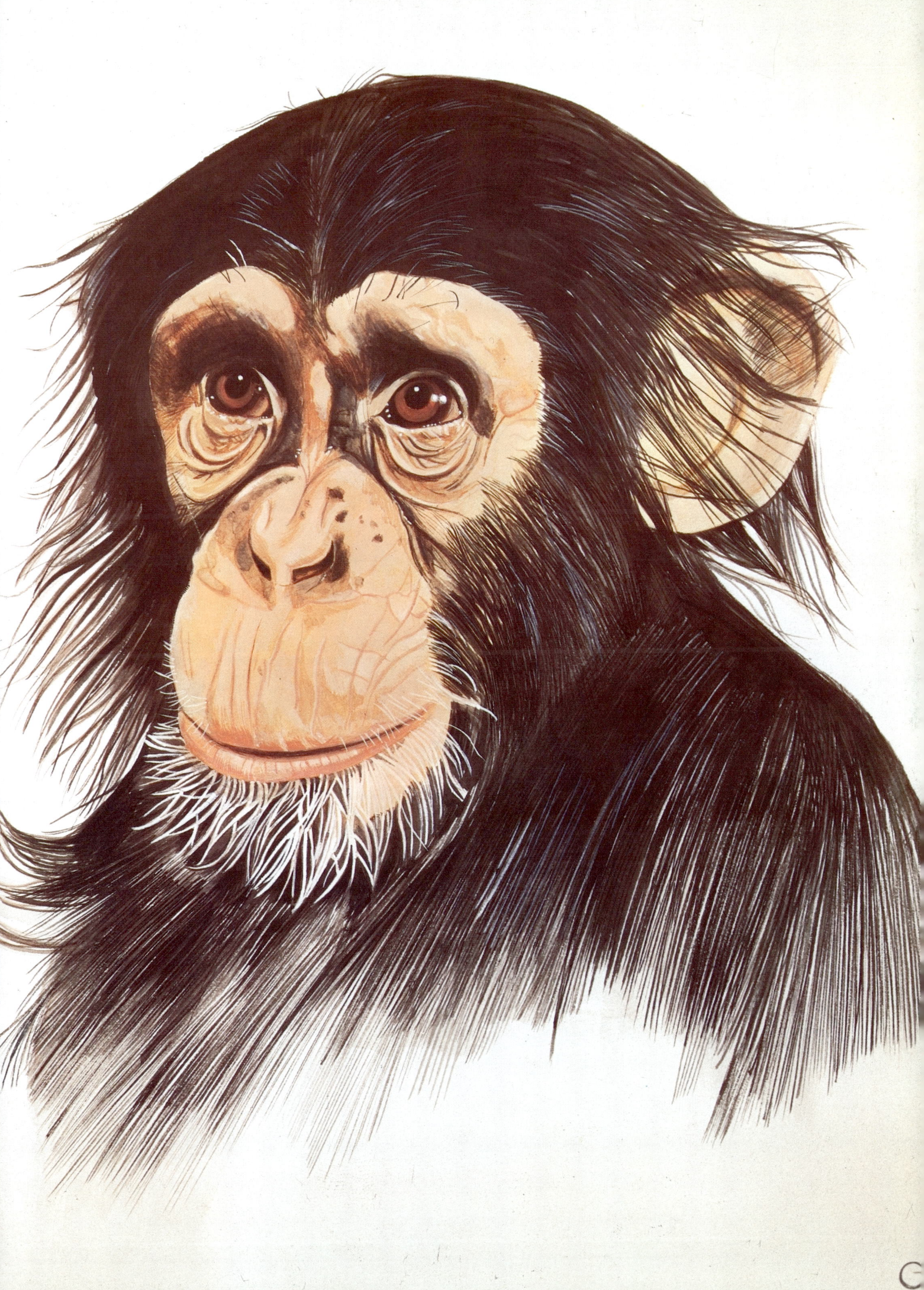

Part Six

Twenty Painting Projects

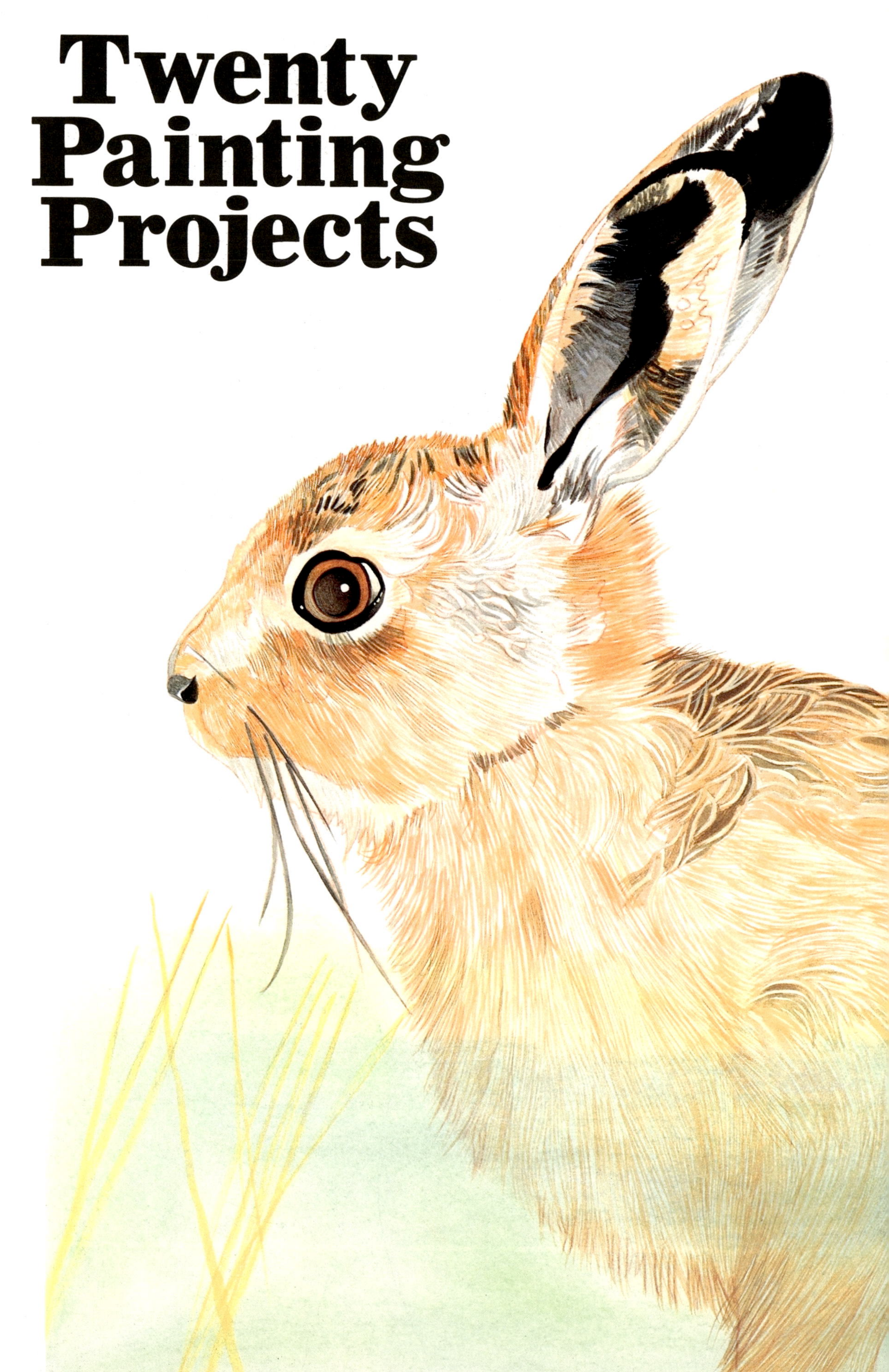

THE NEXT TWENTY PAGES are filled with photographs of animals taken by Heather Angel. Really look at the pictures, for there are countless lessons here for the aspiring artist. Some of the photographs will appeal to you enough to encourage full-scale paintings. Others have been included because they cover areas difficult to practice and master.

I would recommend, before painting any of these photographs, that you run through this checklist:

1. Always look at the picture for at least ten minutes. A great part of the skill in painting wildlife is based on careful observation. It's seeing and recording things other people fail to see that makes a painting special.

2. Make notes about what you've seen right away. Once you get absorbed in the painting process, many of the things you've observed will be forgotten.

3. Do sketches in pencil and make watercolor roughs before you start so that you learn the important lessons the inexpensive way.

4. Don't rush. After all, there's no reason to except in your own mind, and making one good painting is far more important than narrowly missing out on many.

5. Try to achieve a rapport with the animal and its mood by reading about it, or better still, by going out and watching it.

6. Lastly, remember that the animal is shaped by the life it leads and the function it performs. If you don't understand its background, you won't be able to master its likeness.

Lots of luck and happy painting!

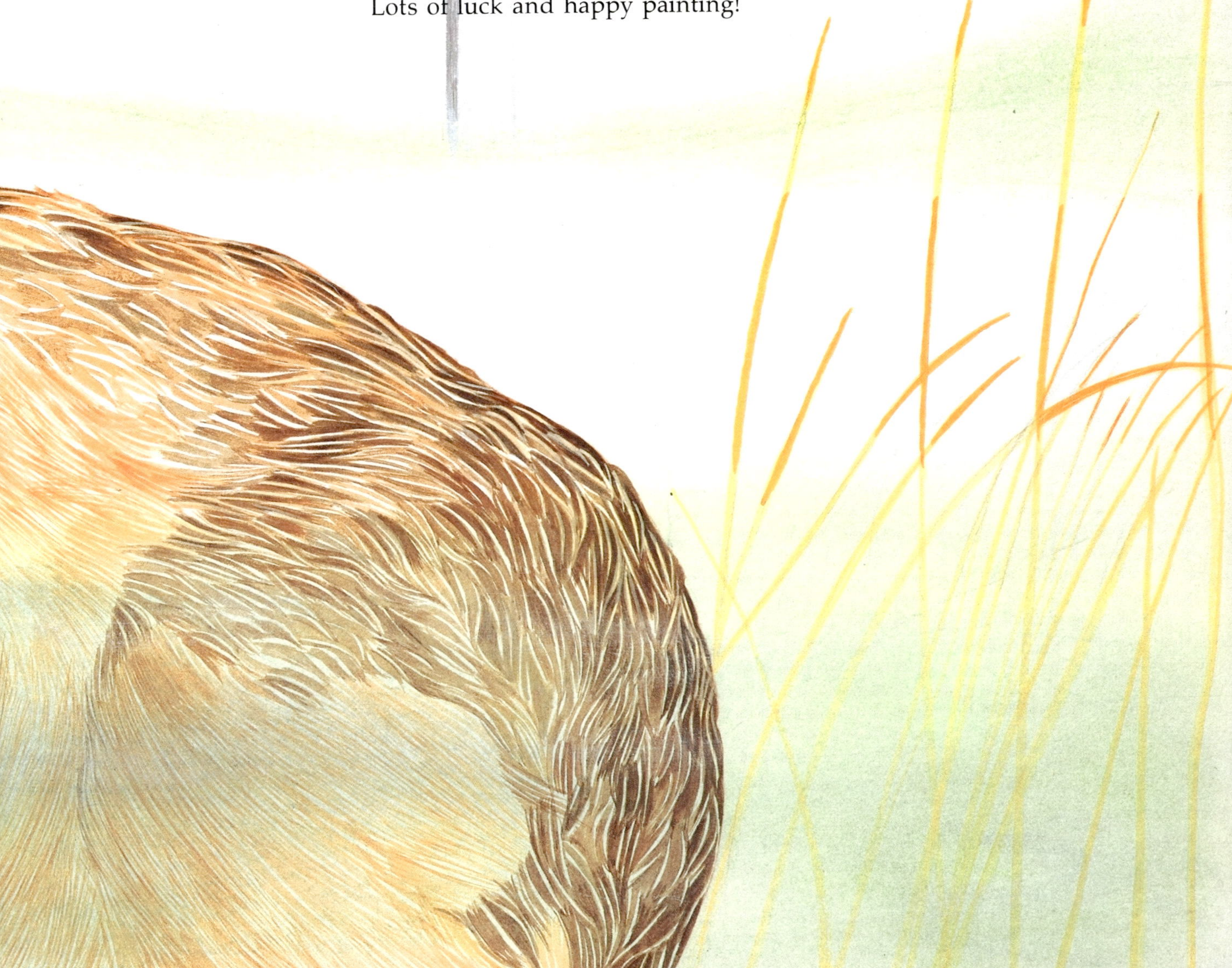

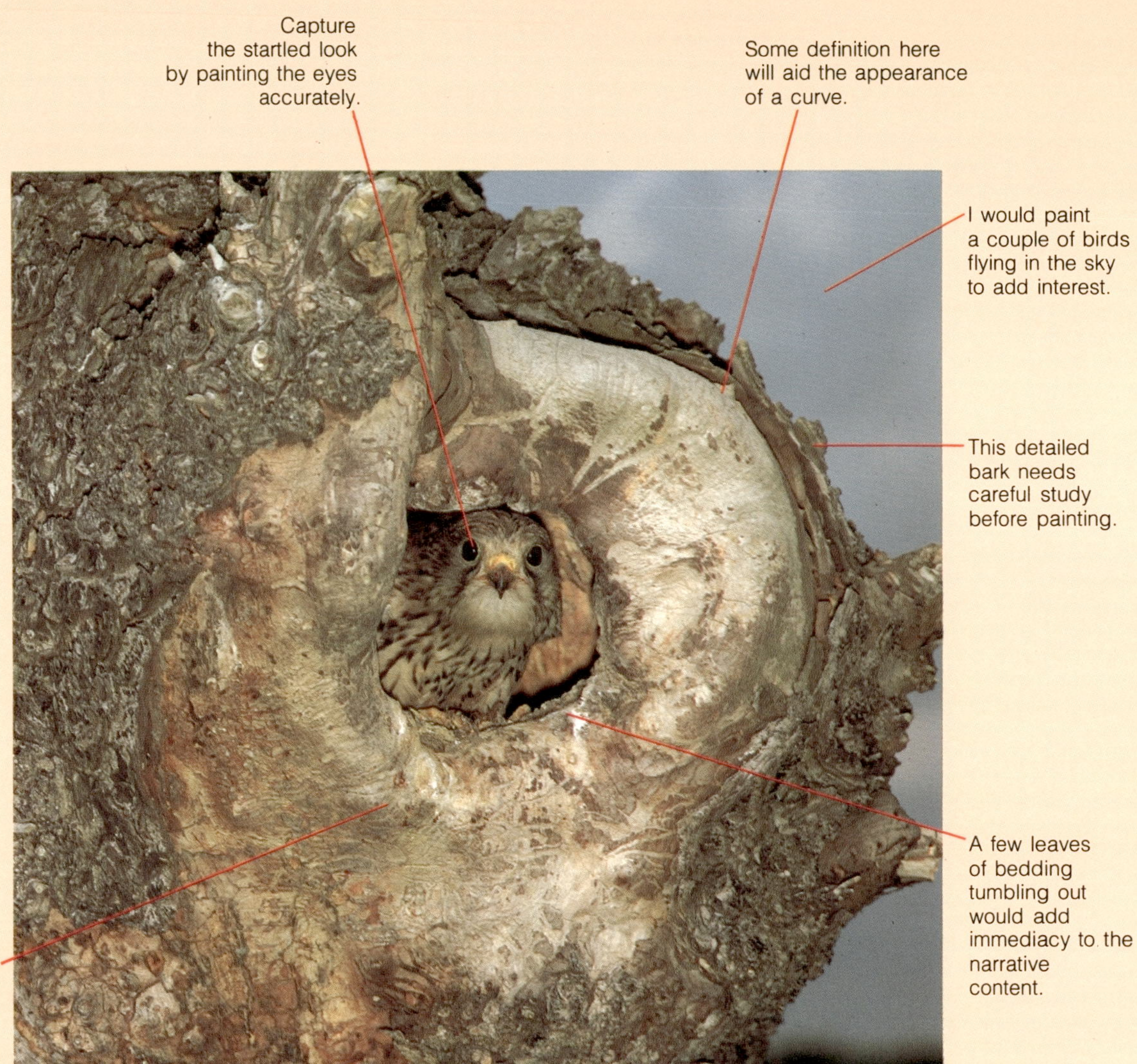

Kestrel

Perhaps it would be more accurate to describe this as a study of tree bark. Though the kestrel takes up a fairly tiny amount of the total space, the way the tree frames it is perfect and is the making of an unusual picture.

A very careful blueprint drawing will certainly be necessary before any painting takes place. If I were doing this, I would crop out much of the tree on the left and extend the tree on the right to show its full curve and at least the beginnings of some branches. (This would also change the composition, moving the kestrel to the left for a more interesting, and less centered, placement.)

The shadows inside the hole have been made stronger than they would actually be by the photographer's flash and these could be softened. Paint the shape of the hole and the area surrounding it in faint colors to get an effect of molding before you start adding the detail of the bark and woodgrain.

Use a couple of pieces of paper to mask the picture and crop it down to the areas that interest you most.

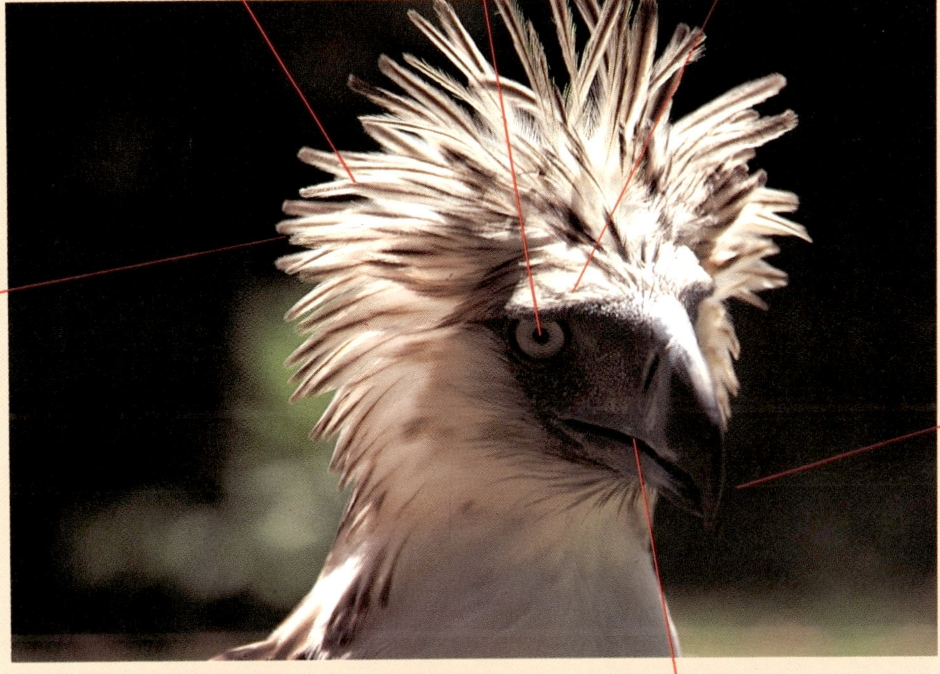

Philippines Eagle

When I was the creative director of an advertising agency, an older and very experienced art director had a favorite and often-used pet phrase, "It's all in the way you crop it." He was, of course, talking about what you cut out and what you leave in on a photograph. He was convinced that a good photograph can be made great by sensitive cropping. I agree with him. Paintings can also benefit from the same careful treatment. The photographer, Heather Angel, felt the same way and concentrated her lens on the essence of this eagle, the fearsome beak and eye and the quite amazingly dramatic crest.

If I were painting this raptor, I would do away with any kind of background and concentrate my attention on the majesty contained within the area of the head.

The position of the various rings alters in angle as the feathers go around the fan.

Study the way the white spines radiate like a design, out from the body, and the way the tendrils of feather follow a direction.

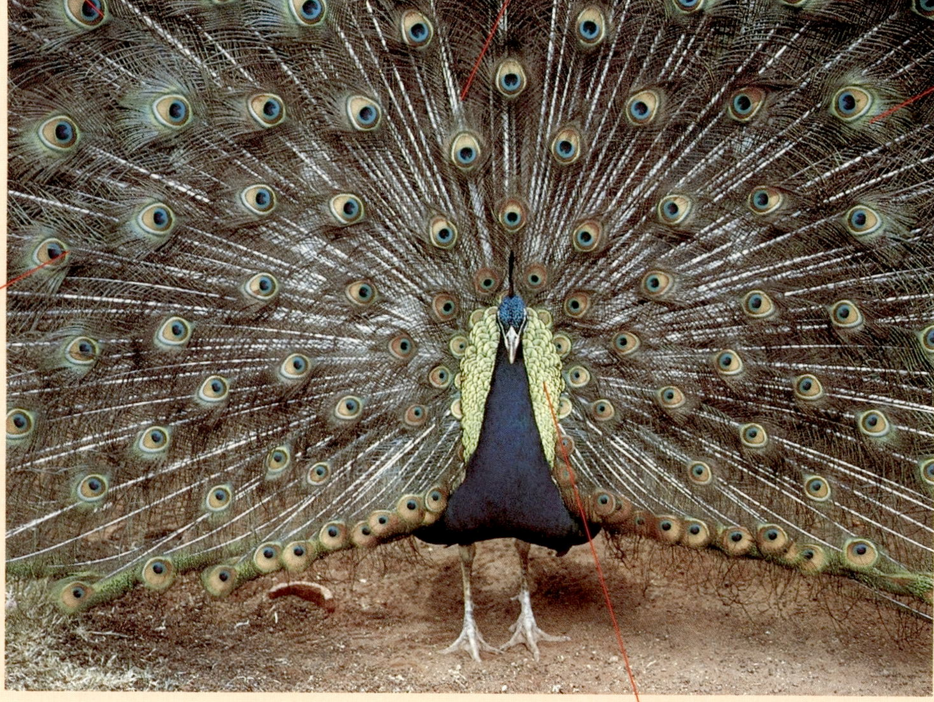

The background between the spines is a bluish-gray. Don't make your painting too green or it will look unreal.

Don't try to paint too much detail into the eyes of the feathers, but do make sure they're all the same.

Study closely the precise, symmetrical effect of the overlapping feathers.

Peacock

I had to paint a peacock some years ago for an important commission, so I studied it very carefully. This is almost an exercise in mathematics, which if not properly mastered, will never look right.

The keys to the pattern are the radiating spines and the eyes of the feathers. I washed the color in between the spines to give myself a dark and contrasting background. In fact, I remember rubbing some pastel into the spaces to give it an airy feel. Each one of the eyes changes its position, with the pointed top end facing the direction that the spine is going in.The fine, hairlike tendrils of feather also follow the direction of the radiating pattern. If you pick a central spine directly above the peacock's head, you can more clearly follow the direction.

This is certainly a study that will reward you for the considerable amount of time that doing it well will take.

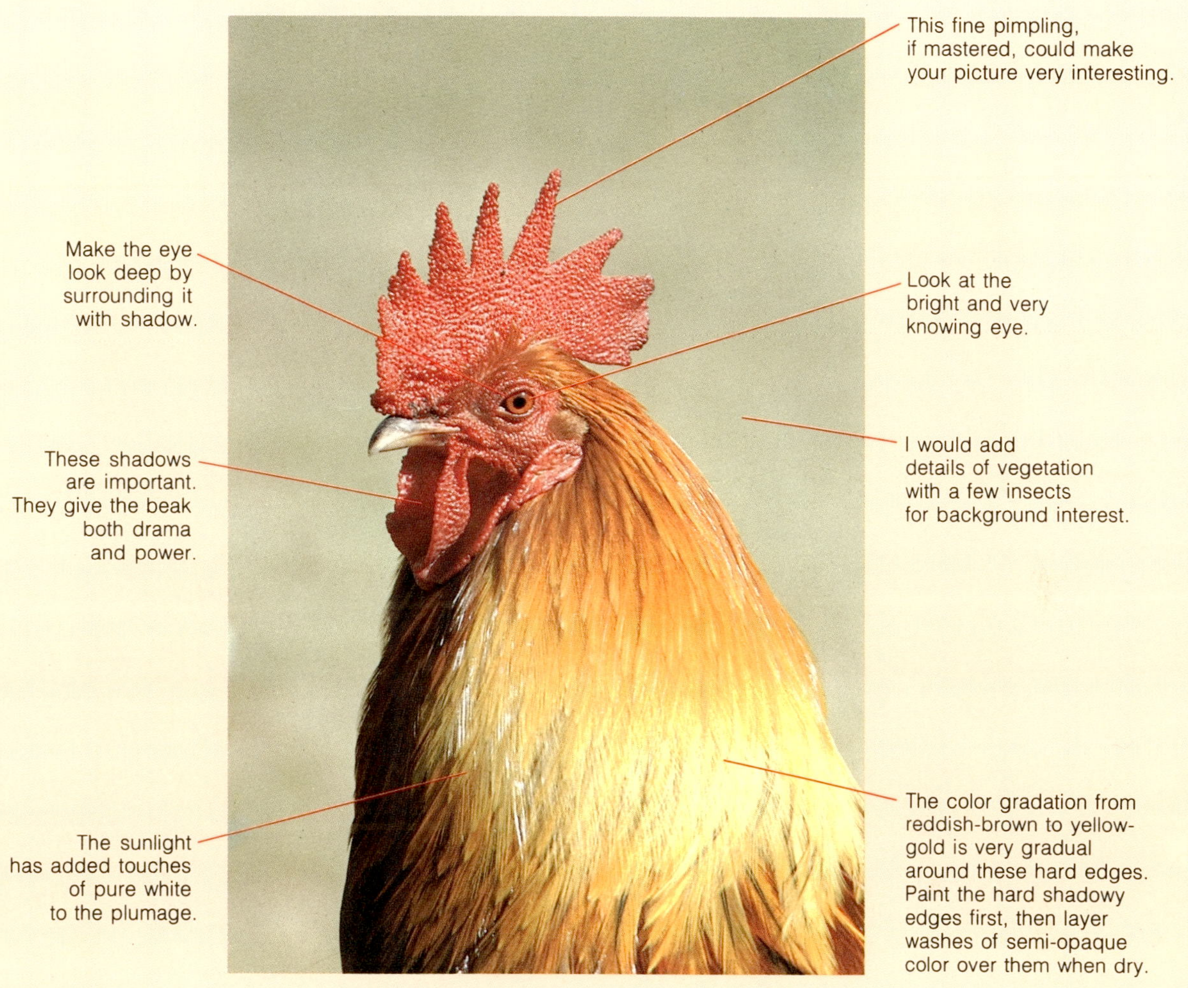

Head of a Bantam Cock

The cockerel is one of the most fiercely masculine creatures in the world. Look at those totally confident and challenging eyes. If you've ever watched one of these arrogant males strutting around his harem domain, you would realize the aptness of the expression, "cock of the walk."

Many of the animals we eat have been depersonalized by the people who encourage us to eat them so we don't feel uncomfortable doing it. That's also why most drawings of them for advertising purposes are toned down—to make killing and eating them more acceptable.

Take a good look at this cockerel. He's well worth painting, especially the magnificent wattle and comb and the fierce eye. You might not enjoy eating him or one of his kind later, but he'll be quite grateful for that—even if it doesn't please you.

Because the heron is on the left of the picture, it is far more interesting than had it been centered. The journey is still to come, the water has yet to be ruffled by its progress forward.

Look at the way the heron is highlighted by the light, which appears to be coming from below as well as above.

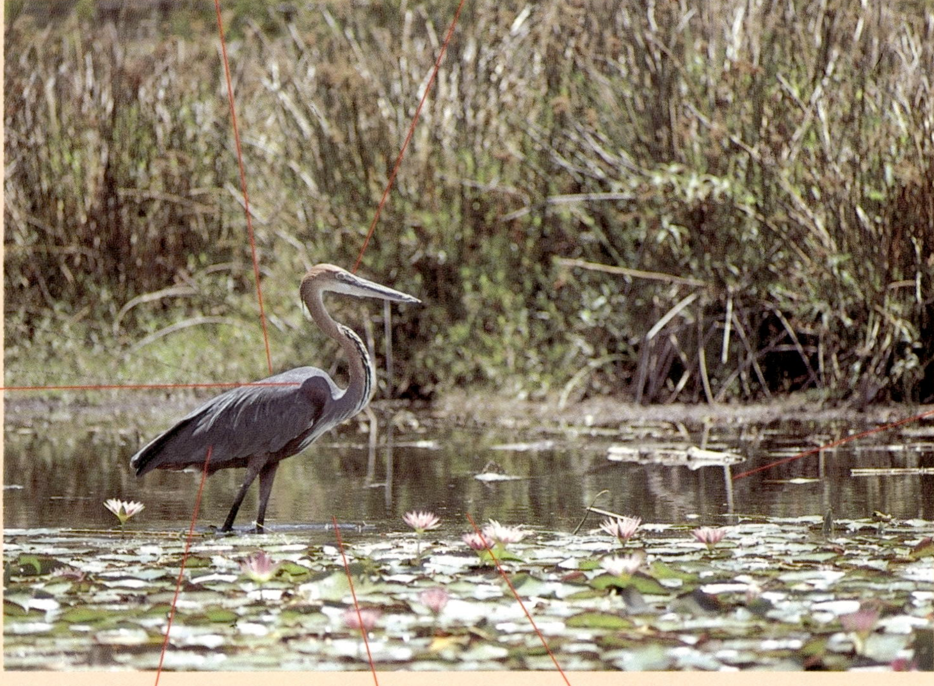

The interesting, curved shadow makes a good design against the line of the back and the powerful, poised neck.

The reflections from the reeds could overly complicate the picture unless they were achieved with a spontaneous and underpainted style.

The feathers are perfect to paint, as they stand out in high relief.

The touch of blue in the water adds emphasis to the bird's movement.

Note how the waterlily blooms break across and into the still-water area.

Goliath Heron

What a masterly example of the photographer's art! Just what would wildlife artists do without cameras or the photographers?

This photograph really excites me, for it is truly beautiful. You ought to paint it . . . . I know I shall! It has enormous variety, and the quality of light sets out the heron in an electric-blue relief that also touches the water below it. The waterlilies add interest and color to the foreground, and the mid-picture band of calm, deep water is framed by the background of reeds.

I think this picture could stand high detail in every ingredient except perhaps the reeds, but it also offers lots of other opportunities. Imagine the front of the picture washed in a vague mist, with the waterlilies emerging from it, or picture a band of mist tendriling its way past the base of the reeds. As a painting exercise, this photograph has everything. I strongly recommend that you experiment with it.

The rushes need to be strongly painted in the foreground with greater contrast, more color, and more detail and treated more delicately in the background.

Look at the wonderful opportunities for value contrast provided by the seed pods of the rushes.

Out-of-focus leaves and twigs can be lightly dropped on at the end with weak colors—or left out altogether if you think they'll be confusing to the viewers.

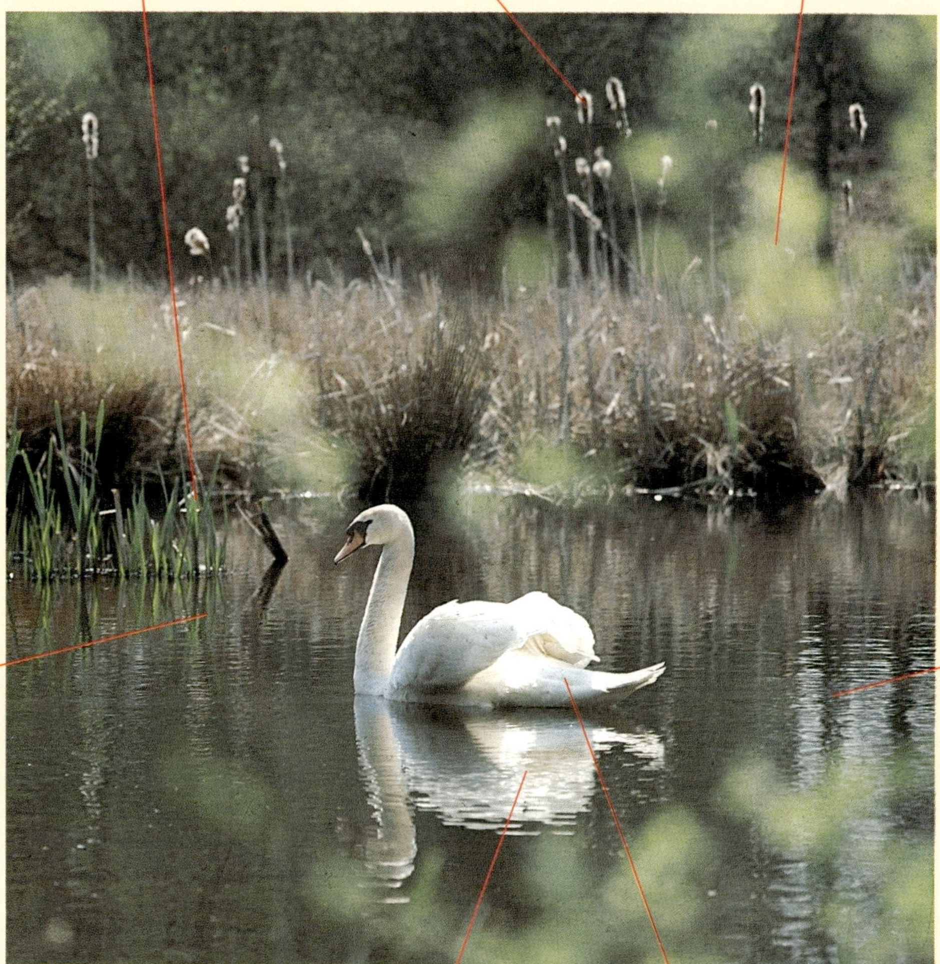

Look at the way the reflections of the brushes and the sky fuse to make perfect painting possible.

The tree shadows distort with the water's movement.

The broken reflection can be painted with choppy strokes of process white gouache with watercolor mixed in or left out of the painted area so that the paper shows through. Look at the tones of color here. Don't be fussy and too careful in painting the reflections or they'll look too labored.

Don't paint the swan in too much detail. It should look as though it's gliding through the water.

Mute Swan

This photograph looks as though it were taken by a devoted watercolorist, as every ingredient that could be desired is here. The painting can be tackled in two ways, either by making a well-defined, crisp picture or a very vague and soft one. I would go first for a rough watercolor sketch before forming preference for one direction or the other. The painting would certainly be suitable for big brushes and lots of wash work.

The shaft of light coming from above could be narrowed considerably to dramatize the static pike.

The light-green plants form an interesting pattern against the background and trace the swell of the water's movement.

The yellow and black eye is the whole center of any indication of life.

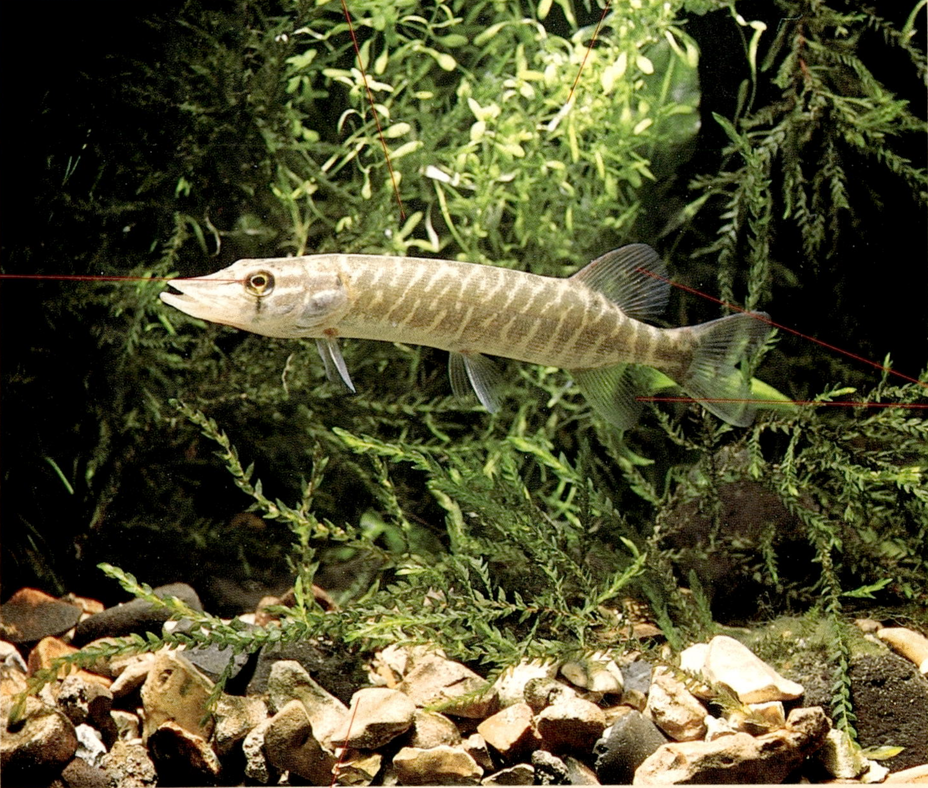

The fins contain quite a variety of colors. Paint what you can see through them before starting to overpaint the fins.

The rocks add another ingredient of interest.

Pike

The predator pike hangs suspended on the current, waiting. It is this quiet, yet tense suspension that makes the picture attractive. The strong line of the mouth and jaw and the glossy, bright, but impersonally blank eye, add moment. The pattern of the body contrasted against the upward spiraling water plants and the dark and mysterious background make it a good painting exercise. The variety of color reflecting into the glassy fins, again contrasted against the dark background, add to the interest.

I would add something else—like a duck's feet or another smaller prey fish—to increase the drama and narrative power of what could otherwise be a too calm and static study. For example, a line with bait suspended an inch or so in front of the pike's nose would give added drama and concentrate the focus of the picture.

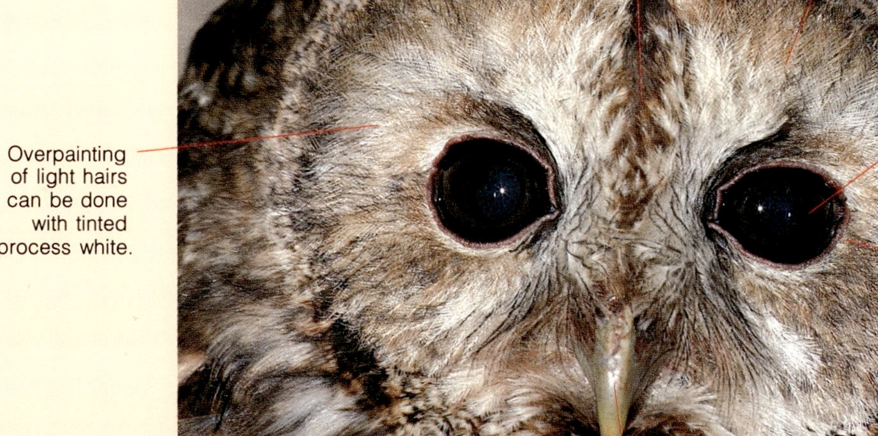

Tawny Owl

This owl is just made to be painted! The wealth of detail on its face will make a most pleasing picture. I would carefully draw a blueprint, and then wash in the darker shadow areas following up with the painting of the fine detail. The areas outside the main part of the face would best be painted with a large, wet brush, building up slowly with layers of paint to achieve the density of pigment needed. Careful patterning here is not that vital. The mere pin-pricks of light reflected into the owl's eye can be put in as a finishing touch with a fairly dry process white on a well-pointed brush, but make sure you place them absolutely accurately. (You can leave a small spot of white as a guide when you are washing in the main color, though this might make life even more difficult.)

The risk in painting is part of its enjoyment. After all, if there was no difficulty in it, it would not be as pleasurable, and the feeling of achievement when you have done it well is incomparable!

Look at the dark patterns that the water creates.

The lines of the hair match the rivulets where water has run off the bear's coat.

The traces of blue in the shadow are quite strong.

The hairs above the water are very defined.

The legs are vague and ill-defined underwater.

There is an actual line that marks the water.

The shadow beneath the water helps to emphasize the actual waterline.

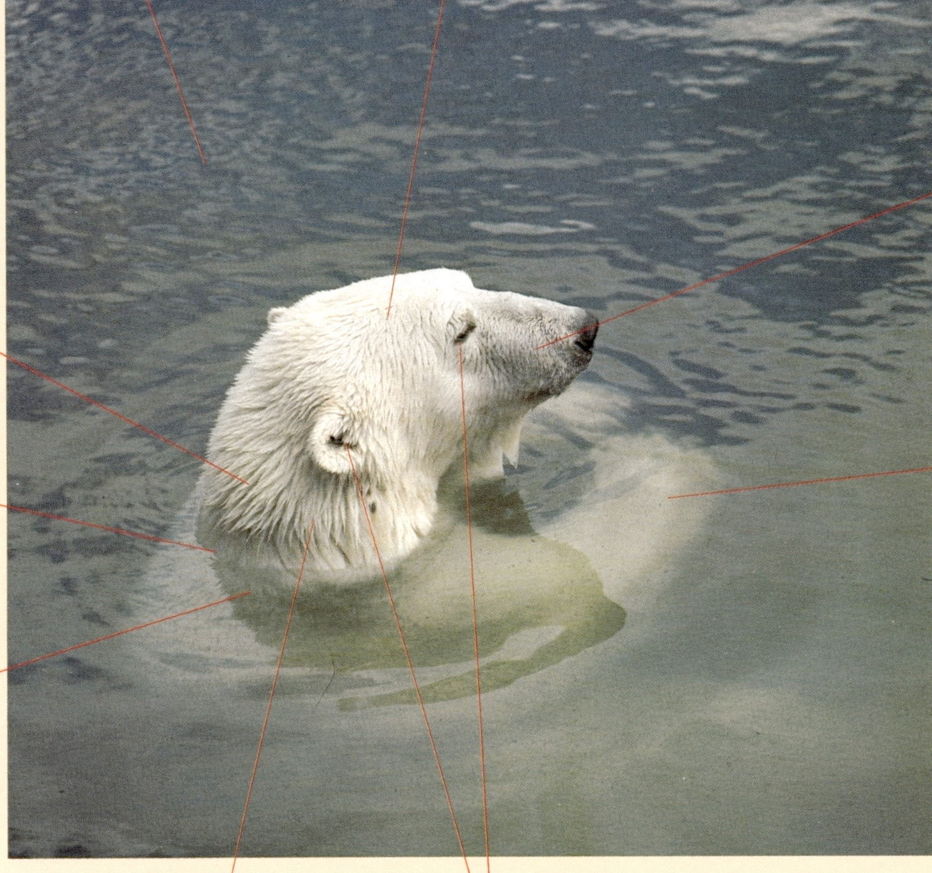

There's quite a tinge of yellow in the fur.

The eye and ear openings are very small to keep out the cold of its native habitat.

Polar Bear

The hardest part of painting this will be getting the water to look natural. If you very carefully draw the darker parts and paint them first, your chances of success will be much enhanced.

Painting the polar bear's head is easier. Concentrate on painting the shadow areas between the hairs so that the wet clumps of hair stand out in relief. All of the hard and clear definition takes place above the waterline. The yellowish tinges can be brushed in afterward with a big, round brush and a very understated and not-too-wet wash.

The difference between what is above and what is below the water can be established by using a fine brush and putting in a lot of detail above the water—and by using a big brush and a looser style of painting below the water. Don't be tempted into painting a hard line for the water's edge against the polar bear's neck, though a very faint and understated line will help show just what is where. Note the way the hair above the water follows the direction of the surplus water running down. Remember to treat the water and the shadows on the water like a blueprint of specific shapes when you're drawing them.

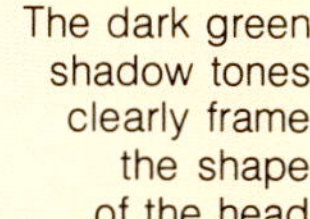

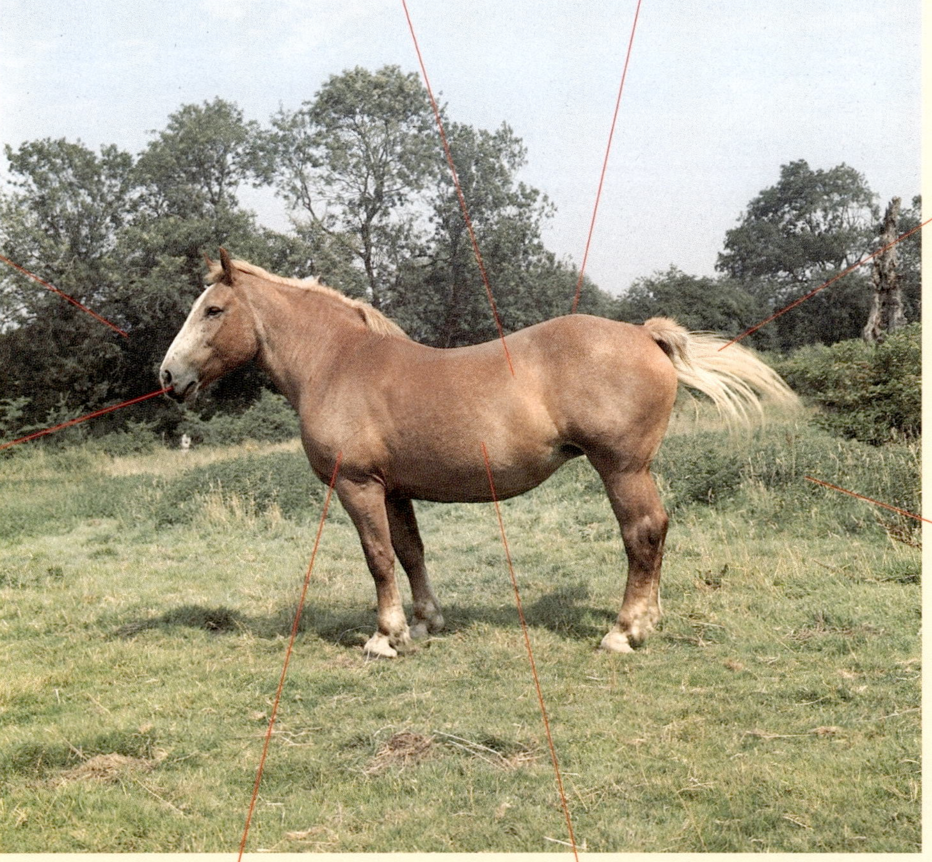

Suffolk Punch

I would enjoy painting a picture of this very sturdy horse. It offers tonal opportunities as well as compositional advantages.

Because of its short, fine, figure-hugging coat, all sorts of difficulties could occur unless you settle early on the technique and board you'll use. I would select a fairly coarse board and treat the horse much the same as the fallow deer in the section on animal textures. The real problem here is the horse's coat. Draw it carefully, showing all of the shadow areas, and take account of the huge, rounded muscle groups.

The background would be more effective if, after drawing it, you flooded the darker areas beneath the trees with very wet washes and built up the density of color slowly. Unless you want to paint every leaf, it would be best to simplify the trees and vegetation or move them farther away so that they appear to be vaguer.

This is a picture to be looked at in a calm, reflective mood, so keep the horse right in the middle of the composition. Moving it either left or right would destroy this calm feeling.

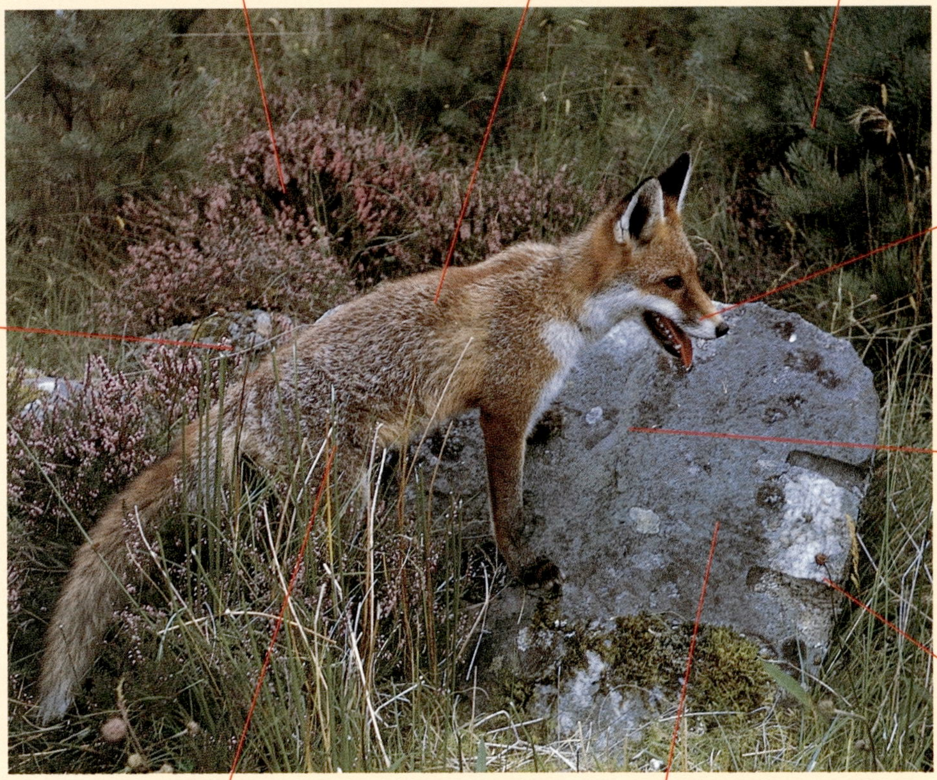

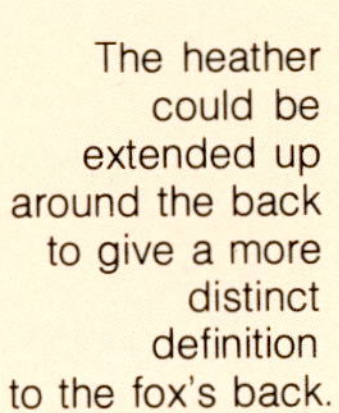

Fox

This study of a fox would make quite a beautiful watercolor. All of the ingredients combine to make a perfect composition and color scheme. The dark green of the background, relieved by the rounded clumps of heather, frame the fox very effectively and give it a mobile "here now, gone in a second" feeling that is certainly synonymous with the animal's nature.

The way the curving grass hides some of the fox and the way it is standing on the bluish-gray rock also add to the drama. The notches cut out of the rock, presumably a gate fixing, give it extra interest.

This picture would certainly benefit from a series of small practice sketches, as so many different painting techniques need to be employed. Make sure you have mastered the stance of the fox before you begin your final painting, as the angle of the rock could give strange results if not carefully studied.

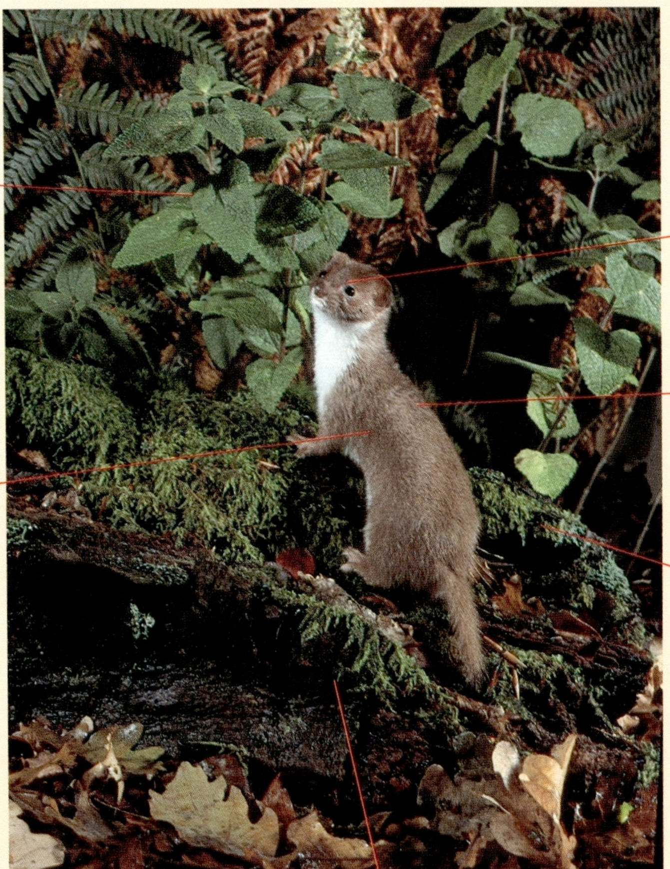

This vegetation, as far as a painter is concerned, is too perfect, too stagy.

Look at the beady, ever-searching, merciless eyes of this super-predator.

Notice the distinct hair direction.

The whole body is alive and tense like a wound-up spring.

The way the moss drapes over the rotting wood gives a nice feeling of form.

The size of the foreground oak leaves tends to minimize the apparent size of the weasel but gives a great graphic effect. Put your hand over the leaves and then decide whether you need them.

Weasel

If there are two animals that terrify me, they are the weasel and the stoat. They also fascinate me.

Weasels are lightening-fast, tense, and very determined predators, undulating across the ground with an air of unstoppable ferocity. When I am traveling through the country roads of Hertfordshire, I often see them snake in leaps across the road, like creatures from an underworld. My brother-in-law tells me of an awful weasel attack he once observed on a pet rabbit. The weasel stood on its hind legs and looked at the unaware rabbit, and then darted in, caught the rabbit by the throat, and shook it. The weasel then retired to a distance of several yards and observed the rabbit for about five minutes, and then renewed its attack. Repeats of this performance went on for twenty minutes or so. The rabbit was three or four times the size of the weasel.

Given that information, I find this photograph though outstandingly beautiful, too pretty to be followed too closely. The photographer is forced to capitalize on the moment, but an artist has the wherewithal to change things. I would reduce the colors of the vegetation and its quantity, and move my focus closer to the weasel. To make the effect even more threatening, I would add rain—but, as you have probably gathered by now, I am slightly biased.

Make sure the grass is drawn in some detail before you paint. It's very easy to lose control of a picture if it's not planned well.

Strong black hairs separate one head from another.

The eyes are a very dark bluish black. A crisp highlight, correctly placed, will give them the right expression.

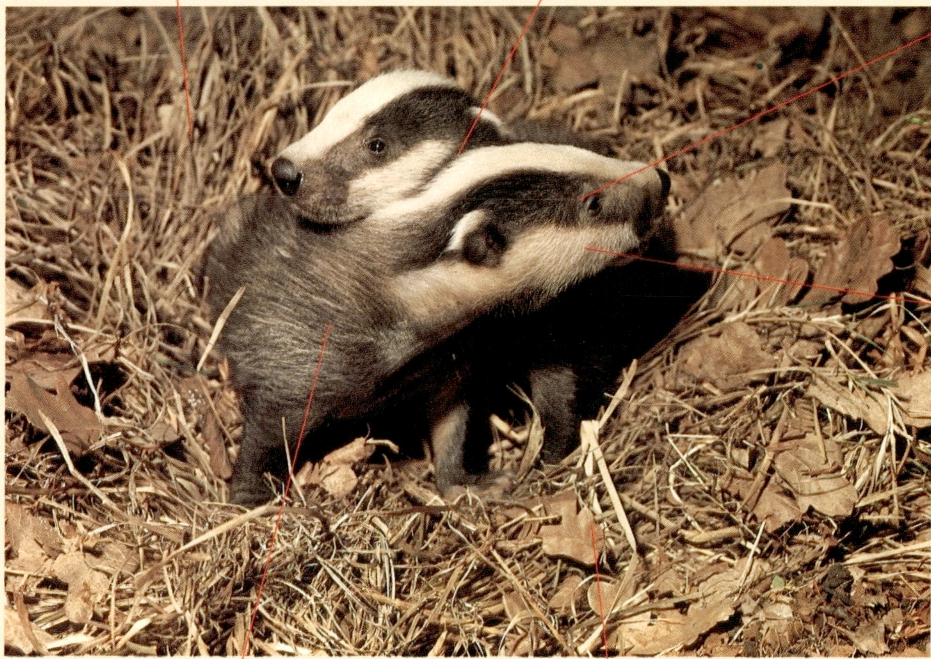

Notice the tinge of brownish yellow on the white hairs. Wash the area with a soft color before putting in the hair detail.

Notice the way the long hairs follow the curve of the shoulder and the twist of the body. Process white gouache in a good, fluid mix will give crisp, white hairs.

The leaf and grass litter is a painter's paradise. Draw the leaf shapes very faintly and then paint the spaces in between them with a mixture of a dark brown and a little black.

Two Young Badgers

The photograph of these two young badgers is already halfway toward providing a very nice composition in painting terms. If I were painting it, I would introduce a few spots of bright color to give the mass of brown tones some relief.

If you choose to paint this subject, make sure your drawing is detailed, especially on the leaves and grass. I would paint the badgers first and only add the leaves when I was satisfied with the animals. The eyes would be a good place to start, as the essence of the animal and the picture is contained within them.

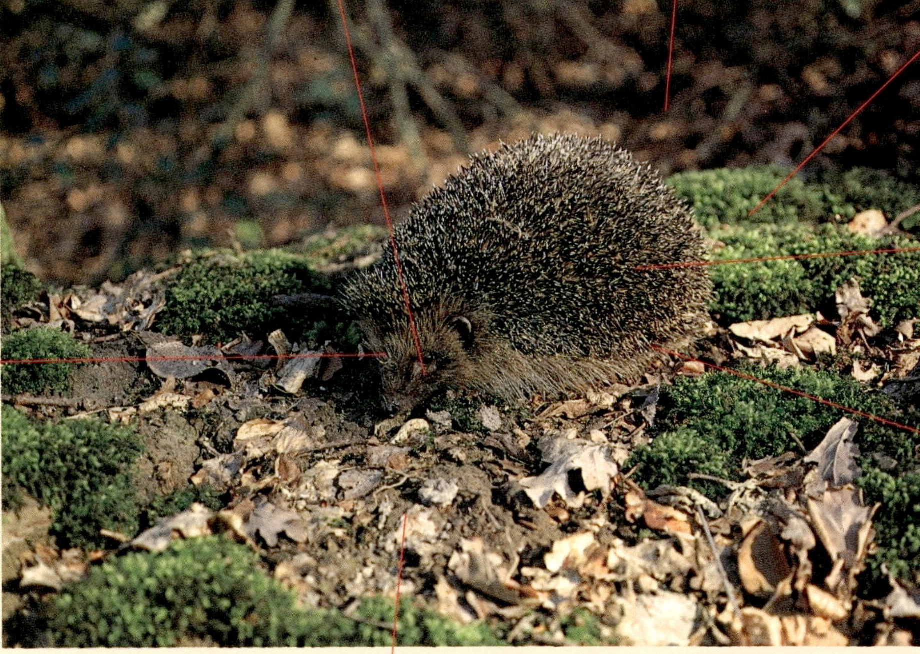

Hedgehog

The hedgehog appears to be one of the most difficult animals to paint. But it's not as difficult as you would think, providing you decide in advance what you'll be doing and work to a plan. In the drawing stage, concentrate on the lighter prickles. Notice that they all move backward, following the shape of the hedgehog's body. Draw every one of them (or give the impression of drawing every single one), and then fill in the gaps between the hairs with dark color.

Some artists prefer to paint the entire hedgehog dark and then add the prickles in afterward with a stronger covering paint. In my view, this is the quick way to doom. If you don't believe me, try it. My children's book, *Spiney the Hedgehog,* was full of color illustrations of hedgehogs, seen from every conceivable angle, and so now I consider myself an expert. The hedgehog shown in the section "Where Different Textures Meet" might help you to see the technique more clearly. (It will also help you paint the leaves and surrounding detail.)

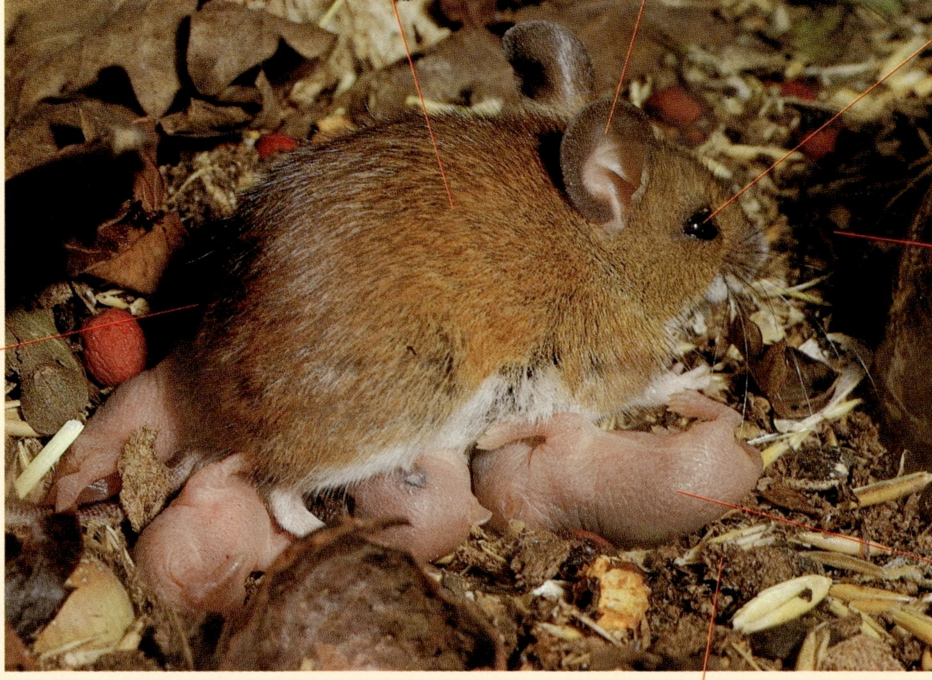

Woodmouse Suckling Its Offspring

This is an interesting study because the woodmouse is actually doing something instead of just apparently posing. There is a lot of evidence of her presence around: empty grain husks, a slightly dried-up rose hip or berry, plus bedding litter that shows that the mouse clearly lives here.

The coat of the mother mouse is a classic example of definite hairs of several colors closely following the body shape. The babies add interest, though for a painting there are too many indistinct shapes, and that could be confusing. If I were painting this, I would confine my attention to the baby that shows most of its body shape. A more complete study would result if you bent the tail of the mouse into a protective curve around the suckling infant. Don't try to put character into the baby because you feel it doesn't have enough—you'll only succeed in turning it into a wizened little monster!

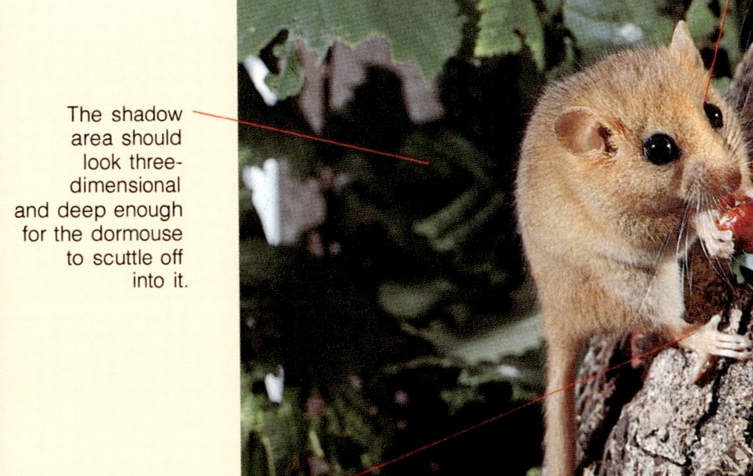

Dormouse Feeding on Hawthorn Berries

This is a beautiful photograph—but that can also create problems. A painting of this dormouse, unless roughed up a little, could look too sweet, the archetypal wildlife painter's greeting card. If you bear the danger of oversweetness in mind, this dormouse can make a very lovely painting.

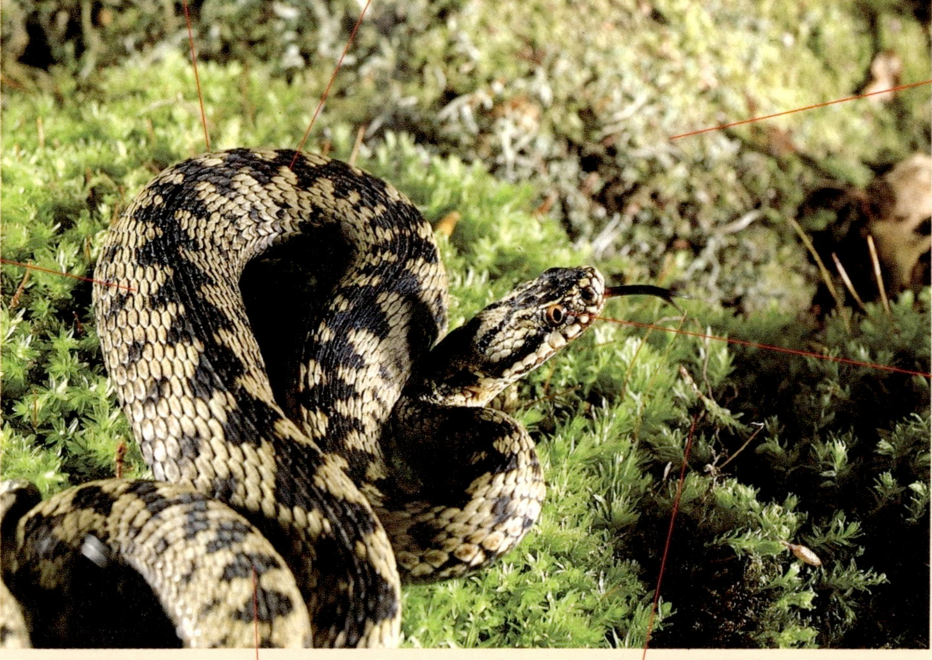

Adder

What a wonderful (and a difficult) painting opportunity this is. It would be essential here to achieve accuracy in your drawing or the adder's power and vitality would be lost. Let your pencil lines be fluid, with strong curves. The time spent at the beginning will save a lot of agonizing at the end. Working out the adder's scales is a big job, but worth every bit of planning. If you get frustrated, slow down. After all, there's no deadline on a good painting, and it's going to last a lot longer than you will—so it's well worth getting right!

Make sure the leaflike divisions of the wings are clearly defined.

This strong, yellowish highlight separates the creature from its background.

Cutting out the background leaves and putting in a flower or a blue sky won't aid the creature's comfort, but it will give you a more visible picture.

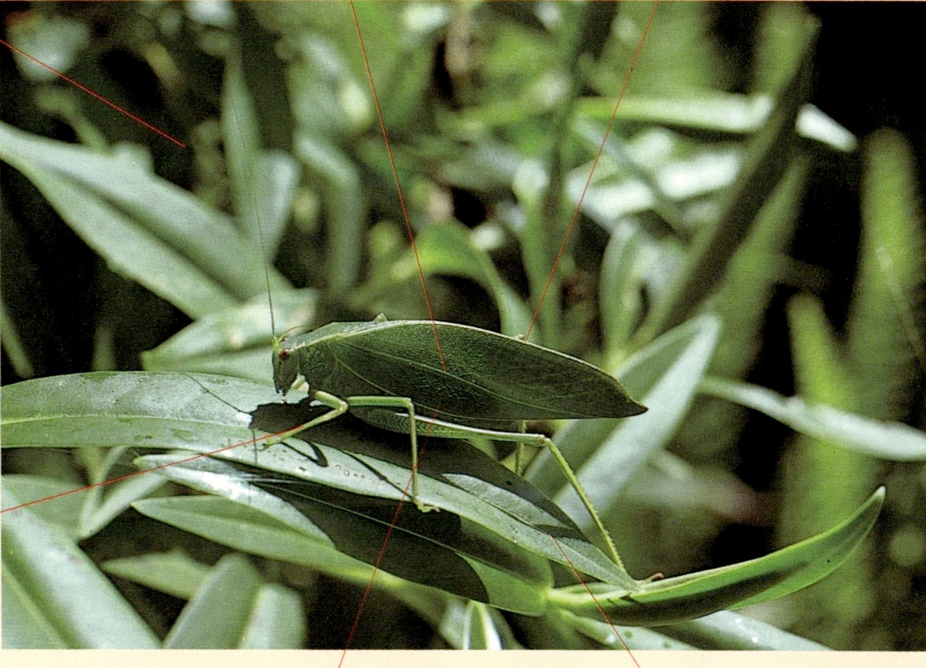

Draw the legs strongly to make the katydid stand out against the leaf.

Make sure your dark color is strong enough to contrast with the legs and give the animal form.

Mix the green first and experiment on a piece of card before touching the actual painting. Make a note of your color mixtures.

New Zealand Katydid

Not knowing what is leaf and what is insect is the whole point of a creature's camouflage. So often in wildlife painting, a creature is so good at losing itself in its background that artistic license in the way you treat it is vital and you may have to reduce some of that camouflage (see "Differentiating Textures").

I would recommend this as a study for the absolute beginner because the shape is not too difficult to draw. But try painting the creature and the leaf it is standing on first before adding the rest of the leaves, and allow yourself some license to fade the background leaves into the distance. In fact, change the color of the leaves by just a fraction to allow the creature to stand out a little more.

If you plan to spend more than one session painting this katydid, make a note of the colors you use to mix the green. Nothing is more infuriating than coming back to a painting and not being able to duplicate the original color.

Place another leaf behind the horns for contrast to achieve definition and avoid losing them in the background.

Try to match the beetle's rich, almost mahoganylike surface by using a big brush loaded in the first washes with plenty of water and kept almost dry in the later stages.

This dark shadow is picking up a lot of green. Don't treat it like a solid curtain. Layer it in gradual washes, leaving the outside edges soft.

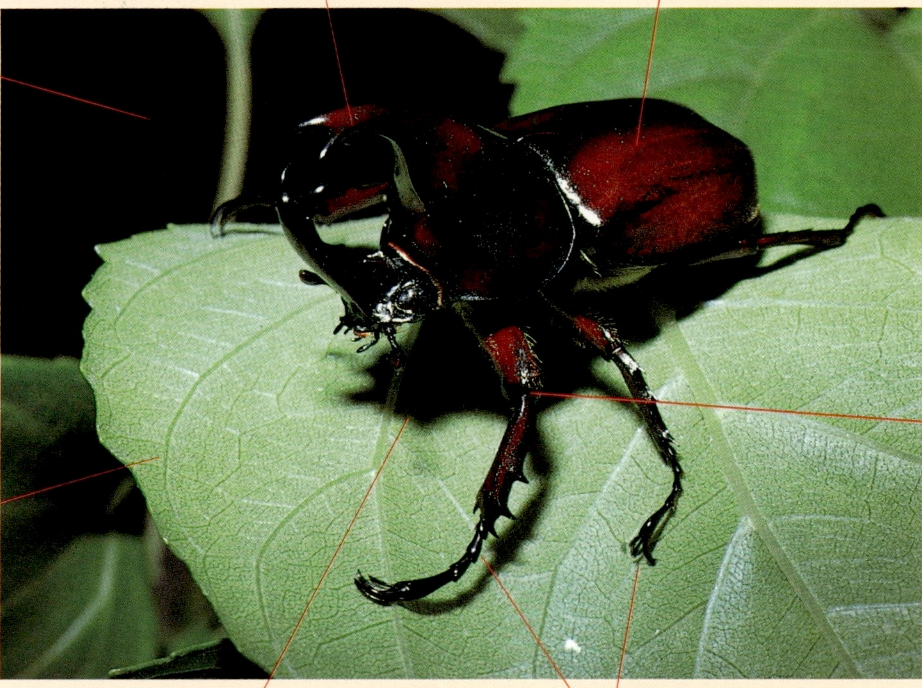

Keep the highlights accurate to give strength and life to the legs.

This leaf is too perfect. For interest add a couple of holes or a battered edge.

The shadow is soft and the beetle is hard. If you don't make this difference obvious, both areas will merge.

Unless carefully drawn, the legs could too easily look as though they are flopping, energyless, on the leaf.

Rhinoceros Beetle

Whenever I paint this sort of beetle, I imagine that it's bigger than an elephant and that the landscape surrounding it is equally vast. Too often pictures of small creatures lose impact because the painter forgot to make the jump from one world to another. Beetles in their own world are massively strong and formidably armored. If you remember this when you're painting them, your picture will achieve some majesty.

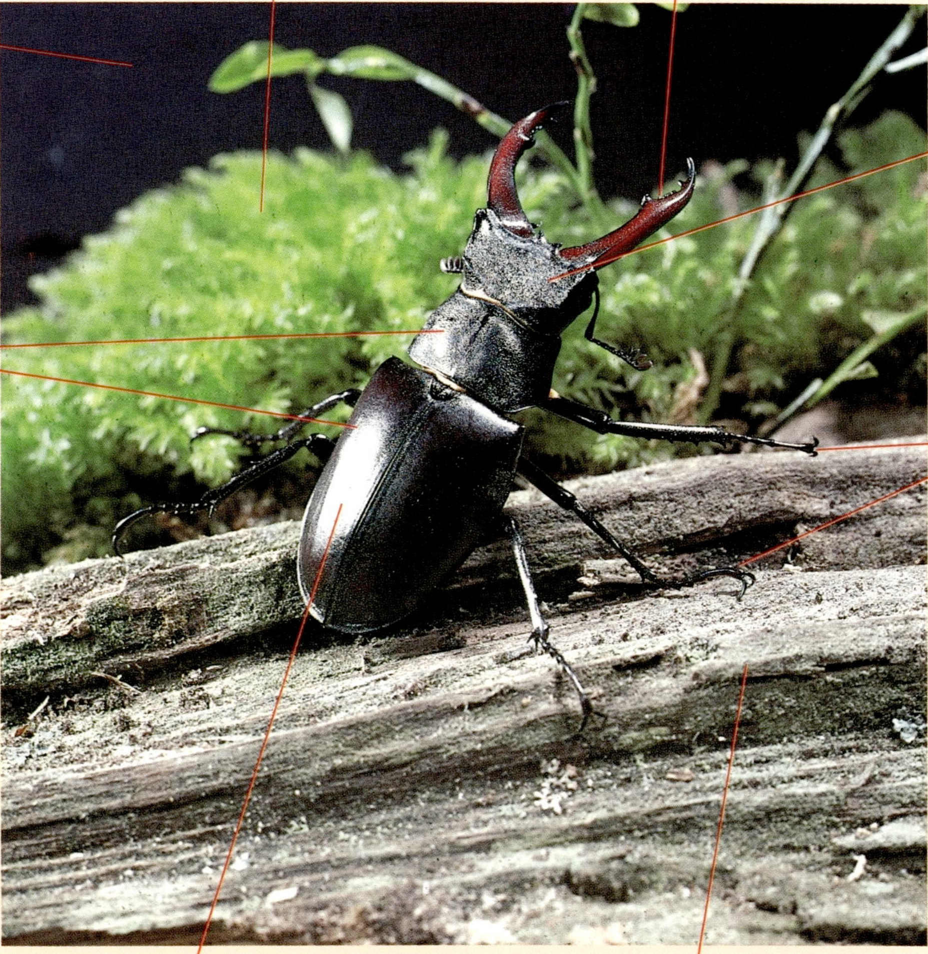

Male Stag Beetle

Most of the call-out points on insects concentrate on increasing the apparent size of these small creatures. As I have already said with regard to the rhinoceros beetle, the danger is making them appear small. The minute I say "beetle," you have an image of something small and this conditions the way you approach the painting. So instead let's call it by its Latin name, *Lucanus cervus,* and pretend that it's 30 feet long and weighs several tons! Imagine the mighty *Lucanus cervus* crashing through the undergrowth, breaking trees as it passes. Imagine it roaring as it comes. Think of it as a hangover from the dinosaur period, and your painting will have some scale and romance to it.

Index